Scarecrow Studies in Young Adult Literature
Series Editor: Patty Campbell

Scarecrow Studies in Young Adult Literature is intended to continue the body of critical writing established in Twayne's Young Adult Authors series and to expand it beyond single-author studies to explorations of genres, multicultural writing, and controversial issues in young adult (YA) reading. Many of the contributing authors of the series are among the leading scholars and critics of adolescent literature, and some are YA novelists themselves. The series is shaped by its editor, Patty Campbell, who is a renowned authority in the field, with a forty-year background as critic, lecturer, librarian, and teacher of YA literature. Patty Campbell was the 2001 winner of the ALAN Award, given by the Assembly on Literature for Adolescents of the National Council of Teachers of English for distinguished contribution to YA literature. In 1989 she was the winner of the American Library Association's Grolier Award for distinguished service to young adults and reading.

Titles in the Series

1. *What's So Scary about R. L. Stine?*, by Patrick Jones, 1998.
2. *Ann Rinaldi: Historian and Storyteller*, by Jeanne M. McGlinn, 2000.
3. *Norma Fox Mazer: A Writer's World*, by Arthea J. S. Reed, 2000.
4. *Exploding the Myths: The Truth about Teens and Reading*, by Marc Aronson, 2001.
5. *The Agony and the Eggplant: Daniel Pinkwater's Heroic Struggles in the Name of YA Literature*, by Walter Hogan, 2001.
6. *Caroline Cooney: Faith and Fiction*, by Pamela Sissi Carroll, 2001.
7. *Declarations of Independence: Empowered Girls in Young Adult Literature, 1990–2001*, by Joanne Brown and Nancy St. Clair, 2002.
8. *Lost Masterworks of Young Adult Literature*, by Connie S. Zitlow, 2002.
9. *Beyond the Pale: New Essays for a New Era* by Marc Aronson, 2003.
10. *Orson Scott Card: Writer of the Terrible Choice*, by Edith S. Tyson, 2003.
11. *Jacqueline Woodson: "The Real Thing,"* by Lois Thomas Stover, 2003.
12. *Virginia Euwer Wolff: Capturing the Music of Young Voices*, by Suzanne Elizabeth Reid, 2003.
13. *More Than a Game: Sports Literature for Young Adults*, by Chris Crowe, 2004.
14. *Humor in Young Adult Literature: A Time to Laugh*, by Walter Hogan, 2005.
15. *Life Is Tough: Guys, Growing Up, and Young Adult Literature*, by Rachelle Lasky Bilz, 2004.
16. *Sarah Dessen: From Burritos to Box Office*, by Wendy J. Glenn, 2005.
17. *American Indian Themes in Young Adult Literature*, by Paulette F. Molin, 2005.
18. *The Heart Has Its Reasons: Young Adult Literature with Gay/Lesbian/Queer Content, 1969–2004*, by Michael Cart and Christine A. Jenkins, 2006.

Portrait of the Artist as a Young Adult

The Arts in Young Adult Literature

Lois Thomas Stover
Connie S. Zitlow

THE SCARECROW PRESS, INC.
Lanham • Toronto • Plymouth, UK
2014

KH

Published by Scarecrow Press, Inc.
A wholly owned subsidiary of The Rowman & Littlefield Publishing Group, Inc.
4501 Forbes Boulevard, Suite 200, Lanham, Maryland 20706
www.rowman.com

10 Thornbury Road, Plymouth PL6 7PP, United Kingdom

British Library Cataloguing in Publication Information Available

Library of Congress Cataloging-in-Publication Data

Stover, Lois T.
Portrait of the artist as a young adult : the arts in young adult literature / Lois Thomas Stover, Connie S. Zitlow.
pages cm. — (Scarecrow Studies in Young Adult Literature ; No. 46)
Includes bibliographical references and index.
ISBN 978-0-8108-9277-4 (cloth : alk. paper) — ISBN 978-0-8108-9278-1 (ebook)
1. Young adult literature, American—History and criticism. 2. Young adult literature, English—History and criticism. 3. Artists in literature. 4. Arts in literature. I. Zitlow, Connie S., 1942– II. Title.
PS490.S77 2014
810.9'9282—dc23
2013024894

Printed in the United States of America

9/30/15

Contents

Preface

A young person's self-discovery—how does it happen? How does involvement in the arts influence the coming-of-age for young adults? What happens if they are struggling with confusion or guilt because they perceive themselves as being different from their families, their communities, and especially their peers? Or, what happens if they are dealing with life-changing experiences, such as a family crisis or tragedy? Would it make a difference if they could express their emotions in the form of art? All young people—including and, in particular, merging artists—have times when they wonder if there is anyone like them. They certainly question if any adult can really understand them. As teachers and parents, we know how important it is for young people to realize that they are not alone in their quest for achieving self-knowledge and finding their ways in the world. In addition, we know what a difference it makes when readers find a book that helps them understand who they are or leads to their knowing more about others.

Several years ago, there was a call for proposals for breakout sessions at the ALAN Workshop to explore the theme of identity and how the question "Who am I?" is answered by all kinds of students in all kinds of ways. We were talking about how important our involvement in music and theater was in our search for a sense of self and place and community. We thought about some of the young adult novels that we had read in which engagement with the arts of any sort helped the main characters stay grounded and find a voice. We compiled a large number of titles about this topic, put together a successful proposal, and, after making our presentation, thought that we had enough material to write an article. Life intervened, and about a year and a half later, we wrote a piece called "Portrait of the Artist as a Young Adult: Who Is the Real Me?" which we submitted to the *ALAN Review*. After the article was published, Patty Campbell approached us during the ALAN Workshop in 2011 and said, "You should do a book about that topic." Would we do it? We sat down over dinner, put together a proposal, and sent it to Patty—and a few short weeks later we had a contract and were on our way.

It has been an amazing experience. Our excitement about the topic and our interest in young adult artists continue to grow. Publishers, to whom we are incredibly grateful, have sent us book after book on the theme of the arts and identity, and the more titles we read, the more we come to realize how rich a topic it is. The amount, variety, and quality of books are impressive, and our annotated bibliography keeps growing. We have also been delighted to find that many of the authors of these books, in addition to being talented writers, are artists of another sort. We have come to know young adults who are painters, photographers, sculptors, actors, composers, vocalists, instrumentalists of all sorts, directors, choreographers, and dancers; some are blowers of glass and makers of origami figures; some paint umbrellas; some are graffiti artists. But regardless of their chosen form of expression, the young people in the titles that we explore in this book either identify themselves as artists or use the arts in intentional ways to help create a sense of self and find a voice through which they can tame the turmoil of their adolescent lives.

The title of this book plays on the title of James Joyce's *Portrait of the Artist as a Young Man*, first published in 1916, a prime example of a Künstlerroman, or artist novel, one that traces the intellectual and educational growth of an artist to maturity. Stephen Dedalus, Joyce's hero, wants to understand art and the beauty it expresses. Even as a young child, he has a love of language and a response to the way that words work, which sets him apart from his peers. At one point, upon hearing the lines of a hymn, "a tremor passed over his body. How sad and how beautiful! He wanted to cry quietly but not for himself: for the words, so beautiful and sad, like music."[1] As he becomes a young man, Stephen distances himself from his family, religion, and the politics of Ireland, in his quest for beauty. Words are his treasures; he crafts the line "A day of dappled seaborne clouds" (166), a line of beauty that gives him joy—and he comes to see that "the object of the artist is the creation of the beautiful." To sustain himself and pursue the beautiful, Stephen prepares to go into exile. His goal is "to discover the mode of life or of art whereby [his] spirit could express itself in unfettered freedom" (246). And yet, while he is prepared for a life of exile and isolation, he is committed to using his art in service to the larger community; he says, "[I want] to forge in the smithy of my soul the uncreated conscience of my race" (253).

The young adult novels that we include in this book are not true Künstlerromans; they do not trace the young people at their centers from childhood to maturity, and they are less philosophical than Joyce's classic text. But the writers of our books were themselves inspired by Stephen's quest, and they give their characters artistic gifts that make them stand outside the norms of teenage life and think about the world and their places in it, in ways different from those of their peers. They often have to make choices like Stephen's—choices that cause a distance between themselves and their families, communities, and friends. But they also find a sense of community and, thus, "self" through their art. The books that we discuss explore the ways that parents, teachers, and other significant adults can nurture the artist's development; the ways that artistic young people connect to friends and peers who do (or do not) share their artistic temperament and goals; and the ways in which the arts provide these young people a way to work toward catharsis and redemption when confronted with tragedy and loss.

We are grateful to the writers who responded to our request to talk with them about their artistic visions and why they choose to write books about young artists. Kim Culbertson is eloquent on this point. In her novel *Instructions for a Broken Heart*, Jessa, an aspiring actress, is dealing with a dramatic breakup as she and her ex-boyfriend are on a school trip to Rome. Jessa's teacher knows exactly the book that she needs to read, and he is willing to give her space to read about Joyce's Stephen and then talk with her about what Stephen learns and what Jessa can learn from him. Asked about her connection with *Portrait of the Artist as a Young Man*, Culbertson writes,

> One of my professors in college gave me that book to read. He, like Mr. Campbell, just knew that I needed to read about another young person struggling with the realization that she saw the world through an artistic lens. I remember after I had read it, had simply lost myself in it for a whole weekend, I took a walk with my professor and he and I had an incredible talk about the artistic temperament and how challenging it

can be sometimes in a world that isn't necessarily artistic, but that it's also such a gift. Interestingly, when I was teaching senior honors one year at a private school in Marin County, I had a young man going through a similar struggle and I gave him my copy of *Portrait* to read. I remember him walking into my classroom one rainy morning and saying, "I feel exactly like Stephen!" He, like I had, realized that not everyone, not even the majority of people, feel things in quite the way he did, in the way I do, and Stephen's epiphany really spoke to him in a similar way that it had spoken to me. I love that a book can be sort of "passed down" in this way.[2]

The idea that books can speak so profoundly to our young people lies at the heart of this book. We hope that through exploring these titles, teachers and parents—and others who care about young adults and who want to support them in their quest to be their truest, most honest selves—will have a resource to help them find just the right book at just the right time: the way that Mr. Campbell provides just the right book for Jessa when she needs it most.

Aaron Copland—one of the best-known and most loved composers of twentieth-century American music—wrote about his art, the meaning of music, and the creative and interpretative mind, in his 1952 book *Music and Imagination*. He understood the need to create, that self-expression is

> the basic need to make evident one's deepest feelings about life. . . . Each added work brings with it an element of self-discovery. I must create in order to know myself, and since self-knowledge is a never-ending search, each new work is only a part-answer to the question "Who am I?" and brings with it the need to go on to other and different part-answers. Because of this each artist's work is supremely important—at least to himself. . . . And just as the individual creator discovers himself through his creation, so the world at large knows itself through its artists, discovers the very nature of its Being through the creations of its artists.[3]

For Copland, music gave meaning to his existence. He found that he even felt a little sorry for those who found no meaning in music and art in general. He could not imagine his life without it. His wisdom reminds us how vital it is not only for young adult artists to realize they are not alone in their need to express and find meaning in their art but also for those who do not see themselves as artists to grow in their understanding of what it means to be artists.

Tom Leveen—actor, director, and writer of young adult novels, including *Zero*—advises young people to find like-minded friends and to stick together. He understands that many "creative types tend to keep their thoughts to themselves, especially at fourteen to seventeen." Readers of his books say, "Yes, yes, that's exactly what it's like!" His protagonist Zero describes what it is like to express emotion in the form of art. When she gets lost in a painting, she sees noise and tastes sound, and "all that matters is each stroke, each whisper-scratch of the stick."[4] Leveen advises all young people to find their passion and work on it:

> You do something—we all do something—that when we're doing it, we lose all track of time. Whatever that thing is—writing poetry, lyrics, or stories; gardening, cooking, reading, playing an instrument, singing, hiking, building, designing, knitting, talking, listening—that's your Thing. Go do it. Do not let anyone tell you that you can't. If you relentlessly pursue that Thing, no matter what your goals might be, you will find other doors opening and opportunities coming up that you never would have even thought of. I didn't know how much I would enjoy doing school visits or teaching writing classes or giving keynote addresses at conferences. Now, it's the best part of my job![5]

But he also has advice for the adults in the lives of these young people, especially about the value of pulling them into the arts. He recalls that he and most of his best friends,

> all of whom are upstanding, tax-paying, successful citizens and parents now, were on a dangerous road until two drama teachers got a hold of us and told us we mattered; who put us to work, worked us hard, and expected the best. Guess what? They got it. Now we're authors, bankers, teachers, master's degree earners, combat medic veterans. . . . Without teachers who invested and told us we could do anything, I shudder to think where we would've ended up.

Tom Leveen has important words for us to remember: "Do not ever doubt how much power your words have in the ears, hearts, and minds of adolescents."

Thus, we hope that our book adds to what a "portrait of the young adult as an artist" can be—that it will support us as caring adults to use the power of our words to help our young artists better understand themselves as well as help their peer group support their artistic needs and unique ways of being in the world.

NOTES

1. James Joyce, *Portrait of the Artist as a Young Man*, critical ed. (New York: Viking Press, 1968), 24. Hereafter cited as *Portrait*.

2. Kim Culbertson, interview via telephone and e-mail with Lois Stover, April 14, 2012, and June 13, 2012.

3. Aaron Copland, *Music and Imagination* (New York: Mentor Books, 1952), 51.

4. Tom Leveen, *Zero* (New York: Random House, 2012), 22.

5. Tom Leveen, interview via e-mail with Connie Zitlow, March 2013.

Acknowledgments

To all the artists, directors, musicians, and teachers of the arts in our lives who have inspired our appreciation of the value of the arts for understanding the self, the world, and others—especially to our grandchildren, who surprise us daily with their creativity and their delight in making art of all kinds.

With thanks to David and Erv for their support and belief, to Patty Campbell for offering us the incredible opportunity to work on this project, to the authors who so graciously shared with us their insights about the value of the arts and their reasons for writing about young adult artists, and the publishers who continue to send us wonderful books about young adult artists, as well as to the Faculty Development Committee and the Department of Educational Studies at St. Mary's College of Maryland for supporting the sabbatical that allowed the time that the project required and to Ohio Wesleyan University. We also thank Steve Bickmore, Jacqueline Bach, and Melanie Hundley for providing the "spark" in their call for manuscripts about identity issues that led us to write the article that subsequently grew into this book.

Chapter One

Identity and the Artist

DEFINING IDENTITY

What exactly is an "identity"? What does it mean to say that adolescents are exploring their identities, that their sense of self is in a state of flux, or that they try on identities the way they try on clothes? How does one go about constructing an individual and unique identity?

In methods classes for future secondary teachers, young adults interested in becoming part of the education profession must consider some key questions about identity, including "*Why* is this time so confusing, difficult, and chaotic?" Invariably, they say that the whole time frame—age thirteen through nineteen—is focused on trying to figure out the answer to the question "Who am I?" It is a time of moving away from parents and other responsible adults—who, up until this point, have made most of the major decisions for the young individuals—to leaning more on peers for a sense of what is important: one's values and how one looks, acts, and chooses to spend time.

Junior, from Sherman Alexie's *The Absolutely True Diary of a Part-Time Indian*, has lived his life on "the rez," where he has long wrestled with the constraints on his identity as a Spokane Indian. He wants more out of life than what he sees offered to his peers, so when the opportunity arises for him to leave his home to attend an all-white school in town, he takes it. But then he feels like a traitor to his heritage and his family. To anchor himself, Junior plays basketball—at which he is very good—and he draws cartoons. His words illustrate why he must draw:

> I draw all the time. / I draw cartoons of my mother and father; my sister and grandmother; my best friend, Rowdy; and everybody else on the rez. / I draw because words are too unpredictable. / I draw because words are too limited. / If you speak and write in English, or Spanish, or Chinese, or any other language, then only a certain percentage of human beings will get your meaning, / But when you draw a picture, everybody can understand it. . . . / So I draw because I want to talk to the world. And I want the world to pay attention to me. / I feel important with a pen in my hand. I feel like I might grow up to be somebody important. An artist. Maybe a famous artist. Maybe a rich artist. . . . / So I draw because I feel like it might be my only real chance to escape the reservation. / I think the world is a series of broken dams and floods, and my cartoons are tiny little lifeboats. [1]

ERIK ERIKSON AND IDENTITY FORMATION

For Junior, his art is a "lifeboat" as he navigates the treacherous waters of adolescence. According to psychologist Erik Erikson's theory of "psychosocial development," outlined in *Childhood and Society* (1963), the central question of adolescents is that of identity. In middle school, as the process of answering this question begins, younger adolescents frequently try on any number of "temporary identities," mostly through the process of changing their style of clothing or hair, as well as strongly identifying with a particular peer group. As they move through high school, older adolescents begin to take a more thoughtful approach to crafting their identities, as Junior is doing by leaving the safety of the reservation and trying to fit into a very different world. He uses his art to explore how he is feeling and to make sense of the confusion in his mind and heart, which arises as the different worlds collide, with their different expectations for who he is and should be. According to Erikson, if a young person fails to grapple with the identity issue or if he or she is not given enough freedom to do so, it will be harder for one to later form intimate relationships and then face the end of life with any clear sense of integrity. Because Junior has his art, he has a way to make the world "pay attention" to him. His art gives him a voice that is otherwise silenced.

The goal of this book is to explore how young adult literature can provide models for young adult readers who identify themselves as artists in their quest to answer the "Who am I?" question. A primary focus is showing how literature might help young artists recognize their niches in the world rather than hide their talents. There are multiple examples in young adult literature of young people who do not necessarily view themselves as artists but are guided to use the arts for cathartic purposes. Many young adult novels show the role of friends in the lives of artists and how adults respond to young artists' desires and achievements. The book concludes with an exploration of the interconnectedness of art and literature.

Building on Erikson

The heart of our argument is that adolescents who identify themselves as artists need to be given models through quality young adult literature about young adult artists. For dealing with Erikson's "identity versus role diffusion" stage of development, note that in recent years his theory has come under fire for several reasons. Dennis, Cole, and Zahn-Waxler (2002) write in "Self in Context: Autonomy and Relatedness" that the theory may not work across cultural boundaries, because some cultures tolerate less initiative in young adults. Kroger reports in *Identity Development: Adolescence through Adulthood* (2000) that young women often seem to need to move into Erikson's stage of intimacy versus isolation before, or as a part of, their identity exploration, and a number of researchers have found that identity does not solidify for many people as early as Erikson's theory would indicate. A character such as Kate, from Zibby Oneal's *In Summer Light*, illustrates such a variation. It is only when Kate falls in love with Ian that she finds the courage to use her artistic gifts and, in the process, solidify her sense of self.

Nevertheless, Erikson and those who have built on his theory clearly indicate the need for young adults to have a teacher who can empathize with them about the uncertainties of this difficult time, while providing the space they need and the security of clear boundaries. We therefore explore the role of a teacher such as Mr. Freeman, the art teacher in Laurie Halse Anderson's *Speak*, who gives Melinda the structure of art assignments, the safety of his classroom, and the encouragement that she needs to find her voice, literally, after she has been traumatized by date rape. In *You Don't Know Me*, by David Klass, John discovers the healing power of music because of the encouragement and support of his band teacher, Mr. Steenwilly. In *Leap*, by Jodi

Lundgren, Natalie gives voice to what so many young adults feel, when she thinks to herself,

> It sucks to be fifteen! . . . We have adult experiences, adult responsibilities, adult worries, but a kid's resources. We need support. We need role models. We need attention and love. . . . But most adults can't even take care of themselves. They just give little kids the illusion that they're in control. At fifteen you see through it and discover you're on your own.[2]

It is her dance teacher Petra who ultimately provides Natalie with the role model and structure she needs to not only find her way as a dancer but also come to terms with her family situation.

By reading young adult books, teachers too can learn about characters who identify as artists or learn about themselves, others, and their worlds by using the arts to explore their emotions and responses to their experiences. In early adolescence, James Marcia, in "Representational Thought in Ego Identity, Psychotherapy and Psychosocial Developmental Theory" (1999), theorizes that many younger teens experience "identity diffusion," a state characterized by what seems to be "haphazard experimentation" with different career plans, sets of friends, activities, and modes of dress. Primarily, this experimentation happens because young teens do not yet have the ability to think abstractly about the future, nor do they have the knowledge about their strengths, weaknesses, and preferences that is necessary to form an identity. During high school and while faced with pressure from adults who have authority in their lives, some young people move into "identity foreclosure," which is, according to Marcia, a state in which individuals adopt the positions of others in "deciding" particular career paths, college choices, ways of dress, sets of activities, or sets of beliefs and values because these are the choices of the parents, ministers, bosses, or admired older siblings.

Sara, from Stacia Ward Kehoe's *Audition*, is a character who in many ways exemplifies this state of identity foreclosure. As a child, Sara discovered her love for ballet, and she quickly became the prima donna of her small rural Vermont town. When her teacher decides that Sara should audition for a scholarship to one of the ballet companies near New York City, Sara agrees without thinking too much about it. Her parents, believing that Sara truly wants to make dance the center of her world, support her after she wins a spot at the Jersey Ballet and then moves south to live with one of the dance teachers and to work her way up through the ranks, to a position of traveling and performing with the junior company. Sara has accepted that she will be a dancer. But after a year in pursuit of dance—a year of many triumphs and much progress as a ballerina—Sara begins to realize that she may have other talents and that it is possible that she may want to change her dream. Sara *is* a dancer; she uses dance metaphors constantly in this novel in verse to explain her feelings, to describe what she is experiencing, but she is learning that she may be more than Sara the dancer.

Audition presents a picture of a young person in identity foreclosure, a person who uses dance and its language to move herself into the healthier state, according to Marcia (1999), "identity moratorium." In this state, the individual is able to say that he or she does not yet have enough information or experience to make an informed choice and is willing to live in limbo for a time while gathering more data. Sara is not about to give up on dance, but after being encouraged by an English teacher about her writing skill, after being exposed to a more rigorous curriculum than what she experienced in her small rural school, and after scoring high enough on the PSATs to be a National Merit finalist, Sara begins looking at colleges that have both dance programs and interesting liberal arts majors.

According to Marcia (1999), Erikson's "identity formation" will not occur until the individual has experienced a period of crises and decision making that lead to the ability to make an independent commitment to a particular path through life. In reading a book such as Emily Franklin's *The Other Half of Me*, young adults and teachers, too, gain insight into how movement through these states can work and how a young person can use his or her art in this exploratory process. Jenny feels herself to be the outsider in her family; she is a half sibling to the rest of the children, conceived by her mother through sperm donation before her mother met her father and had the other three. Her siblings and her parents are athletic and shine at sports; Jenny does not see the point of sports and is longing to find out more about her "other half," her biological father, in an effort to figure out where she belongs. She takes a painting class, and through the comments of her teacher, which lead her to some insights about herself, she is finally able to move beyond "foreclosure"—with an identity as the "outsider"—into "moratorium," accepting that she has a lot to learn before she makes any final decisions about what path to take through life.

Some researchers—such as Bettis and Adams in "Landscapes of Girlhood" (2005) or McLeod and Yates in *Making Modern Lives: Sub-*

jectivity, Schooling and Social Change (2006)—note that the movement into increased independence is a cause of uncertainty for young adults. As young people rebel and then take more responsibility for themselves and their actions and as the adults in their lives learn to deal with these changes, conflict can flare up.

If the adolescents have low self-esteem or if the responsible adults in their lives are overbearing, conflicts can intensify. For instance, in Maria Padian's *Jersey Tomatoes Are the Best*, Eva wins a place in a prestigious summer ballet academy that can lead to a position in a New York dance company. The pressure from her mother to do well is intense, and Eva finally succumbs to anorexia because her weight is one of the few things in her life that she feels she can control. As soon as she gets to camp, the voice in her head talks to her, particularly when she is in front of the "unforgiving mirror." "*I'm the biggest in the class. Tallest. Fattest. A giantess in a room full of pixies. You suck, and they stuck you in a class with girls two years younger.*"[3] In the end, Eva finds her way on the path toward recovery, though the path is clearly precarious. Her doctors finally decide to allow her to dance for an hour a day. She says it feels "amazing" because there is no mirror where she dances.

> I became obsessed with the reflection, with relying on the mirror to tell me whether I was doing it perfectly. And you know what? There's no mirror on the stage. There's no mirror during a performance. If you want to dance, *really* dance, you have to just cut loose and feel it. So the fact that there's no *barre* here? No mirror? No Madame DuPres? Just me and the music coming from some crummy CD player? It's been . . . pure. (340)

Self-Concept and Self-Esteem

According to Schunk, Pintrich, and Meece in *Motivation in Education: Theory, Research, and Application* (2008), "self-concept" has to do with how the individual describes his or her physical appearance and skill, cognitive and academic abilities, and social skills. Many adolescents have a difficult time being comfortable with themselves, particularly as they confront transitions and challenging situations. The sense of self-esteem drops during early adolescence as young people face challenges of puberty, changes in school, and a redefinition of their relationships with both family and peers. If a young person thinks that there is a wide discrepancy between the ideal self and the real self, then his or her self-concept suffers.

It is easy to imagine that if Lutie, from Caroline Cooney's *The Lost Songs*,[4] were to self-assess, she might think that she could be a better friend, but she knows that she is taking Doria under her wing. She is aware that she is a lot better at music, especially singing, than a lot of other kids and that she is doing OK in school. Lutie has a positive social self-concept, a decent academic self-concept, and a less positive physical self-concept but overall seems to feel all right about herself. When she faces some challenges to this sense of self as she learns about her mother, who ran away from the family, and as she reaches out to a childhood friend who is on the verge of exploding in ways that could land him in jail, Lutie has to rethink her identity. She has to build on her strengths to arrive at a positive resolution of the crisis facing her to retain her sense of self-esteem, or self-worth.

Lina, in Ruta Sepetys's powerful *Between Shades of Gray*, demonstrates the power of a positive sense of self, rooted in identifying herself as an artist in the face of challenges way beyond those that most young adults face. Lina's world is shattered when, in 1941, the Soviet secret police arrive at her family's home in the middle of the night, separate her father from them, and send Lina, her mother, and younger brother to a prison camp. The three ultimately find themselves north of the Arctic Circle, huddling with a ragtag group of fellow Lithuanians, Estonians, and Finns in a dirt hovel, fighting for the strength to survive just one more day.

It is art that gives Lina that strength. Throughout her harrowing experiences, including the death of her beloved mother and the news that her father, too, has perished, Lina draws. Before the arrival of the Soviet police, Lina had been preparing to attend art school. She uses that artistic talent not only to document what is happening to her family and peers but also to honor her family, anchor her convictions that a future is possible, and give herself the will to live. Based on the experiences of the author's family, Lina's story speaks to a part of history seldom taught or discussed, and Lina says that her art was intended "to create an absolute record, to speak in a world where our voices have been extinguished."[5] Her story does accomplish this goal. But even more powerfully, Lina shows just how important art is to her belief that she can and will hang on through what becomes twelve years of exile in horrendous conditions. She draws to maintain her sanity and her life. It is her sense of identity and self-worth as an artist that provide Lina with a lifeline to the future.

Individuals with high self-esteem feel good about themselves and feel that they are inherently worthy of others' positive regard. A number of researchers—such as Baumeister, Campbell, Krueger, and Vohs in "Exploding the Self-Esteem Myth" (2005)—have found that those with poor self-esteem in adolescence are more likely to face poor health, engage in criminal behavior, and have fewer economic options as adults. So it is important that teachers find ways to provide their students with realistic assessments of their strengths and performances. According to Choi, in "Self-Efficacy and Self-Concept as Predictors of College Students' Academic Performance" (2005), teachers need to provide opportunities for students to build their academic self-concept, which is related to academic achievement, and to create safe and supportive environments in which students can develop their talents and interact with peers. Thus, as teachers, we can all learn from Mr. Bates in *The Lost Songs.* The organ teacher who works with Doria and gives her advice about whether to graduate from high school a year early gives her goals for her playing, offers her advice about ethical issues, and while pushing her musically, generally reassures her about being who she is. He understands her, so when she tells him that she is not making any friends in her new school, he responds, "Some people aren't good at being kids. . . . It usually means they'll be good at being grown-ups. You are so grown up, Doria. I can certainly imagine a gulf between you and the other kids, because they're still children" (52).

SO WHAT?

In an issue of the *ALAN Review* focused on identity in adolescence, our article "Portrait of the Artist as a Young Adult: Who Is the Real Me?" begins,

> Because young people have concerns about their identities, it is important for those of us who work with adolescents to consider how young adult literature addresses its readers' search for self-knowledge. As part of our exploration, we have been interested in the issues faced by young people who are artists, wondering whether their art makes life more confusing and whether, in their search for self, it could be helpful to read about other artists. How might reading about young people who use art in crafting their identities help these students better negotiate their real worlds and find a place where they fit in?[6]

With more specificity, the rest of this book explores young adult literature about young people who identify themselves as artists and use the arts for purposes of self-exploration and catharsis. There are ideas that teachers can learn from their counterparts in young adult literature, and there are myriad examples of activities that English language arts teachers can employ to pull their artistically oriented students into the worlds of books, thus increasing their motivation to succeed and providing a scaffold for them to make sense of the texts they are reading. When teachers use such texts and teaching strategies, the world of the English classroom becomes a more hospitable one for all students and a place in which teachers can better achieve the goal of fostering appreciation for diverse points of view, diverse ways of being in the world, and diverse individuals with a multitude of strengths and interests.

NOTES

1. Sherman Alexie, *The Absolutely True Diary of a Part-Time Indian* (New York: Little, Brown, 2007), 5–6.
2. Jodi Lundgren, *Leap* (Toronto, ON: Second Story Press, 2011), 128.
3. Maria Padian, *Jersey Tomatoes Are the Best* (New York: Knopf, 2011), 87.
4. Caroline Cooney, *The Lost Songs* (New York: Delacorte Books for Young Readers, 2011).
5. Ruta Sepetys, *Between Shades of Gray* (New York: Philomel, 2011), 338.
6. Connie S. Zitlow and Lois T. Stover, "Portrait of the Artist as a Young Adult: Who Is the Real Me?," *ALAN Review* 38, no. 2 (2011): 32.

Chapter Two

Crafting an Identity as an Artist

How does involvement in an artistic field help young people who are artists deal with the confusion of adolescence? Are there ways in which self-identifying as an artist adds to their confusion? Is reading about other young people who are artists helpful? Does reading about characters who use art to create their senses of self help student artists navigate their real worlds as they search for ways to find answers to Erikson's question of "Who am I?"

In the Newbery Award winner *Out of the Dust*, by Karen Hesse, playing the piano is not only the lifeboat in which Billie Jo takes refuge from the painful aspects of her life in Oklahoma during the Dust Bowl and Depression. Playing the piano is also central to her sense of self. The windblown, barren landscape in which she lives is a metaphor for the barrenness of Billie Jo's life after her mother dies and her father retreats into himself. Making music gives her some sense of peace:

The music / springs straight out of me. / Right hand / playing notes sharp as / tongues, telling stories while the / smooth / buttery rhythms back me up / on the left. Folks sway in the / Palace aisles / grinning and stomping and / out of breath, and the rest, eyes shining, / fingers snapping, / feet tapping. It's the best / I've ever felt, playing hot piano, / sizzling with / Mad Dog, / swinging with the Black Mesa Boys, or on my own, / crazy, / pestering the keys. / That is / heaven.

January 1934[1]

Billie Jo uses her art to claim a place in the world. Her art allows her, at least for a while, to make order out of the chaos of her life and ultimately create a sense of self that is positive and strong.

Sibilance T. Spooner in *Midnight Hour Encores*, by Bruce Brooks, is a young person who identifies herself as an artist, a talented musician. At sixteen, "Sib" is a world-class cellist. She knows that her hard work has made her a musical prodigy. Because her mother abandoned her at birth, she sees herself as self-made—with a little help from her father, Taxi. She says, "I play the cello. I'm very good. If it means anything to you, the circle of international music critics puts me about third or fourth in the world right now."[2] With her father, Sib travels to California to take part in a competition and find her mother. As a result of her journey, she learns a great deal about who she is and what role her music plays in her identity.

Sib and Billie Jo have quite a different relationship to their music than do Cooper Redmond and his friends in *Beat the Band*, by Don Calame. Coop and company enjoy hanging out together, and they have fun messing around, playing guitar and drums. But they do not really practice. When the "Battle of the Bands" competition is announced and they decide to participate as a way of looking "cool," they are starting from the beginning. While they do get better and actually gain some fans for their antics, the comments from the audience have to do with their "big junk" performance, deemed as "interesting" and "having balls." For Sib and Billie Jo, being a musician is something central to how they interact with the world, as opposed to being something that they just do for fun or to pass the time, like Coop and his band.

BUT SO WHAT?

Why is it valuable for teachers to know the stories of Junior, Billie Jo, and Sib? Many teachers find that they can relate most easily to students who have interests similar to those that they themselves pursued as teenagers. Our backgrounds as members of musical ensembles and the casts of various theatrical productions help us when reaching out to students who act, sing, and play instruments in band and orchestra. Our interest in the topic of the young adult artist comes in part from our personal awareness of the importance of such activities.

But neither of us can draw anything more recognizable than a stick figure. While we enjoy visiting art museums and can identify our favorite painters, photographers, and sculptors, we do not have that same sense of what it is like to really *be* a visual artist. However, when we read about Kate in Zibby Oneal's *In Summer Light*, we can begin to have that deeper understanding because Kate is, first and foremost, a painter. Taking a hike along a rocky shoreline, Kate sees the craggy surface as a giant canvas and feels propelled to "paint," using the wet clay of the beach:

> She scooped up a handful of clay and made a first great swooping curve low down on the smooth surface. . . . She made a series of curves, scooping clay and sweeping it higher on the rock, using the palms of her hands and her fingers like brushes. . . . She scooped and painted, laying down great overlapping strokes, interlocking curves, spiraling patterns. She did a series of snail whorls that she remembered having seen on a Cretan vase. Then a sort of free-form octopus shape. Shapes and patterns came to her from pictures she'd looked at, from pottery she'd seen in glass cases in echoing museum rooms. . . . Her whole body became a brush. . . . She wanted to keep climbing, to keep painting, to go on and on painting her way into the layers of blue above her.[3]

We have never felt anything remotely like what Kate experiences, and yet because Oneal is able to give voice to the way that Kate paints from her soul, we now have a language to use in talking with our students who see the world as Kate does: as artists for whom the surfaces and images of the world invite exploration with paint and clay, chalk and charcoal, steel and stone.

INSIGHT FROM AUTHORS

Kim Culbertson is a fifteen-year veteran of teaching who is also an author of several young adult novels, including *Songs for a Teenage Nomad* and *Instructions for a Broken Heart*, both of which center on young adults who see themselves as artists and who use their engagement in the arts as a way to make sense of their life experiences. She says that she writes about young adults who identify themselves as artists for these reasons:

> Over the years, I've had people shy away from supporting their children in the arts because they'll "never make a living at it," but I think that's applying way too much emphasis on career path and financial outcome. I like to argue that in exploring our passion for things, in the actual act

of creation and love of something, we do, in fact, "make our living" because self-expression and the joy of an artistic process make one's life more enjoyable, more defined, more fully realized—no matter what we end up doing to pay the bills. [4]

Reading young adult literature centered on characters who use art of any sort to make meaning of their worlds, to "make a living" as Culbertson says, is a useful endeavor for artistic students, who can feel validated as they see themselves in the pages of such books. It is useful for teachers, who can step into another way of being in the world and thus better connect with artistically inclined students.

It is also useful for students who may scoff at their artistic peers as "weird" outsiders, for being driven by their artistic visions, because such books can help them bridge that gap between self and other that good literature so often accomplishes. The young adult artists in these novels often discuss the nature of art in ways that help those of us who are less artistically inclined better understand how to look at art and what it means to be an artist. For instance, Vanessa from Liz Gallagher's *The Opposite of Invisible*, describes "Fountain," by Marcel Duchamp, which she sees while on a school field trip. Vanessa is interested in breaking forms and says that she loves Duchamp for his "ready-mades" of which "Fountain," a urinal, is an example. Alice says, "I should be grossed out. But it's pretty cool in an ironic sort of way: the most basic everyday thing, which is also totally private, out there for everyone to see. To admire. Or at least think about."[5] Vanessa tells the other students the story of how Duchamp came to exhibit it. She says, "Totally scandalous. . . . Totally different. I adore it. . . . Because being different . . . means being interesting. And that will always be hot" (17).

In Jon Skovon's *Struts and Frets*, Sam knows that he is meant to be a musician, but he is finding it hard to deal with his band and with his mother's fear of what an artistic life means in terms of stability. But Sam's grandfather understands him, and as Gramps explains to Sam what artists do, he helps Sam's readers better appreciate this internal drive that the artist feels and must honor. He tells Sam about one night when, as a jazz pianist, he had the chance to sit in on a gig with Chet Baker, a jazz horn player and vocalist, on a night that he felt like he "touched the moon."

Sam asks why it has to be so hard, and Gramps says, "Because that's an artist's job, Sam. To take this steaming shit pile called life and transform it into something beautiful."[6] Gramps continues, advising Sam, "You have to risk everything. . . . Do all the things that scare you, learn from them, and then translate them into something for the world" (163). Gramps says that the world will probably not appreciate the gift but "[you] can't help yourself."

Another author's insight underscores the point about the value of this literature for validating young people who "can't help" themselves, who *have* to make art. Rosanne Parry is a violinist whose book *Second Fiddle* is the story of three girls whose music is the basis of their friendship. One reader not only saw herself in Parry's story but came to better understand herself after reading the book. In recalling a conversation with this reader, Parry makes an important point about the value of books in which young adults are artists:

> I had a conversation with a reader recently who said that Jody in *Second Fiddle* had inspired her to practice her piano every day instead of fighting with her mom about it and practicing only two or three times a week. She'd been playing piano all her life, and although she loved music, she wasn't sure the piano was the right instrument for her. Her mom had chosen piano for her many years before and she was feeling a little stifled in her musical routine. We had a nice chat about how a musician finds her voice and style of music. She felt like she was ready to make her own decisions about what she wanted from her music, and the book helped her have that conversation with her mom. I *love* that about books. I think the conversation that happens in a family because of the book is far more important than anything that is actually in the book.[7]

It is clear that there is tremendous value in such literature and multiple reasons for teachers and librarians to know these books and help young people find them. In the following pages, we explore in detail novels in which the main characters' relationships to their art is a core element of their identities.

THEATER

My Most Excellent Year: A Novel of Love, Mary Poppins, and Fenway Park

Young men who find joy being onstage often face peer pressure from those who view them as not being "manly" enough to enjoy sports. Having books in the classroom and the library about young adult males who are involved in positive ways with drama is an important way to provide them with role models of how to navigate the world. Young women, too, who delight in being part of theatrical productions and prefer taking drama courses to AP calculus can be helped to face parental objections to their choices. Thus, a book such as Steve Kluger's *My Most Excellent Year: A Novel of Love, Mary Poppins, and Fenway Park* is an important addition to a teacher's classroom library.

There are three young adult voices in Kluger's story. TC is a star baseball and soccer player who has fallen for the new girl at school and who, as a result, takes a risk and becomes involved in a talent show. The talent show is directed by Augie, TC's best friend, who also plays soccer but has been a huge fan of musical theater since he could walk—and who also finds himself falling for another guy, somewhat to his surprise, even though TC and his parents have long wondered when he would discover that he is gay. The surprise big star of the talent show is Ale, the object of TC's affection. Ale, short for Alejandra, is daughter of the former U.S. ambassador to Mexico, but she does not want to enter the family business of politics; she, too, has dreamed about dancing and singing but has hidden this aspect of who she is from her parents, who she fears will be disappointed and dismissive.

Ale feels that she has "become a disappointment"[8] to every one of her relatives because of her inability to hobnob with ambassadors and diplomats. Thus, she resolves to compensate by getting straight As in honors classes, winning creative-writing contests, and keeping her mouth shut so that when she has to join the diplomatic corps, she will have the credentials to do so. *But*, two things happen to her that turn those plans upside down. First, before the start of this novel, she got the flu and could not eat. Her bodyguard Clint bought her the DVD of *Damn Yankees* to take her mind off her stomach. Ale tells us, "Until I recovered enough to return to class, I was glued to the television screen watching Gwen Verdon dance a tango and a mambo again and again until I could match her step for step" (12). Then her father took the whole family to see *Fosse*, "where for two and a half hours, the most beautiful men and women imaginable used their bodies to create sheer magic. By the time the curtain had come down, my eyes were wet and I was absolutely certain I knew what I wanted to do with the rest of my life" (13).

She feels like an outsider at school as well as at home; it is only in the dance studio that she feels that she can be herself. In the journal that she is keeping for her English teacher, Ale writes to Jacqueline Kennedy, telling her that when she dances, she

> can't imagine anything half so intoxicating, especially when Mrs. Salabes shows us a four-part combination—including an arabesque—and I'm the only one who gets it right. . . . Did you know that your body can say more with eight bars of music than you could possibly write in a fifteen-page essay? (65)

Ale is smart. She does earn all A's in honors classes, but it is dancing that gives her that sense of self that she can find through no other activity, and it is through her developing friendship with Augie and her budding romance with TC that she finds the courage to let her family know who she really is.

Augie befriends Ale, who is one of the first people to ever truly get all the references that he makes to musicals as a way to express his thoughts and feelings. Augie uses phrases such as "my mood was right out of Sondheim" or song titles such as "We Need a Little Christmas" to describe how he is feeling. Augie and Ale are cast in the school's production of *Kiss Me Kate*. Augie says of himself—as he is playing Bill, a straight guy scoundrel who tends to gamble—"the kids are so used to my Katharine Hepburn, they never knew what kind of range I had before" (240). But his penchant for musical theater creates a problem for him with his boyfriend Andy. When Augie tells people that in his last life, he was the Andrews Sisters, Andy gets intimidated. That is enough for Augie to cut things off with him, feeling as though he cannot change himself to be with someone and telling his friends that Andy just does not get him. Andy has not been as comfortable in his own skin as Augie has been in his, which is why the two break up; but as Andy gains confidence in himself and misses Augie in his life, he asks if they can get back together. When Augie relents and tells Andy that they can get back together, Augie says, "If I'm in the mood to be Pat Suzuki in *Flower Drum Song* for five minutes and you even *think* of blushing, it may be the last thing you ever do" (312).

Augie is lucky in that his parents have always supported him in his choice of activities and that they accepted him as gay before he even recognized this aspect of himself. It is with this acceptance and support from his parents and TC—who is a strong, likeable, handsome straight guy—that Augie is eventually able to figure out his true calling. Augie is on his way, and the reader feels that he will receive Tony nominations for best director before he is thirty.

Ale's parents come to realize that it is useful to have a daughter on the stage when they are circulating among the diplomatic elite, and, even more important, they come to recognize that she is a natural, with a big bluesy voice that is part Merman and part Minnelli, with kicks to match anything that Fred Astaire or Gene Kelly could produce. So, somewhat reluctant but ultimately with true love, they applaud her as a performer. Ale, too, will garner her share of Tony Awards. Both these young people have the courage to be themselves and to live their dreams, in spite of some external pressures to pursue other options; thus, they are strong role models for those young adults who identify themselves as actors and actresses and who use the roles they play to continue gaining insight into who they are and how to deal with all that life throws at them.

In some way, though, it is TC who is the character of real value for those students who have some talent onstage but probably not enough to make it in the harsh world of the theater. TC has grown up with Augie's references to musicals and accepts his friend's penchant for breaking into song or citing Broadway. But TC has not had much desire to be onstage himself, although he has a developing interest in politics and social justice issues. So he decides to perform in the talent show to get Ale's attention. She admires JFK, so he decides to present Kennedy's famous inaugural speech from 1961 about a new generation of Americans. To prepare, TC watches the speech over and over and practices taking breaths when JFK does, moving his hands when JFK does, and punching the words exactly the same way. When he performs, he is sensational.

While TC has given this performance to show Ale that he is serious about politics, about social action, and about her, he is invigorated by the experience of being onstage, of moving an audience, an experience that gives him insight into the passions of both Augie and Ale. TC is a terrific foil to Augie and Ale because he has been onstage; he understands what it takes to do well in the spotlight and so is a better audience member, a better friend—and a good role model for young males who might be interested in testing out the waters as an actor just to have a new experience.

DANCE

Leap

Natalie in *Leap*, by Jodi Lundgren, is fifteen and is at the end of her junior year of high school in Victoria, Canada. She has been part of an elite dance team run by an ogre of a teacher, Ms. Kelly, who has an old-fashioned sense of jazz, hates modern dance, and runs ballet classes like a dictator. While Natalie's identity has been wrapped up in being a member of the team, in being a dancer, she has begun to contrast her body to those of her peers who seem to be Ms. Kelly's favorites, and she has started to feel concern that her stockier, less lithe build is not well suited to the elegant ballet moves and sexually charged jazz moves that Ms. Kelly uses in her choreography. Natalie is happy that she will be with her friends for their summer intensive workshop with Ms. Kelly, but she is not as excited about the prospect as she has been in past years.

But things change for Natalie when, on the first day of summer class, Ms. Kelly introduces the dance team to a former student, Petra, who is now a professional dancer with the Vancouver Ballet. Ms. Kelly has invited Petra to choreograph a piece for the team's senior showing. Petra is different from Kelly right from her entrance to the studio. She begins class in the center of the room, something that has never happened in the collective memory of the girls, who always start, under Ms. Kelly, with exercises at the barre. Natalie is entranced. As the class progresses, she is led to question not only the ballet and jazz conventions that are so much a part of her but also the teacher–student relationship against which she has felt herself straining over the past year.

Petra introduces the class to modern dance. She tells them to let the impulse to move come from within, to pick one body part and let it "lead." She understands that as advanced dancers with years of study in set moves and sequences of motion, their bodies might feel programmed to move in a certain way, but she asks them to think about what their limbs might say if they broke out of their traditional moves of pliés or jazz isolations, if the dancers released their limbs "from the grooves of habit."[9]

Natalie finds herself stuck in routine, as Petra predicted might happen, until the teacher gives more cues: "Improvisation will help you to develop a new dimension to your dancing. . . . You, as dancers, will [be] co-creators" (51). Petra ends by making eye contact with each girl and thanking her. Ms. Kelly asks Natalie if she enjoyed herself, and Natalie says that the class was OK—actually, though, she's "soaring" inside. The next day, while doing ports de bras, Natalie tries to apply what she has learned from Petra. She lets her torso loosen, her fingertips sweep the floor, then she rises fluidly, in one motion, her arms stretched above her head to frame it, then she arches backward, her shoulders wide and her chest open. Ms. Kelly gives her a weird look; a senior girl tells her she looked beautiful, and Natalie is hooked.

The more Natalie studies with Petra, the more confined she feels by Ms. Kelly's approach to dance, which she decides makes her feel like a sex object. During performance, Natalie lets herself get swallowed by the music in new ways, which scare her:

> When I crossed the stage alone, I staggered, disoriented, searching the ceiling. Loneliness welled to the surface and sapped my strength. . . . I was rooted to the spot. . . . This wasn't choreographed. I was wrecking the dance. I lagged behind the music until, with a panicked surge of effort, I propelled myself to the other side. (75–76)

Natalie, heart pounding, goes on to describe how the crowd responds; at first, audience members make no sound but finally rouse themselves to applaud because "this wasn't the packaged entertainment they were used to. It was art" (77).

Natalie still does not quite realize how good she was. She is apologizing to Petra about her crossing, when Petra says that she made the audience feel her struggle: "Do you know how hard that is? Most professional dancers never get there. It's one thing to be pleasing to look at; it's another thing to move the audience. You moved us!" (77). Lance Irving—another professional dancer and choreographer and a friend of Petra—attends the show. When he sees Natalie, he tells her that he is moving to Victoria and hopes to offer dance classes; he asks if she would consider working with him.

Natalie gets invited by Petra to fill in for a dancer who has twisted an ankle just as Petra is teaching the company the dance for a choreography festival. She welcomes Natalie into the company of professional dancers and, with encouraging words, helps her make the transition into being part of the group. When she is not rehearsing, Natalie takes Lance up on his invitation to take a Martha Graham–based technique class, and Natalie feels herself blossoming as she learns this new approach.

Lance tells the class that his goal is "to teach you to dance from your emotional center. I want to make you feel safe enough to express what's in your hearts. With passion and accuracy" (128). Natalie finds the whole experience spiritual. He tells her that she has great potential—but she doubts herself. Lance emphasizes, "Let everything you're feeling spill into the dance. Even the doubts and fears. If you try to shut down your emotions, you'll look dry and academic. . . . But if you welcome them in, you'll be convincing" (128).

Lundgren provides an amazing description of Petra rehearsing a dance, in which she goes from being shut in darkness to dancing with a beam of light, almost as a partner, while Natalie is surreptitiously watching. Natalie's response to Petra teaches the reader what a dance well performed should ask of the audience. In response to Petra's ability to demonstrate naked vulnerability, Natalie "wanted to wrap her in my arms and hug her; I wanted to join hands and skip with her; I wanted to fight my way into the technicians' booth and learn how to shine the light she longed for and deserved. By the time it was over, I'd been on a journey" (142). After watching Petra, Natalie realizes that Ms. Kelly's view of dance is a mechanical, stilted one, designed to make the performers sexual objects or eye candy. Petra's solo stirs Natalie emotionally, and this is what she now wants from dance.

When Lundgren has Natalie describe how she feels during the professional performance, readers come to understand how the dancer moves individually and as part of the company:

> Eye contact and synchronized breath joined us into a larger organism. We gave weight and received it; we lifted each other. . . . As we spoke in our own directions, I felt the thrill of near-collision. These women commanded the space. (146)

Natalie struggles to keep up with their power. She continues,

> I was surrounded by darkness, stripped of support, forced to rely on myself. . . . Safety came only from solitude. But solitude brought pain. I filled that solo with so much emotion that I almost lost control. (146)

The dance at this point is a metaphor for Natalie's life—her feeling of distance from friends and family. The reader understands not only how Natalie feels but how being onstage, being a dancer, and letting the dance itself call to her deepest emotions helps her come to terms with those feelings and find release from them in constructive ways. As she begins to settle into her new identity as a modern dancer, she is able to settle into new relationships and gain perspective on herself, her abilities, and her future.

PHOTOGRAPHY

Exposed

Liz Grayson identifies herself as a photographer. She is sharp, focused, and confident in what she sees through her camera lens: "Nobody needs to tell Elizabeth Grayson, Photogirl, to focus."[10] Her story— from Kimberly Marcus's 2011 debut novel, *Exposed*—is powerfully told in first-person free verse. When Liz graduates from high school, she hopes to go to the Parsons School of Design. She is the first to get to photography class and eager to enter the darkroom with her chosen negative, a picture that she took of her best friend, Kate, "Mistress of Modern Dance." In the picture, Kate is doing a perfect, soaring split in the Dance Express studio, which has been Kate's second home since she was four. Liz is certain that Kate was born to be a famous dancer and that the two of them will be forever best friends.

Kate is such a good friend that she even understands when Liz is in "PMS," described by Liz as her

> "Preparing My Shot" mood, / where everything goes quiet / and I turn in
> on myself, camera poised, / waiting for the perfect moment / to click.
> (10)

Liz recalls becoming a photographer when, for her twelfth birthday, her beloved brother gave her a camera. Liz describes Mike as a track star, a partier, and a bit of a chauvinist pig. After Mike leaves for college, he comes home, smelling like stale beer, just to do his laundry: faded jeans and smelly running gear.

Liz works for her dad, "Captain Robert Grayson, King of the Ferry, Noble Seaman of Nantucket Sound" (7). His nickname for his daughter, "Lizzie-Lou," shows his affection for her. After her Saturday shift, she likes to stay on the island, take pictures, and then catch a later ferry home. Liz tells Mrs. Pratt, the photography teacher, about her plans for putting together a portfolio:

> I'm thinking of focusing / part of my portfolio / on Vineyard portraits, /
> Not of day-trippers or rich summer folks / but off-season shots / of
> what-you-see-is-what-you-get / year-round islanders. (38)

When Mrs. Pratt looks closely at the completed portfolio, she picks up "a perfect shot" and says, "Liz, you can go places" (50).

Liz's dad shouts his response to the great news from Mrs. Pratt over the blare of the ferry horn: "WAHOO! That's my girl!" (6). But Liz cannot tell Kate the wonderful news because Kate is avoiding her, and Liz does not know the reason why. Liz wonders if it could be a result of the fight they had at their last Saturday-night slumber, which has always been a once-a-month tradition with just the two of them. When Kate tells Liz that she still loves to dance but does not want to do it professionally, Liz responds with what they always fight about: "You're just scared you can't make it, but you can" (14).

Kate says,

> Just because I don't want to dance professional, / just because my plan
> for my life isn't *your* plan for my life— / that doesn't mean I'm afraid to
> take a chance. (17)

Liz's response is that she would never let *anything* get in the way of her taking pictures. When Kate jabs her with the words "That's because you can hide behind your camera" (18), Liz leaves Kate downstairs and goes upstairs to her bedroom to sleep.

The next morning Kate is gone, and Mike comes out of the laundry room with stale beer on his breath, saying he got home late after a party. Liz tries to call Kate—no answer or message—but is told that Kate went home at dawn feeling sick. All week Kate pretends not to see Liz but spends time with their other friends. Liz thinks,

> She's not returning my calls, / She's making plans without me, / She's
> pretending she doesn't see me / when I pass her in the hall. / I've been
> consumed with her. . . . / And except for a few times / every few
> minutes, / I hardly think about Kate / at all. (61)

A friend declares that she knows why Kate will not talk to Liz: "Callie told Dee that Mike told Tanner that he and Kate were doing the wild thing at your house last weekend while you were asleep" (62). At school the rumors fly, and Liz tries to be the firefighter, "putting out tiny rumors before they have time to grow and spread" (71). When she finally catches Kate at the bottom of the stairwell, Kate is silent a long time and then tells her why what happened was such a big deal, but Liz has trouble accepting Kate's version of things. Liz says,

> My brother is a track star. / My brother is a partier. / My brother is a bit of a chauvinist pig. / My brother, even when he annoys me, / is someone I love. . . . / My brother / is not / a rapist. (76)

Mike says it was sex; Kate says he held a pillow over her head. Who is telling the truth?

When Mike is arrested, their parents are devastated and want Liz to convince Kate to take it all back. For Liz, "nothing is steady / except for the feeling / of my camera in my hand" (116). What would she do without something to cling to, her camera, and the support of Mrs. Pratt? When thinking about Mrs. Pratt's assignment to create a self-portrait, showing her point of view, Kate wonders if she is "Photogirl" or "Sister of a Rapist" (156). She blames herself for leaving Kate alone in the living room that night and wonders if she will ever feel the PMS mood again. Her father stops her as she slams her camera against a wooden pylon at the beach.

Sitting in the courtroom, Liz realizes that she no longer sees things in crisp black-and-white contrasts anymore but rather recognizes that "some things come in shades of gray" (237). Mike is found not guilty. He thinks that he did nothing wrong, but Liz is not sure. After her acceptance letter from the Parson School of Design comes, he calls and congratulates her. Liz does not know how to be a sister to him anymore, but she thinks maybe someday they will sit across from each other in a therapist's office and try to find a way to be okay. Liz is pleased to learn that Kate is going to Cornell with plans to major in history and minor in dance, but she does not hear the news from Kate. On Memorial Day at the beach when she finally sees Kate, Liz approaches her, gripping her camera like a lifeboat, and tells her that she is sorry about that trial. Kate tells her that she is sorry that Mike was not convicted but not sorry that she testified. Liz realizes that this girl, who she thought would never take a risk, took one.

In this carefully written story with a painful but genuine conclusion, author Kimberly Marcus gives readers much to think about, including the role of art in a young person's life. Readers of *Exposed* know that Liz sees life in terms of her art, photography, which is to her what dance is for Natalie in *Leap*. In these beautifully written and powerful stories, the young adults' identities are inseparable from their art.

MUSIC

Second Fiddle

The same anchoring of self in art occurs for the musicians of the historical fiction novel *Second Fiddle*, by Rosanne Parry. It is May 22, 1990, in West Berlin, seven months after the Berlin wall has come down, and the border between friend and enemy is not clear. Three young eighth-grade girls, who identify themselves as musicians, begin the day like every other Tuesday afternoon. Jody Field, the narrator, is taking the S-Bahn with her musician friends Giselle Johnson and Vivian Anderson to their music lesson in downtown West Berlin. The three are students in the American School on the army base at Zehlendorf and have studied music with Herr Müller since they were ten. Their story shows the power of music for young people who live with the challenges of army life.

Music is so important to Jody that when she is on the train, she usually takes out her music notebook and works on songs she is composing. It has taken her three months to finish her "Canon for Three Friends," but she is not satisfied with the cello part. She has felt close to Giselle and Vivian when they play a piece of music, especially a hard one that they have really worked on. Yet they are strangers to her because they spend time together only when playing music.

Although her parents do not really understand the importance of music in her life, Jody has clung to music as a way to feel stable and rooted. When her family is set to move back to the States, she wants to be sure that they pick a house where there is a high school nearby with an orchestra. Her father has promised her that they will put orchestra on the list of criteria for picking a place to live, but he has jokingly said that her little brother Tyler wants to move somewhere with dinosaurs, so Jody has competition. Her response says much about how she sees herself: "Great. Second fiddle again."[11]

When the novel opens, the girls have only five days left before the big Solo and Ensemble Contest in Paris. Together they have been working on their competition piece, Pachelbel's Canon, since Christmas. It will be the last time that the three of them perform as a trio, because in less than a month the army will move Giselle and Jody back to the States. The trip to Paris is Jody's way to keep from thinking about saying good-bye to Giselle and Vivian—one last trip for just the three of them. Being in Berlin, where she has been in the same school for three years, has been the longest that Jody has been stationed anywhere in her whole life. She has known Giselle and Vivian longer than she has known anyone, except for her little brothers. As the girls travel on the train, they talk about what they want to see and do while they are in Paris.

Herr Müller is to be their chaperone, but when they arrive for their lesson, he tells them that he cannot take them to the Solo and Ensemble Contest in Paris, because he needs to have surgery. What will they do? Their parents had agreed to let them go only if Herr Müller would be with them. None of their parents can go because of an important military ball. The girls decide that they cannot think clearly without ice cream and head to a new shop on the other side of the Brandenburg Gate. Surrounding the oasis of the Gelato Mario, with its red tables and sparkling clean windows, are drab empty storefronts, shuttered buildings, and street peddlers with trays of communist souvenirs, which they are trying to sell illegally. Except for the peddlers, the street is almost empty.

As the girls are eating their ice cream, they witness the attempted murder of a soldier. Two men in uniform jump out of an army jeep and shout angrily in a language that is not English or German. They drag a third man along the iron grating beside a railroad bridge, hit him in the head, and heave his severely beaten body off the bridge to drown in the river. The girls see the men's red stars and realize that they are two Russian officers, who then quickly drive away.

The girls decide that they must rescue the injured soldier. After they pull him out of the water, Jody uses what she learned in CPR class, and he slowly starts to breathe. They learn that his name is Arvo and that he loves to sing. He tells them that he is not Russian but was forced to serve in the Soviet Army as a translator:

> Estonia is my home. I am alone in the Soviet Army. I am the only one from Estonia in Berlin, and they hate me for it. They spit in my food. They steal my letters to my family and the money I send to them. They never speak to me but to curse. . . . It has always been so for Soviet soldiers who are not Russian. (67)

For days, the girls scheme to go back to East Berlin, where they take food, medicine, and warm clothes to Arvo as he hides under a bridge.

They all ignore the danger, but Jody is particularly determined: "I wanted to save Arvo from those men who tried to kill him. I wanted him to be free. I wanted to play music with my friends, and I wanted to go to Paris, not for a family vacation but just for me" (87). The girls decide that the only way they can get to Paris is to have Arvo pose as Herr Müller.

They successfully make it to Paris with Arvo, who has told them that he can find other Estonians hiding there. They notice strange-looking men in black turtlenecks and wonder if they are being followed, but their focus is on the music contest. Before it is their turn to perform, another group plays the same piece by Pachelbel that they had prepared. When it is their turn to play, it is announced that the Berlin American trio has made a change and will play the debut performance of "Canon for Three Friends," by Jody Field. As Jody describes the piece, it is clear that she uses the language of music to make sense of her emotions and her world:

> The piece began shy and quiet, because that was how our friendship began when I was ten and even more shy than I am now, and also because when I started writing the song, I wasn't at all sure I could finish. The beginning was not my favorite part of the piece; . . . at least it was easy to play and followed all the rules of a canon. . . . Then came the main theme. We played it together with no harmony part because I wanted it to be like the first time we really listened to each other and the sounds we made as a group. In the third part we had a musical argument. Vivi played the theme in double time, and then I played it at the regular tempo but with ornamentation, and then Giselle plucked out the theme on her cello and looked at us like we were so lame for arguing. I couldn't help smiling, because she really got what I was trying to say in the music. The last part was lots of long, strong cello notes: Giselle walking away from us in her long strides after our fight. Vivi and I played runs of scurrying notes, and now Vivi was smiling, because it was like us running to catch up with Giselle. In the very end we each took a turn playing the theme. Giselle's variation was very forte and strong to fit her take-charge personality, and Vivi's was dreamier, a thinking girls' variation. Mine was the bridge, like always. A little bit like Vivi's, a little bit like Giselle's. (116)

After their performance, Jody realizes that she has never felt closer to Giselle and Vivian than at that moment. One judge gives Jody her business card, suggesting that Jody apply for a scholarship to her school because they are always looking for musicians who can compose. The judge tells Jody that it is a competent, balanced piece. A British judge asks to see the composition because he wonders if it is a copy of some little-known piece. Jody reluctantly gives him her notebook.

The girls do not even hear the judges' results, because they realize that Jody's wallet, with all their money, has been stolen. They rush out to look for Arvo but cannot find him. They wonder how they will eat, where they will sleep, and how they will get back to Berlin. They realize that the French police seem to appear wherever they are, but they are not aware that their adventure has prompted the involvement of the KGB, police forces from four countries, and the Supreme Allied Commander. Their twenty-four-hour escape comes to an end when they are found and taken to the American Embassy, where they are greeted by their worried parents

Rosanne Parry has created in Jody a young woman who knows that she is in love with music and who has found two best friends, a singing soldier, and a competition judge who have all told her that she has talent. As the story comes to a close, it is clear that being a musician is central to Jody's sense of self and that no matter where her family ends up, she will always be a musician.

VISUAL ART

Irises

What music is to Jody, painting is to Mary in Francisco X. Stork's *Irises*. She wants only to stay home and paint. Mary does not think that her father and her sister Kate, who is bound for college to study medicine, take her art seriously, but she knows that her mother admires her talent. Mama proudly saves Mary's drawings and paintings to show Papa when he comes home and has even framed Mary's picture of an eagle to be on Papa's desk. Painting is simply something that Mary does without thinking, and people are amazed at her work. Art is as important to Mary as becoming a doctor is to Kate.

Mary and Kate live in El Paso with their loving, happy mother and their solemn father, who is a preacher. In the prologue to the story, Mary is painting a portrait of Kate, who does not want to sit still much longer. Their mother reveals that to get her to sit for a portrait, she promised to take Kate on a special trip before she starts high school. They will go visit Aunt Julia in San Jose, California, where Kate's mother grew up. But as a result of an automobile accident that occurs after they are back in El Paso, their mother is in a vegetative state, basically lost to the family. Their life becomes very different. After the accident, Papa seems to change his attitude toward Mary's art. She knows that he thinks that people who paint are weak and unable to survive in the harsh world, and he is afraid for her. Mary realizes that the act of painting has become a duty rather than a joy. Yet she continues to paint because her sense of loss is less when she is painting.

Their mother lies with unfocused eyes barely open. One day as Papa sits in the shade and talks with Kate, he tells her that he is worried about the state of her soul, her faith:

> After your mother . . . entered her current condition, after the accident, I tried to get you to be self-sufficient. I have endeavored to make you strong. I wanted to fortify your heart against sorrow. I believe I succeeded, but I might have been overzealous. [12]

He tells Kate that maybe he should have been more lenient, but he wants the girls to be able to take care of themselves. He wants to be sure that Kate, as the older of the two sisters, knows that if something ever happens to him, she will have to put family first. When Papa walks in the house, Mary notices him shuffle toward the bedroom with trembling legs.

Mary hopes to go to an art exhibit that afternoon, but she is left to stay home and take care of her mother while Kate goes to her boyfriend Simon's to study for an important test. Mary is disappointed about missing the exhibit but decides that she will work on her painting. To learn more about Van Gogh's techniques, Mary has been copying as many of his paintings as she can, but she has been struggling with his *Irises* for a long time. When she goes to check on her mother, lying on one of two single beds, she sees her father resting on the other bed. She realizes that he is dead, and she calls Kate to come home.

Kate recalls that just three hours before, she and her father were in the backyard, and she had barely listened to him. "She felt a wave of tears in her chest ready to explode" (13). The tears come as she wonders if she has misinterpreted his love. At the same time, she tries to order her thoughts: "*Now you are free,* they said to her. *You can leave El Paso. You can go to Stanford*" (14). But if Kate leaves, how will it affect Mary and her desire to have time to paint? When the nurse cannot be there, what will they do? Kate is determined to continue her studies, still volunteer at the hospital on Saturday, and work at the restaurant owned by Simon's father.

After the funeral, Mary goes to Papa's studio to look for the framed drawing of an eagle and other pictures that she had given him. Deep down she wants to believe that he valued her painting. When she realizes that he has thrown them all away, she feels a terrible and dark loneliness. The following morning, Kate tells Mary that she will have to come home after school to help Aunt Julia care for their mother. Mary will have to give up spending time in the art studio, and she is devastated.

Years before, Mr. Gomez—Mary's freshman art teacher—had told Papa that Mary has an extraordinary gift. Mr. Gomez had convinced him to let her stay after school. Now this week is to be Mary's last time to spend an extra hour in the studio. She wonders why she is still pretending she wants to paint:

> Why didn't she just admit that she had stopped *liking* to paint since Mama's accident? It was a show she had been putting on. A show for whose benefit? What was the point of creating colorful forms when Papa didn't want them, when Mama would never see them? Papa was right to throw away all her paintings when Mama became ill. What did painting irises have to do with the sadness of the world? (50)

Yet she is not looking forward to saying good-bye to Mr. Gomez. When she thanks Mr. Gomez, he tells her that he has learned more from her than she from him. He tells her that her gift is a "way of seeing and feeling that he has never encountered in a young artist before," that her "painting is so much more than knowing" (80–81).

When Mary learns that Kate has been accepted to Stanford and given a full scholarship, she tries to be happy. Kate finally tells her about her promise to Mama, who had dreamed of going to Stanford herself when she was in high school. It had become both their dreams. Anger is not an emotion that Mary is used to feeling, but she realizes that it creeps up more frequently when she thinks about Kate going off to Stanford and leaving her alone with Mama.

Everything seems to be changing. Aunt Julia tells Mary that she has breast cancer and needs to go back to California. What will they do when she leaves? The church council and deacons want Kate and Mary to move out of the parsonage so they can keep the new preacher, Reverend Soto, who is already considering an offer for a different position. Kate realizes that she is attracted to him. Yet she responds with anger when he suggests that there are decisions that she needs to make, because her mother is no longer alive, she is "just a body that breathes" (137). Kate is aware that these are words that she has wanted to say all along, but "the thought that she wants to let Mama go for her own convenience sticks in her head like a painful splinter she cannot remove" (156). Papa had thought that ending Mother's vegetative life was a sin. Kate thinks that her father hid underneath church doctrine and God's will as his way of keeping her mother alive, because the accident was his fault. He had gone through a yellow light, thinking that he could make it, but he did not.

One day when Kate sees streaks of rose and vermilion in the sky, she thinks about how Mary would like those colors. She is filled with love and pride as she thinks about her little sister, whose gift to create beauty is as important as Kate's powerful desire to be a doctor, something that she has not always honored. How painful it must be now for Mary to be without seeing the light in things and people, that joy in painting that came from Mama. Because she knows that Mary will never leave Mama, not even in a skilled nursing facility, Kate finally decides to see a lawyer to find out what steps need to be taken to end her mother's life support. She has been repeating to herself, "*It's what's best for Mary, so she can see the light, so her own light will shine*" (246). It is very difficult for Kate to suggest to Mary that they let Mama go, but Mary finally realizes that, even in the hospital, there had been no light in Mama.

The narrative takes up again a year later. Mary is living in San Jose with Aunt Julia, who has responded well to treatment. Kate visits often from Stanford, and they talk about how they miss Mama and Papa. It is the anniversary of their mother's death, and they are finally at peace. Mary is grateful that Kate had waited and given her time to get to that place. Mary looks at the painting that she is doing of a lemon tree behind Aunt Julia's house. She gazes at the tree and waits. Then she sees a soft light shine among the leaves. And she paints.

There is much to think about in this complex and thoughtful story; yet, throughout the book, the focus is on Mary's extraordinary gift and what her art means to her. Her identity is that of an artist. She responds to everything through her art, her ability to see the light in what she is painting, and how she feels about the results of what she creates.

THE GIFTED AND TALENTED YOUNG ARTIST

What makes the young people described in these novels different from their peers is that being an artist is central to their identities, and they have a skill, knowledge, and commitment to their art that set them apart. As Sib, from *Midnight Hour Encores*, shows, true artists understand themselves as artists: "I'm not modest at all if you mean by modest that I deny my talent. I am a great cello player" (205). Sib and the other young people described in this chapter fit Renzulli and Reis's (2003) definition of giftedness as having three components, including above-average general ability, a high level of creativity, and the level of motivation and commitment to their chosen discipline that is necessary to be successful. The No Child Left Behind Act of 2002 also discusses giftedness as including high-achievement capability in a creative or artistic endeavor by those who need "services or activities not ordinarily provided by the school in order to fully develop those capabilities."[13]

Young adult characters who are artists talk about needing to engage in their chosen artistic form almost as much as they need to breathe. In *A Time for Dancing,* by Davida Willis Hurwin, Jules (Julianna) is actually dying of cancer, undiagnosed until it has reached stage 4. Jules pushes herself to be a part of the spring showcase, saying,

> Never in my life have I worked as hard. Each count of eight seemed endless, every part of each step harder than the last. The audience was hungry and sucking every last bit of effort out of me. They didn't think I could do it. No one thought I could. . . . It wasn't important. I was dancing for myself because . . . I couldn't *not* dance.[14]

Benjamin Bloom's (1982) study of gifted individuals revealed that they engage in focused and intense practice; they take suggestions from teachers and coaches whom they admire as experts and work hard at mastery.

In *Bunheads*, by Sophie Flack, Hannah, the main character, questions whether she has the commitment that ballet demands. She appears to be successful; at nineteen, she has earned a place as a member of the corps de ballet for a prestigious New York company. But she ultimately decides to leave the field because she is not sure she wants this life. Dancer, painter, actor, or classical/jazz/rock musician—it does not matter: the true artist—and the young adult character who identifies as artist—cannot imagine life without the art. They crave those moments when they find "the zone," that suspension of time when they become one with their artistic creation. When Eva, a ballerina from *Jersey Tomatoes Are the Best*, is in a lesson, she loses track of time, loses track of everything except the particular movement she is rehearsing. She is in what she knows that her friend Henry, a gifted athlete, calls "the zone," where her heart quiets and her shoulders loosen:

> Then, at *grand battement*, it happens. . . . Each time my foot goes a little higher, the joints relax a little more, and on the third *grand battement a la seconde* I feel completely loose, I see my foot soar above my head, the leg scissors down, straight, and I realize: it is the best, most perfect *grand battement* I have ever done. I feel this . . . rush . . . of elation. . . . Something lovely, beautiful, created just for me. Only for an instant, then it's gone. But this is why I dance.[15]

Young artists understand that life may be difficult for them financially and emotionally. Sammy, from *Struts and Frets*, talks to the leader of one of his favorite indie bands who happens to work days behind the counter of a coffee shop:

> See, you don't do it to become rich and famous. If that's what you want, go do something else, because for every one band that makes enough money off their music to live—and we're not talking a lot of money, just enough to live . . . there's ninety-nine that have to work crappy day jobs just so they can pay the rent. This is something you do because you love music and you gotta get it out there. (206)

It is a fact that these young people who identify as artists spend hours with paintbrush or camera in hand; it is the fact that they spend hours at the dance studio or in front of the music stand that makes the adults in their lives take notice and provide the special expertise and other opportunities necessary to nurture their gifts. Because gifted and talented young people can often feel themselves to be outsiders as a result of their single-mindedness and sense of purpose, it is important that they have opportunities to be with others who share this focus. Thus, Natalie needs Petra; Jody needs Giselle and Vivian; Augie, Ale, and TC need one another. And gifted and talented artistic students need these characters in their lives so that, if they feel themselves to be alone in the music practice room or onstage, they have models of ways to navigate their journey toward self and evidence that their hard work can pay big dividends.

Involvement in the arts can help us all be more attentive to the world around us, more in touch with our own and others' emotional landscapes, and more aesthetically oriented.

NOTES

1. Karen Hesse, *Out of the Dust* (New York: Scholastic, 1997), 13–14.

2. Bruce Brooks, *Midnight Hour Encores* (New York: HarperCollins, 1998), 16.

3. Zibby Oneal, *In Summer Light* (New York: Viking, 1985), 91–92.

4. Kim Culbertson, interview via telephone and e-mail with Lois Stover, April 14, 2012, and June 13, 2012.

5. Liz Gallagher, *The Opposite of Invisible* (New York: Wendy Lamb Books, 2008), 16.

6. Jon Skovon, *Struts and Frets* (New York: Amulet Books, 2009), 162.

7. Rosanne Parry, interview via e-mail with Connie Zitlow, April 22, 2012.

8. Steve Kluger, *My Most Excellent Year: A Novel of Love, Mary Poppins, and Fenway Park* (New York: Dial, 2008), 12.

9. Jodi Lundgren, *Leap* (Toronto, ON: Second Story Press, 2011), 51.

10. Kimberly Marcus, *Exposed* (New York: Random House, 2011), 1.

11. Rosanne Parry, *Second Fiddle* (New York: Random House, 2011), 56.

12. Francisco Stork, *Irises* (New York: Scholastic, 2011), 3.

13. Anita Woolfolk, *Educational Psychology*, 12th ed. (Upper Saddle River, NJ: Pearson, 2013), 156.

14. Davida Willis Hurwin, *A Time for Dancing* (New York: Puffin, 1997), 228.

15. Maria Padian, *Jersey Tomatoes Are the Best* (New York: Knopf, 2011), 88–89.

Chapter Three

The Arts and Loss

The arts are powerful vehicles for exploring traumatic events large and small, for making some order out of the chaos—both the physical and the emotional—left in the wake of violence, death, destruction, or loss. Thus, it is important for teachers to understand the key role of making available to their students books that portray young adults who engage in artistic expression as a way of dealing with traumatic circumstances. Having an opportunity to read such books is particularly relevant when a student has lost a parent, sibling, or friend. Reading about such characters can be cathartic—and can help a reader better empathize, as a result, with individuals who are facing the trauma of losing a loved one.

According to Belifiore (1992), *catharsis* is a term first used by Aristotle in his *Poetics*. As he applied the concept to the dramatic arts, catharsis is an "emotional cleansing" experienced by a character in the play as well as by the audience, in vicariously living the character's experiences of strong emotion, such as sorrow or fear, and then having those feelings better understood and released, freeing the character and the audience to return to a more balanced emotional state. Strickland reports in the 2000 *Gale Encyclopedia of Psychology* that in the nineteenth century, Josef Breuer (a colleague of Sigmund Freud) used the term *cathartic* in describing his use of hypnosis for patients who were suffering from hysteria and could recall traumatic experiences, express the emotions that they had repressed, and then feel an emotional release, leading to relief from their symptoms. Freud and modern psychoanalysts use the term to describe the concept of exploring profound emotions from the individual's past, helping the patient fully experience and then express those emotions in ways that allow for release.

Caitlin in Kathryn Erskine's Newbery Award winner *Mockingbird* poses the question that young people ask when they are dealing with loss: "Do you know how to get to the state of experiencing an emotional conclusion to a difficult life event?"[1] Caitlin's mother died of cancer, and her brother was killed during a school shooting at his middle school. Caitlin wants to find a way to reach some kind of closure—she wants relief from all the sorrow that has overshadowed her life and that of her grieving father. Many of the characters in the novels discussed here want the same thing—relief and closure—and they use their involvement in the arts to accomplish this important task. In some situations, the searching for closure can involve the need for redemption on the part of young people who feel some guilt, warranted or not, for the tragedies and losses they are facing. Following these selected stories about catharsis are books where protagonists find no relief for their sorrow until they can be redeemed for the guilt they feel.

THE ARTS, YOUNG ADULTS, AND CATHARSIS

In young adult literature, there are myriad examples of characters who use various art forms to foster catharsis and healing in themselves and others, as well as order their worlds. These characters are not necessarily artists in the same way as some of the young people described in earlier chapters. Although some of them have the capacity to become artists, they do not, at least initially, see themselves as painters or photographers or dancers; instead, what is important is that they find self-expression through the arts at crucial times in their lives, when they need to deal with difficult emotional situations. On their way to catharsis, these young people use their art to move through Kübler-Ross's five stages of grief (Kübler-Ross and Kessler, 2007). Although the stages of grief are not always experienced in a lockstep process that is the same for everyone, her ideas are informative when reading stories about what young people experience after a traumatic loss. Often, when stories begin, protagonists are in denial about some traumatic event (stage 1). Through their art, they confront their anger (stage 2); they might bargain with themselves or with others (stage 3); they express their depression (stage 4) and finally come out on the other side of their grief, accepting what has happened to them and ready to move forward with their lives (stage 5).

DEATH OF A PARENT

Sister of Glass

For instance, in Stephanie Hemphill's historical novel in verse, *Sisters of Glass*, Maria Barovier is the daughter of a master glassblower on the island of Murano, part of current-day Venice. After her father dies, she is forced to become a "lady" and entertain possible suitors as a way to bring more money into the family coffers. She is dealing with the loss of her father and the loss of her youth, and she says,

> Comfort comes only one way— / When I start at the second fornica / And imagine myself inside its warmth, / Then pick up my chalk. / My sketchbook fills with pictures, / Like a carafe overfilling with water, / Like a garden blooming boatloads / Of flowers.[2]

Later, as Maria comes to term with what she thinks will be her destiny, she does so by deciding that she will use her art to "find less horror" in traveling across the sea to become part of a new family. She says, "I will focus and not speak / out of turn, just capture the scene / for my canvas / and show it all, one day soon / to my dear gaffer" (101). The gaffer is a friend who works in the glassblowing furnace. As so often is the case in the process of acceptance, once Maria agrees to her fate, she becomes free to tell her older sister exactly how she feels about the impending marriage. This breakthrough pushes the two young women to work together to find loopholes within their father's will and the betrothal papers that allow Giovanna to take Maria's place in Venice at the hand of the senator. Maria can stay behind at the family home, helping in the fornica, supplying the gaffer (who becomes her husband) with perfect batches of glassmaking material, and using her sketching skills to add enameling to his glass.

Pieces of Georgia

In Jen Bryant's *Pieces of Georgia*, another novel in verse, Georgia, like Maria, is struggling with her feelings. She has been sad and lonely since her mother, an artist, died. She knows that her parents met at the Savannah College of Art and design, but her daddy turns away from her and does not say much when he sees her holding her sketchbook. Georgia is an introvert who takes solace in solitary activities, such as walking the dog, caring for horses, or writing in her journal, so silence is the norm in her very small family.

Shortly after Georgia's thirteenth birthday, an anonymous writer sends her a letter that includes the gift of free admission to the Brandy-wine River Museum in Chadds Ford, Pennsylvania. As she learns more about the work on display there and the artists who created it—the Wyeth family of artists—Georgia is pushed to see the world in new ways and try different techniques for her drawing. For instance, Georgia thinks that she knows what a portrait is, but then she sees Jamie Wyeth's portrait of his wife, Phyllis, "and all that's in the picture / is a straight-backed chair, some kind of wild, red-berried plant / and a broad-brimmed hat."[3] She is, at first, confused, but then she thinks,

> Maybe Jamie wanted you to / *imagine* what his wife was like, / and those were his hints. So I pictured her— / thin and blond and a bit serious (the chair), but also little / wild inside (the red-berried plant), but kind of elegant, too (the hat). / It was a neat idea, painting someone without the person / being there. (58)

Thus, when Georgia attempts to do a portrait of her father, she sketches his work boots and tool belt, "leaning against each other near the door, like two old friends" (97), and she adds a magnolia tree to represent his Georgia roots. In the end, Georgia is really pleased with her results.

Then her art teacher, Miss Benedetto, shows the class paintings by Georgia O'Keefe. Young Georgia assumed that her parents named her for the state where she was born, but when she looks at O'Keefe's works, she remembers her mother's sketches and wonders,

> If maybe you named me Georgia / for the artist who painted flowers and bones / so that you see them fresh, / like they are secret worlds you can lose yourself inside / if the real one gets too bad. (15)

Georgia's teacher convinces her to apply for a special program for gifted artists, and Georgia is torn. She really wants the experiences that the program will provide, especially field trips and time to talk with others who are serious about their art, but she knows that her father will be upset. But her longing to immerse herself in her art wins out; she finds a way to slip the permission form under her father's pen as he is signing other school paperwork. When she learns that she has won a spot in the program, she finally confesses what she has done. At that point, her dad says that she must think he is "one mean s.o.b." (159), and she says no, just sad, which she never wants to make worse. Then, he shows her that *he* was the anonymous person who gave her the museum pass. Georgia does not know what to say, but she describes how

> Daddy put his arm around me and hugged me, / And I buried my nose in his scruffy old robe, / And for the first time since the day you died, / We both had a good, hard cry. (159)

At the art show, Georgia's dad talks a long time with her art teacher, learning more about his daughter's talents. Georgia tells him how she tried to learn as much as possible about drawing from looking at the work of the three Wyeths, whose paintings are the center of the Brandywine River Museum collection. On the way home, they stop at a convenience store to get something special for breakfast the next morning, and Georgia's father gives her a dozen red roses with a card saying, "Georgia—I am so proud. Love, Daddy" (161). This lyrical novel by Bryant is an excellent example of how art helps a young person face the physical loss of her mother and the emotional loss of her father and find catharsis for herself and her dad.

A Little Wanting Song

In *A Little Wanting Song*, by Australian Cath Crowley, Charlie—short for Charlotte—deals with circumstances that resemble Georgia's in many ways. When Charlie was seven, her mother was hit by a truck while she was crossing the street. Charlie carries her mom around with her, talking to her, feeling as though she is getting advice from her. So, at sixteen, she is not really all that sad any longer about the lack of her mom's physical presence in her life. What does make her sad is that she feels abandoned by her father, a gifted chef, who has wrapped himself in his grief over the loss of his wife. He seldom communicates with Charlie, seldom laughs. When her father's mother dies, Charlie's beloved grandmother, he retreats even further into his own world—a world in which he drinks a fair amount to keep the pain at bay.

Over Christmas break during the first summer after her grandmother has died (the novel is set in Australia), Charlie and her dad visit Charlie's grandfather, who runs a general store in the small town where Charlie's dad and mom grew up. As Charlie helps her grandfather around the store, it is clear that her presence is helping him to move beyond his grief and out of the lethargy that he has experienced since the funeral of his wife, which makes Charlie see even more clearly how distant her own father is. Charlie has coped for years with her loneliness by playing her guitar and writing songs that express her longing for connection. During vacation, she begins to make friends with some local teenagers, including a young man to whom she is attracted. The novel is actually told through the dual voices of Charlie and Rose, who longs to leave the town and hopes that, if she can get into Charlie's good graces, she might be able to stay with her. She wants to attend a special school focused on science in the city where Charlie and her father live. Charlie describes her moods in musical terms, as in feeling "E-flat. Low and hollow. Soft and sad."[4] In those moments, she composes songs, like the one for which the book is titled:

> It's just a little wanting song / It won't go on for all that long / Just long enough to say / How much I'm wishing for / Just a little more. (47)

Through her music, Charlie gradually makes connections with Rose and Dave and moves from "E-flat" to something brighter, to a "cello" mood—a "song played late at night by wishful fingers." When the novel ends, Charlie says,

> I like how I never had the call before / To use the word "adore" before / But now I do. / I got a little piece of what I want with you. (257)

Charlie and her father connect through a song that she writes for him, and they finally talk about her mother's death and slowly begin to push away the silence in which they have lived for so long. By the end of the novel, it becomes clear that Charlie may be able to become a professional musician because she has a great deal of talent. But what is even more clear is that Charlie would not have survived her mother's loss, the subsequent loss of her father, and the ups and downs of the summer without channeling her emotions into her music.

Shizuko's Daughter

Yuki, in Kyoki Mori's lyrical novel *Shizuko's Daughter*, has also lost her mother but to suicide in the wake of a dismal marriage, which leaves the twelve-year-old bereft. Suicide is considered taboo in Japan, where Mori's novel is set, so the silence surrounding Shizuko's act is deafening. Only a year after her death, Yuki's father marries again. He is distant with his daughter, while her stepmother, with whom her father had an eight-year-long affair, is openly antagonistic to the young girl. Mori follows Yuki through seven painful years during which Yuki works toward catharsis by painting pictures of happier times. She recalls how she and her mother enjoyed the beauty of nature, the colorful flowers in her mother's garden, and the collection of beautiful pottery. By the time Yuki is in college, she has fought her way to a sense of fragile peace and independence. She turns her beautiful memories into art and comes to terms with her mother's death. Her art has served her well on this journey toward understanding, and it is a way that she can connect with those few people she gradually comes to trust.

* * *

In Allen Zadoff's *My Life, the Theater, and Other Tragedies* and Maria Boyd's *Will*, high school students Adam and Will, respectively, have lost their fathers rather than their mothers. Following the deaths, they have withdrawn inside themselves. Their mothers feel as though these young people have lost their senses of self, which is true. Will and Adam have encased their hearts, trying to protect themselves from any more pain, but in doing so, they have distanced themselves from their peers and their remaining family members.

Will

After the death of his father, Will, in Boyd's *Will*, describes himself as wrapping his emotions in bubble wrap. He keeps himself distant from his mother and begins getting into trouble at school as he engages in antics designed to make his mates laugh so that he does not have to talk to them about his loss. As a result of his escapades, Will is told that either he will take the role of the assistant to the musical director, retired Brother Pat, playing his guitar and working with the younger students or he will not be returning to school. When Will hears his sentence, he thinks,

> Years of cultivating my ranking at St. Andrews instantly shattered. The school musical was always on the fringes of geeksville, but to be involved with the band was the lowest. At least when you were acting in the musical you got to hang out with the girls. The band was full of losers. [5]

Will's first day with the cast and crew of the play challenges his stereo-
types:

> It seemed like everyone had traded in their egos and were actually
> getting worked up about being involved. It had the same feel as when
> the boys and I were just about to go onto the soccer field. You weren't
> thinking about yourself, you were thinking about how you were going
> to win the game and annihilate the opposition. (92)

As rehearsals continue, Will starts to feel "smack bang a part of it"
(166) in a way that he had not before. He thinks about how the geeks,
his term for the band guys, can be annoying and how the chorus girls
giggle, but he also becomes aware of how hard everyone's been working. He realizes, "It was like we had all been through a really painful,
exhausting, superlong training session and now we were getting ready
for the semis" (167). So he starts to think about the fact that a lot of
creative people do not get to do anything with their gifts, because they
are told that it is not a real job, because they are perceived as a "dropout
or wanker" (167) if they even try, and because if they make it, they are
perceived as being full of themselves.

It is partly music that breaks the bubble that Will has wrapped
around himself for protection from those emotions. It is also partly the
experience of the opening night and its attendant celebrations that affect him. When the curtain closes on the production, he knows, "There
was no way anyone could not be lifted and carried around by the buzz
in the room," and he can feel himself being "carried away with everyone else" (227). Because of this experience, Will wants to make things
right with everyone that he has crossed over the past few months,
including Mark, the male lead, who was known as a gifted footballer
(soccer in America) and who turns out to be gay. Will also wants to
make amends to Elizabeth, the female lead, who turns out to be smart
as well as talented, and to his best friend, Chris, whom he has long
judged to be totally stable, an emotional rock, but who reveals that he
too has been torn up by the loss of Will's dad. It is after the play has
ended and most of the participants are celebrating with friends and
family that Will, watching his mother stand by herself, realizes that *she*
needs to talk about his dad. So, he begins a long-overdue conversation,
during which he is touched to hear her say that what he has accomplished, especially in motivating the younger boys, makes her see his
dad in him. Through this musical theater experience, Will and his

mother achieve a kind of catharsis that lets the reader know that they will be OK.

My Life, the Theater, and Other Tragedies

Unlike Will, Adam from Zadoff's *My Life, the Theater, and Other Tragedies* has definitely chosen to be part of the theater group. Sixteen-year-old Adam has been struggling with an increasingly paralyzing fear of the dark that he has felt since losing his artist father, a painter, two years earlier. He has taken refuge in being a member of the tech crew for his high school's theatrical productions, and he has discovered that he has a knack for lighting—both the design and the technical work involved in making such a design come to life.

Adam loves being on the catwalk, "surrounded by lighting instruments and cable, watching the actors get a tour of the set down below."[6] Although the actors do not know the names of the kids on the crew and they say dismissively, "He's just a techie," the techies say it "with pride" (7). Adam thinks about his lights with fondness, musing about the instruments he is about to hang:

> I think about the type of light each one throws. The soft fuzz of the Fresnel, the tight focus of the Leko, the bright wash of the PARcan. Then there are the gels—translucent colored sheets placed in front of the lights to change the color of the beam. I love setting up lights. Cold metal in the air is all potential, like stepping outside right before dawn when you know the world is about to change. (11)

As a techie, he is not supposed to think about light in general; he is supposed to think about *a* light, the one he is operating. Adam, however, is a designer, enough so that he recognizes errors on the part of the student who has been allowed to do the set and light design for *A Midsummer Night's Dream*, the current show.

When Derek, the student designer, has his father buy the theater a new spotlight and it arrives, Adam sees it and immediately wants to run it. But Derek wants his girlfriend of the day to operate it. Adam is worried because Mindy is not trained and has no skill. His crew members tell him to let it go, that Derek set this all up himself. But Adam, on further reflection, realizes that it is not actually the spotlight he cares about; in reality, he cares about the show. Disaster strikes, though, because the spotlight, operated inexpertly by Mindy, burns right into the eyes of the actress playing Helena as she is delivering a speech, and she tumbles offstage, breaking her leg. Of course, Mindy is not accused of causing the problem, and Adam finds himself ostracized even more than usual by the actors, who think that he is trying to kill them.

But Adam has an unusual opportunity to break out of his shell when he is alone on the catwalk, after rehearsal breaks up, finally getting a chance to see what the spotlight can do. A girl named Summer, on whom Adam has developed a crush, is still in the theater; she is one of the fairies but is going to audition for the role of Helena. They have their first conversation through the light. She calls out, asking if anyone is still there. He wiggles the spotlight to show his presence, and she steps into the light:

> Startled, I move the light off her, about two feet away to the side. She puts her hands on her hips like she's pissed. Then she hops to the side, landing in the center of the light again. I laugh. . . . I move the light away from her again. She slides to the right, keeping up with me. I move it forward and she moves forward, then I move it back and she moves back. Almost like we're dancing. Dancing with the light. (91–92)

The moves with the light break the ice, and they begin to have a conversation. They agree to practice together.

As Summer runs Helena's lines, Adam uses the spot to create the mood that the lines suggest. He thinks about his father and one of his dad's paintings, of a woman reclining at night:

> It's a large expanse of white and yellow with the barest hint of a woman lying off to one side, her skin nearly the same tone as the rest of the painting. It's like a pun on the idea of night, because instead of seeing nothing because of the dark, you see nothing because of the light. I imagine what it would be like to go home and tell Dad about this girl, tell him how I thought about his painting when I was looking at her. (95)

Summer inspires Adam as he watches her rehearse. He imagines her delivering her lines to him instead of the guy playing Demetrius. Then the actor puts his arms around her, and that brings Adam back to reality, knowing that he will never actually get the girl; instead, it is his job to make sure that she is lit properly:

> So that's what I do. I pull the lever to slide a gel into the spot. Not just any gel. The amber one. The special color I chose. A subtle rose hue

blooms on Summer's cheeks. Now she is even more beautiful in Wesley's arms. (96)

Derek, the student designer, is outraged by the change—but Mr. Apple, the teacher in charge, says that he likes it, and Derek takes credit for the change, which Adam does not contradict.

Summer asks Adam why he loves tech. He loves the collaborating on a team, doing the hard work: "The way every situation is a riddle you have to solve, and you can't just solve it any old way, because in tech, the simplest solutions are usually the best. So you have to be kind of ingenious about it. And then there's light" (200–201). He goes on to talk to Summer about illusion and the way that he can create it with light, how he loves taking the audience "to another place. They go because they want to. And because the techies made them believe it. We constructed it" (201).

However, Derek has the nerve to add additional lighting equipment at the last minute, thereby overwhelming the transformer so that on opening night, when the lights are supposed to go up on the play, the transformer blows, leaving the whole theater in darkness. In that darkness, Adam connects with the spirit of his father, finding a way to light the actors with a trick that he learned from his dad, who once took him into the woods, cut open glow sticks, and shook them onto trees, using them "like paint, transforming the dark woods into a green speckled abstract" (243). Adam quickly hands out the glow sticks that he carries with him to ward off the dark and finds headlamps, flashlights, candles, and lanterns. The actors get into the concept of an improvisation, and the play goes forward.

In the end, Mr. Apple, who has a breakdown and abdicates responsibility for the show, supports Adam's vision of how to make the show go on. Mr. Apple has the inspiration to have Puck blow out all the candles lit for the final scene, and he makes sure that Adam is in the audience to see this ending and the change of meaning it creates. When the last candle goes out and darkness falls, Adam's fear—the fear of the dark that has been affecting him for so long—does not descend with it for the first time since his father's death. Instead, through his involvement with the play, through his ability to create a vision and carry it out, and through coming to understand his father better because of his experiments with light, Adam achieves the catharsis that helps the reader realize that, like Georgia or Yuki or Will, he too will be OK.

GRIEF AND THE NEED FOR REDEMPTION

Dealing with the death of a loved one is especially difficult for young people when the identity search is overshadowed by the need for redemption. Atonement involves being delivered from guilt and bondage, somehow finding a way to make amends for mistakes or to forgive wrongs committed by others. This need for redemption is particularly strong when individuals feel as though they are responsible for an event that resulted in the loss of a loved one. Young people who are still finding out who they are and what their place is in the world are filled with guilt and rage when they feel that there is no escape from their sorrow and no way to atone for what they did. How can they repair a wrong that led to a tragedy that they think they might have prevented? How can they escape the desperation that threatens to destroy their lives and possibly those of others in their families? Their lives seem to be on hold as they wonder if there is a way out of their confusion and doubt, especially if those closest to them do not even seem to know who they really are or what they are experiencing. Because of the emotional deprivation that they experience, they feel alone, desperate, and helpless.

Out of the Dust

Billie Jo in Karen Hesse's *Out of the Dust*—a diary-like story written in strong first-person free verse—is an example of a young person who feels lost and alone, certainly in need of redemption. She struggles to learn how to forgive her family, nature, and, most of all, herself for the dire circumstances of her life. She and her parents, who live in Oklahoma in 1934, deal with dust everywhere. Her best friend has moved away, gone west to get out of the dust that has settled in the wake of long-term drought. Coupled with poor agricultural practice, these conditions eventually decimate one hundred million acres of prairie land, primarily in Texas, Oklahoma, New Mexico, Kansas, and Colorado, which leads to a large migration of individuals to other states, where conditions are little better because America was in the grip of the Great Depression.

Billie Jo finds some relief in playing the piano. Tragedy strikes when an accident results in her mother's death, and Billie Jo feels responsible. She wonders how there can be any redemption, any way to atone. Billie Jo's father had put a pail of kerosene in the kitchen, and her ma thought that it was filled with water when she put it on the stove. She had originally run from the resulting flames but then decided to turn back, to put out the fire, when she was suddenly engulfed in a column of flames, as the pail of burning kerosene that Billie Jo was heaving from the house hit her. Overwhelmed by his guilt and sorrow, Billie Jo's father runs from the house and goes into town, leaving Billie Jo with her pregnant mother, who lies dying from her burns. Billie Jo tries to give her water to drink but cannot even squeeze the cloth because of the blisters and pain that she has sustained in her own hands, in trying to get rid of the burning oil.

For many months after they bury Billie Jo's mother and unborn son, Billie Jo cannot even look at a piano, especially not the one that was her ma's. She wonders if there is any way to escape the dust, the loss, the grief when she cannot even play her beloved piano with her stiff, scarred, deformed hands. After several months, she can sit at the school piano and make her hands work in spite of the pain and stiffness. She practices until her arms throb. "It's the playing I want most, the proving I can still do it."[7] When she finally plays in a competition, at the packed Palace Theatre, she drops right inside the music and does not feel anything till after the clapping starts. She earns third prize, ignores the pain running up and down her arms, and feels like she is part of something grand.

This event is the catalyst for Billie Jo to begin to move beyond her pain and sorrow. She forgives her father for having the pail of kerosene in the house and herself for the rest. He even has the piano cleaned and tuned. Through her involvement in her art form, Billie Jo reaches the catharsis that leads her to a feeling of redemption so that, in spite of their difficult circumstances, she and her father will be able to live with themselves and with each other.

MOVING BEYOND CATHARSIS TO REDEMPTION

As Billie Jo's story shows, catharsis is often not enough; redemption must follow for the young person to move forward on his or her life's path. Losing a parent in any way can be devastating, and as Billie Jo illustrates, it is even harder when the adolescent feels responsible. But in some ways, it is even harder for a young person to lose a beloved sibling, especially if the one still alive feels guilty for what led to the death, which seems to be a common plotline and thematic focus in several powerful young adult novels featuring young artists. One learns fairly early in life to expect that parents will predecease their children, but when a sibling dies, the natural order of things is upset, and the sibling left behind is faced with the fact of mortality. That grief is intensified if the young person believes, rightly or wrongly, that he or she contributed to this tragedy. Thus, it is important for parents and teachers to know about and share stories of young people who use the arts to stay connected with their siblings and find redemption in the wake of tragedy. Without working through both their grief and their guilt, these individuals will not have an opportunity to experience happy adult lives.

In stories about young people searching for answers after a life-changing event, the arts can be redemptive for young adults who are talented musicians, painters, or photographers. These young people find some relief when they are practicing a piece on the piano or guitar, working on a drawing, changing the colors in a painting, using a camera lens to record what is too painful to watch with the naked eye, or finding the right materials to finish a sculpture. The arts then have a crucial role in helping young people rebound as they find a way out of their guilt and confusion, escape their loneliness, take steps toward their atonement, and finally feel as if there is redemption.

Adios, Nirvana

In *Adios, Nirvana*, by Conrad Wesselhoeft, Jonathan loses his sibling, his twin brother, Telemachus, at the end of their sophomore year. Now, during his junior year, he is losing his grip on reality, in part because he believes that he is responsible for Telly's death. Jonathan had been sick with a nasty cold and asked Telly to get him some medicine; on his way to the store on his skateboard, Telly was hit by a truck and fatally wounded.

As the novel opens (after Telly's death), it is a snowy night in Seattle, and Jonathan lets his hands loosen from the rails of a bridge, and he feels as though he is falling to freedom. But his "thicks" will not let him go. After he plunges twenty feet into the snow, Kyle, Nick, and Javon take him home to the Reverend Miriam Jones, "Mimi," his mom. Her most recent gentleman friend hears Jonathan playing the guitar and joins him for a jam session that seems to help spark in Jonathan a desire to move forward with his life, which is in shambles, especially at school. His junior English teacher comes up with a plan that will allow

Jonathan to make up for his disastrous academic performance. With his mom, his friends, and the school principal all urging him to take advantage of this offer, Jonathan spends time at a hospice, listening to blind World War II vet David Cosgrove recall searing memories of being on a sinking ship under attack by the Japanese. Through writing an epic poem about Telemachus, through learning a guitar solo that the school principal demands he perform on the guitar that Seattle musician Eddie Vedder left to the school in Telly's honor, through crafting the memoir, and through painting the house so that his mom can open a wedding chapel, Jonathan slowly finds his way back into some sense of hope for the future.

In general, Jonathan realizes, after Telly's death, "something changed. Music started to come easier. For some reason, I got better. . . . If you apply the same principles to music that you do to poetry—namely, intestines-dragging-the-ground honesty—you will get better. Play it that way, and you can go far with a few chords."[8] Jonathan's work with Cosgrove also helps him with his music. Cosgrove is trying to help Jonathan understand his blindness. "In darkness, everything is different. Time. Place. Tone. . . . The world is quieter, not so frantic. Your imagination awakens and begins to full the canvas. You come to see that blindness is not a locked door but a different door" (77). Something about that first conversation with Cosgrove inspires Jonathan to create a piece of music that will honor his brother; it ends with two juxtaposing chords: "But those two chords are like poetry. Side by side, they clash perfectly. Jagged glass and butterfly. Light and dark. Chiaroscuro" (83). Jonathan says that tune captures Telly, all his sweetness and complexity, "a strawberry dipped in balsamic vinegar" (83).

When Jonathan's best friend, Nick, says that it is time to move beyond Telly's death, he opens the door to Telly's room, gets out Telly's guitar, and hands it to Jonathan. He then sets the whole group of guys jamming. Jonathan is finally ready to face his loss. He thinks, "Everything sounds fuzzy, sloppy, incoherent" (190). But "incoherence can be a form of coherence. Just as jagged edge can be a form of butterfly. That is the lesson of art, whether music or poetry" (190–91). The guys make him play a solo, and he shares with them his unfinished "Tune for Telly." For Jonathan, the music "starts a train, and I jump on board. In my mind, we're eight again, rushing down the trail to Longfellow Creek, Grandpa limping and cussing behind us. Then we're in our toddler days, flying the zip swing at Lincoln Park. Days of aching perfection. Glimmering immortality" (92). The novel ends with the feeling that Jonathan will be OK, because he is thinking, "Who knows how many good days we have in us. But there are miracles in moments" (234). Wesselhoeft's poetic, powerful language gives readers that sense of "miracles in moments," the sense of the catharsis and then redemption that Jonathan feels and guidance for finding ways through grief by trusting oneself to use whatever artistic means of expression one can tap.

Revolution

In her personal revolution, Diandra Xenia Alpers, who changed her name to "Andi," finds herself transported through time back to the French Revolution in the novel *Revolution*, by Jennifer Donnelly. In the present time, Andi grieves the loss of her brother Truman, a tragedy for which she feels responsible, and relies heavily on drugs prescribed by her doctor for her depression. She is a senior at St. Anselm's, Brooklyn's most prestigious private school, and she feels that Vijay Gupta is her best and only friend. Andi is a gifted musician, but her emotionally distant father tells her that she is a genius and so pressures her to do well in school and pursue a degree at an elite college. Instead, she skips classes and goes down to the Promenade, where she plays her guitar for hours until her fingertips are raw. Andi's rage, grief, and guilt threaten to destroy her life.

The day before winter break, when Andi is headed to her music lesson, the headmistress calls her to the office and reminds Andi that she has not submitted an outline for her required senior thesis. Andi will be expelled if the outline is not submitted when school resumes. She has not done the outline, but she does have a subject for the thesis: tracing the musical DNA of an eighteenth-century French composer, Amadé Malherbeau, who was the first to write predominantly for the six-string guitar. Andi wants to trace Malherbeau to Jonny Greenwood, a contemporary musician. Instead of sitting in the office, Andi wishes that she were hearing the notes and chords of Bach's Suite no. 1, a piece written for cello and transcribed for guitar. She wants to be playing it at that moment with Nathan, her seventy-five-year-old music teacher who lost his family at Auschwitz and who understands Andi's grief in ways that others cannot. When Andi finally gets to her lesson, she and Nathan play music for hours.

At home she sees her mother painting another picture of Truman. There are hundreds of them, some even nailed to the ceiling. Her mother, Marianne LaReine, is French. "Sometimes she speaks English, sometimes French. Most of the time, she doesn't speak at all,"[9] due to the depth of her own grief after losing her child. Around Andi's neck is Truman's key, which she has worn since he died. She remembers the night before Truman found it. Her parents were arguing loudly about the fact that her father was never home, working all the time as a scientist. Her mother asked her father what it is he wanted, to which he replied, "I want the key . . . the key to the universe. To life. To the future and the past. To love and hate. Truth. God. It's there. Inside of us. In the genome. The answer to every question. If I can just find it. That's what I want. . . . I want the key" (28). The next day, when Andi, Truman, and their mother are at a flea market, Truman finds a key, which he buys, polishes, and gives to his dad, telling him that it is a special key, with "L" on it for love. With the argument still in his mind, Truman tells his father, "It's the key to the universe, Dad. You said you were looking for it. . . . I found it for you so you won't have to look anymore. So you can come home at night" (30). A few months later, their father receives a Nobel Prize and is home even less. One night Truman goes into his study and takes the key back. He has it with him when he dies.

Because Andi is failing everything except music, her father checks her mother into a hospital and insists that Andi go to Paris with him for the winter break. She is to take her laptop to work on her thesis outline. In Paris, they stay with her father's friend, "G—a round man in yellow jeans, a red sweater and black glasses . . . a rock-star historian. . . . [who] wrote a mega-bestseller on the French Revolution" (60). While waiting for dinner, Andi looks through boxes and crates and trips over a long wooden case, the kind that guitars come in. In it, she finds the most beautiful guitar that she has ever seen, made of rosewood and spruce with an ebony fingerboard. G's wife, Lili, tells Andi that it is from the late seventeen hundreds, that it was made in Italy, and that Louis XVI had owned one just like it. Lili had bought it from a man who found it in the catacombs, lying under some headless skeletons. G insists that Andi play it, but she is afraid because it is so fragile. G probably assumes that the guitar will be some kind of therapy, she thinks, "but I'm really bad at being helped." She tells G that she brought her own guitar and does not need this one. He replies, "Perhaps it needs you" (68). After fixing the old strings, Andi plays a combination of songs on the guitar, and Lili is impressed with her talent.

Andi then notices an old photograph of a glass jar with something in it. G tells her that he is sure it is the heart of Louis-Charles, son of Louis XVI and Marie-Antoinette, the lost king of France. Andi realizes that the purpose of her father's trip to Paris is to do DNA testing on the small heart to see if it belonged to the child king. He had not told her about this project, out of fear of upsetting her. When G asks Andi what she will be doing while her dad is working, her dad responds that she will be working on the outline for her thesis. G is excited to learn her topic because he has books on Amadé Malherbeau and tells her where she can find his papers and some of his original scores.

The next day when Andi finds a score written by Malherbeau, one that she has not seen before, she plays it on the old guitar and is amazed by this eighteenth-century tune. Her dad asks what is so special about this composer, and she wonders if he is really interested. But she explains that Malherbeau broke a lot of rules, refused to write pretty harmonies, defied convention, and used a lot of minor chords and notes. She can even hear sounds of Malherbeau's guitar music in Franz Liszt's piano works and in American blues and jazz. Her dad wants to know how she will demonstrate these comparisons. She explains that she will do so with examples, "bits of music, phrases from the pieces she will reference as part of a PowerPoint presentation" (86). Her father thinks that it sounds risky and hard to pull off, telling her that she should just write a paper instead so that she can get a good grade, graduate, and maybe offset the failed classes in the eyes of college admissions officers. Andi stops listening. She wishes that he "could see that music lives. Forever. That it's stronger than death. Stronger than time. And that its strength holds you together when nothing else can" (87). Her father tells her that music just is not enough; it will not pay her bills.

Andi wants to go home, but the only way that her dad will let her leave is if she completes her outline, and it has to be worth an A. As she reads about Malherbeau, she wonders why one of his compositions is called the Fireworks concerto and why he quit writing the music that had made him famous. As she is thinking about the mystery, she looks at the old guitar case, wondering about its secret locked compartment. She decides to try Truman's key and panics when it gets stuck. She twists and pulls until it finally turns. Beneath the opening, Andi thinks that she is looking at Truman's face but realizes quickly that it is not an image of Truman; it is a boy with blue eyes and blond curly hair like Truman's, but this boy is wearing an old-fashioned lace-collar shirt and gray jacket. Next to the portrait is a little muslin sack with a small book in it. The first date in the diary is "20 April 1795." In it are words about the boy, who is a prisoner in the Tower. Andi cannot get the diary out of her mind. She becomes obsessed with the plight of the young writer, a girl named Alexandrine, "Alex." Stuck in the diary is a newspaper article about a Green Man terrorizing the citizens of Paris with destructive fireworks.

In Paris Andi searches the archives in a library and takes pictures of music and photos of Malherbeau's house and personal papers. She even finds the score of Malherbeau's Fireworks concerto. One evening she meets a young man named Virgil, with whom she plays music and exchanges music CDs that they have each made. But Andi cannot give Virgil her full attention; she is drawn back to the diary and has to know more. She learns that Alex had been hired to entertain Louis-Charles with her puppets. She was the Green Man, who set off the fireworks for Louis-Charles to see when he was locked in the tower. At one point, Alex is almost captured but escapes into the catacombs. Andi knows enough about the French Revolution to realize that Alex is in the midst of those tumultuous events, and she wonders "what happened to Alex after Versailles fell. Did she stay with Louis-Charles?" (183). One evening Lili and Andi watch a television show on which G and her father argue about whether the preserved heart could be that of Louis-Charles. Andi becomes determined to learn more and decides to tour the catacombs, where she sees piles of dead bodies—which seem alive to her. She wonders what is happening to her mind, but she assumes that she is hallucinating as a result of fatigue and her depression pills.

Andi works on her PowerPoint presentation until she feels that she must finish reading the last few entries in the diary. She is devastated when she reads that Alex witnessed the massacres. Andi thinks that she might have had a role in them. She realizes that Alex saw history up close and personal, and what she saw made her insane. Andi is afraid to read more. She wants Louis-Charles to have escaped, and she hopes that her father and G find out that the heart did not belong to the child king.

Her work on her outline about Malherbeau progresses, and even her dad seems satisfied. When Andi finally feels that she is ready to read the last diary entry, dated "1 June 1795," she sees that there is blood smeared across it. She realizes that the guards got to Alex, who survived just long enough to write one last entry. Just then her dad and G walk in, looking tired and upset as a French secret serviceman waits for them to get ready to tell the president what they found. All the genetic testing of the mitochondrial DNA has proved that the heart is that of Louis-Charles. Andi does not want it to be true. She wanted the young boy to live. She asks her dad to pretend just once that he is not a scientist but a human being. He answers that as both a scientist *and* a human, he believes that the heart belonged to Louis-Charles.

Andi opens the diary for the last time and sees that Alex's last entry just stops. She faces the fact that "a little boy died in Paris, long ago, alone in a dark, filthy cell. And another boy died on a street in Brooklyn, his small body bloodied and broken" (344). Andi thought there would be more in the diary's pages than sadness and blood and death. But she realizes that she already knew the ending—hers and Alex's. She goes to the Eiffel Tower with plans to jump but is too late to be on the last elevator for the night. Virgil finds her sobbing and asks her what she is doing at the tower.

Andi finally tells Virgil about Truman—that he was killed on his way to school. Each day, she and Truman would pass a welfare hotel where a schizophrenic named Max lived. He would yell at them and carry on about a revolution that was about to start. Truman was afraid of him. On that tragic day, Andi was supposed to be with him, but she had stopped to talk with Nick, a guy she liked who was starting a band and wanted her to play in it. So Truman went on alone. As he passed the hotel, the police were evicting tenants. Max yelled at a woman in a fur coat and lots of jewelry who was walking by; a cop grabbed him, and Max snapped. He seized Truman and held a knife to his throat. When Andi heard the sirens, she ran to the spot. As a rookie officer drew a gun, Max bolted into the street with Truman, and they were hit by a delivery truck. Andi tells Virgil that she keeps trying to find an answer or some solace—with a shrink, with drugs. It used to be that her music kept her going, but she is past that now.

Virgil convinces Andi to join him and some friends to play a gig at a party hangout on the beach where they can sneak into the catacombs. When they are chased by the police, Andi falls and hits her head. Suddenly, she finds herself in the catacombs, back in the eighteenth century, where she meets Amadé Malherbeau, who thinks she is Alex. He tells her that he came to Paris in 1794, changed his name from Charles-Antoine, and wrote silly music for the theater, nothing like what he had composed before. Andi thinks that the mystery about Malherbeau is solved.

The section "Paradise" begins as Andi opens her eyes and Virgil tells her that her forehead is bleeding. She had been dreaming or hallucinating about her trip back in time. Virgil calls one of his taxi-driving friends to come and pick them up, saying that his friend is hurt and needs to go to a hospital. While they wait, Virgil sings a song they were playing earlier called "My Friends." Andi looks up, sees the stars, and is finally ready to live.

In the epilogue, a year later, Andi is in a Paris hospital where she works with music therapists once a week and plays music for children who have been traumatized. Andi's mother has sold the Brooklyn house, moved back to Paris, and is painting again. She and Andi share a flat. Andi has graduated from St. Anselm's because of the thesis, which earned an A+. Her premise about the DNA concept of a musician drew lots of attention, especially the ending, where she explained that Amadé Malherbeau was really Charles-Antoine, the last Comte d'Auvergne, whose groundbreaking use of minor chords and dissonance came about because of the grief that he felt over his parents' death at the hands of the revolutionaries. Andi is now a student studying for a degree in classical and contemporary music at the Paris Conservatory. She and Virgil spend lots of time together. She has moved past her grief, and her "heart feels so full that it hurts. Full of love for this man I've found. And for the brother I lost. For the mother who came back. And the father who didn't. Full of love for a girl I never knew and will always remember. A girl who gave me the key" (472).

A Map of the Known World

The redemptive power of art—found and created—is the focus of Lisa Ann Sandell's book *A Map of the Known World*. Unlike Andi, Cora Bradley does not feel responsible for her brother's death, but her grief and isolation are like that which Andi experienced. Cora wants to know what led to her older brother Nate's death. Who is responsible? Her story begins with words that reveal the eye of an artist: "Somewhere else, life has to be beautiful and vivid and rich. Not like this muted palette—a pale blue bedroom, washed out sunny sky, dull green yellow brown of the fields. . . . I am suffocating."[10] She wants to escape from Lincoln Grove to a world "where colors and smells and winds are fresh and delicate, vibrant and new" (3). Cora looks at maps of other places that seem exotic and alluring and draws elaborate colorful maps of this unknown world, as well as maps of her known world.

Cora's family is turned upside down after her reckless older brother Nate is killed in a car crash, and because of Nate, everything has fallen apart. She grieves the loss of her brother, is saddened by the lack of affection from her parents, and misses their ordinary yet warm dinner-time together. At dusk, her distant and angry father comes in the house without a greeting and will not come to the table for dinner. Her mother arrives home from work, slams the door, calls anxiously to Cora, throws a frozen dinner in the microwave, and quizzes Cora about her day. Cora's place of escape is her room, her refuge where she takes out a tablet of drawing paper and stares at places far away.

As Cora begins her first year in high school, she is sure that everyone thinks of her as the girl whose brother died. She looks for her best friend, Rachel, and tries to avoid the "Nasties," a group of girls who used to be her friends. "Advanced Art" is the one class that Cora is looking forward to, but the color drains from her face when Damian Archer comes in as the bell rings. He was Nate's best friend and had been in the car with Nate—but walked away. Her parents blame him for influencing Nate to do terrible and foolish things.

When the new teacher, Ms. Calico, tells the class about summer art programs, Cora assumes that the teacher is talking to the upperclass students and not her. But she does want to do things—things that will mean something, that will matter. More than anything else, she is terrified that she will not have the chance. Cora has a hard time keeping up with her classes, but art is different. Art class is where she feels like she is really learning, and she enjoys the challenge and mess of charcoal and pastels. Cora is surprised when Ms. Calico tells her that she would like to recommend Cora for a summer program in London, where they have a cartography class. Cora badly wants to win a spot, but she knows that her parents will never allow her to go, even if she were accepted.

One day Damian approaches Cora and offers her a ride home. At first she refuses, but after he repeatedly makes the offer, she accepts, knowing that she is breaking her mom's "Rule #3," which is not to get into a car with anyone under the age of forty—not to mention that he is the person in the world that her mom hates the most and trusts the least. Before Damian takes Cora to her house, he shows her a barn that he and Nate were allowed to use as a studio. There she saw "a jungle of sculptures, . . . twisted metal and torn wood, . . . wire and slabs of stone.

Giant canvases covered with thick, violent slabs of oil paint, and other *things* hang on the wall" (63). She had never even thought that Nate was an artist or that he and Damian might be capable of creating such beauty, when they were so often in trouble for stealing things. Cora sees a large round stone with a tall metal pole poking from its flat top with boards nailed together nearby. It is unfinished: Nate's last piece. With this surprise discovery, Cora's healing slowly begins. When she is back home, she thinks about going into his bedroom but cannot do it yet. It is too much—discovering that she never really knew Nate at all and learning that he was an artist who made beautiful things and then was lost to her.

When Cora finally does decide to explore Nate's room, she finds a black case hidden under his bed. In it is a collection of pencil sketches, and they are beautiful, delicate and strong:

> Scenes of a mother and her son resting beneath a tree, a cat balancing on a fence post. . . . So many tiny, ordinary pieces of life. . . . Nate rendered these moments so intimately, so truthfully. The lines of his pencil brushed across the pages with sensitivity, with empathy. I can see that. Feel it. (88)

In a tube hidden in his closet, Cora finds a series of watercolor paintings—of tree branches, birds, flowers—and she realizes what a truly great artist he could have been. She smuggles all his things and hides them in her room.

In her anger and grief, Cora runs outside and rides her bike out of Lincoln Grove to a country road. She stops by a creek, where she falls down hugging a weeping willow tree and sobbing: "*What was the point of your dying when the rest of the world keeps going? We have to keep living without you, Nate!*" (95). She sees the sun setting, the moon rising, and, at the edge of the creek bed, a slender white bird. She feels a sudden peace descend and is moved by the beauty. "This is the world. . . . I can use my pencils and charcoals and pastels and paintbrushes and capture this moment. . . . There is so much beauty. . . . *Art* is the point" (97). She decides that she will map the world that she knows, the places that she shared with Nate, and she will mount her map on the pedestal that he built. The following Sunday, as Cora begins drawing and sketching, she feels the pieces of her heart coming back.

Cora feels that she must find a way to get to London for the summer art program that Ms. Calico told her about. One night, when she feels that she must talk with someone, she calls Damian and crawls out her bedroom window to meet him at a diner. She tells him that she wishes that she could be strong like Nate, who would speak up to their parents. Damian's response is not what she expected:

> All Nate and I could do was act like royal nightmares. . . . And look how we ended up—dead and a dead beat. . . . We were afraid that to be smart, to be talented, to like art. . . . To be even a little bit responsible or mature wasn't cool. It was easier to be bad, dangerous, to drive really fast, to not listen to anyone. We were just scared. . . . No one could tell us what to do. . . . The worse we behaved, the less everyone expected. . . . We didn't know that we could be creative without destroying everything around us . . . including ourselves. (150–51)

Because he and Nate were so rebellious, Damian feels that everyone has given up on him. Because he thinks of himself as a misfit, a loser, he is surprised when Cora tells him he is talented, that his work she saw in the barn is beautiful. She tells him that he should show it to Ms. Calico, who, as a new teacher, did not know Nate.

When Cora goes home, she feels a new sense of determination. She fills out the application for the London program and puts together her portfolio. In it she includes the maps that she has drawn of faraway countries. Ms. Calico is impressed when she sees the finished work and says that Cora has an excellent chance to be accepted. Later, when a letter arrives from the United Kingdom stating that Cora has been accepted, it includes a permission form that parents must sign.

Helena, another student in the art class, befriends Cora, and one day they talk about Damian and Nate and the sculptures and paintings in the barn studio. Helena has a wonderful idea. They will have a gallery opening, a party, for the yearly art show and include Nate's sculptures as the centerpiece of the show. Cora spends increasingly more time with Damian and finds that she really cares for him. But one day, her mother sees them together and is furious that she would spend time with the boy who, in her mind, is the one who killed Nate. Cora shouts back that Damian did not kill him. "Nate took care of that all by himself. . . . Nate was a beautiful artist . . . but it was you and Dad who pushed him and made him feel like a failure, like a screwup. It's *your* fault he died!" (212).

With the art teacher's and the principal's approval, Helena and Cora design posters and paste them all over school, inviting all artists to bring their drawings, paintings, sculptures, and any other works to a celebration of art and life. At the barn, Cora works at her map where pieces of Lincoln Grove spring from the pine surface. When the deadline is near for a parent's approval to go to London, Cora forges her mother's signature but feels both horrified and exhilarated.

On the one-year anniversary of "The Accident," Cora realizes how much she still misses Nate. But she also thinks about what has changed since that night: her parents act like zombie prisoner-masters; she started high school and has been kissed by Nate's best friend; she and Rachel are not speaking, but she has a new friend, Helena. Something amazing happens at school that morning, as Cora watches at least two dozen kids from various classes bring paintings, sketches, prints, collages, sculptures, mobiles, and other assorted works for the gallery opening of the art show. "It seems every clique is represented . . . like a high school rainbow" (247). After school, people file into the room. Ms. Calico tells Cora that her brother was talented, with an original and exciting sensibility. Certainly, with two such talented children, her parents must be proud. Furthermore, she is happy that Cora is going to London, where she can receive more formal training. Cora winces as she thinks about forging the signature on the form. She looks at her map, standing on the metal-and-stone base that Nate had constructed, which "has become a three-dimensional, topographical, touchable, living thing" (254).

Cora whirls around when Damian says that her parents just walked in. Instead of anger, she sees tears in her mother's eyes. When her dad reaches out to Cora, the three stand in a huddle. Then her mother sees Nate's painting of a mother and son. She thanks Cora for doing this: "for this gift, even if we didn't know we needed it" (257). Cora shows them her map. They are amazed. The memory of what she has done comes rushing back. She tells them that she has done something terrible and she is sorry. But her mother knows. The letter had come back with insufficient postage. They will make the decision about the trip at home. At Ms. Calico's request, Cora speaks to the gathering, thanking everyone for coming and helping her to celebrate her brother's art, which is shown alongside all of theirs. Cora can take comfort in what Nate left them: a piece of himself in his art.

Trash

In Sharon Darrow's *Trash*, the relationship between the siblings Sissie and Boy—whose mother did not even care enough about them to give them real names—is close. They are shunted from one foster home to another. Their first placement is with Mrs. Clay, a retired art teacher who gives them materials for drawing, tells them stories about art school, and inspires them so that in art class, "Boy painted wall murals / & I covered benches with mosaics / made out of tiles smashed with hammers."[11] But after Mrs. Clay has a stroke, they move several times until they land with Lannie and Big Daddy, who are trash pickers. They make Sissie and Boy go with them as they make their rounds of the trash and garbage dumps, finding what Lannie calls "treasures." Sissy begins to search for such items herself, thinking about the people behind the broken bits and pieces: "a silver ring so tiny only a fairy child could wear it / barrettes some mama had sewed ribbons and lace on" (19).

Eventually, Big Daddy becomes abusive, and Sissy and Boy set out to find their older sister, Raynelle. While on a bus heading into St. Louis, where Raynelle and her family live, they catch their first glimpse of spray-painted screams of identity:

> silver arch shines like / dawn on red bricks / spray-painted names: / *GRAAT ZELLZ ARCHER* / huge jagged letters / across railroad bridges / water towers & billboards / graffiti blooms / lights up / boy's eyes. (55)

With Raynell, they find a home; she puts them in school, where they catch up in their classes, but both like art class best. They connect with two other teens, Tyrone and Dolores, who say that they will teach Boy and Sissy about "urban art," about how to make the kind of graffiti that calls so much to Boy. They love the tagging, being "art bandits" (61). Sissy learns that

> Tyrone says / Artists should / be free / Art should / Rage over / Every blank / Wall every / Train car— / Boy and Tyrone / Dolores & me / Paint worlds / Turn rust / to silver / & brick / To gold. (63)

But tragedy strikes one night when Boy fails to clear a leap from a rooftop as they are spray-painting, and he tumbles to his death. Sissy is arrested and spends four months in prison for crimes against property and resisting an officer. While there, she gets her GED but is wracked with guilt, feeling as though she should have been able to save Boy. She is wracked with anger, too, about why he did not look closely before making the leap. When she is released, she cannot face life with Raynelle. Really, she cannot face life without Boy, and she descends into homelessness and grief. Her school friend Dolores finds her and gives her money that she says she owed Boy. With the money, Sissy buys ten dollars' worth of spray paint, which she uses to spray his tag all over the city—*Atenz, RIP*—on every wall or Dumpster or sidewalk she can find. In doing this painting, she finds enough consolation that she decides to also paint the surfaces of the abandoned warehouse where she is living with other homeless folks. In that act of adding color to their walls—a turquoise sea and golden galaxies—Sissy begins to find some hope. She begins to give all who are there the "room of their dreams" (123), from an igloo to the Taj Mahal. Reaching out through the art, she learns the names of the homeless people. She shares her story of Boy and learns their stories in return. On the back of Boy's gravestone, she paints an artist's studio with a mountain view and imagines the two of them together, giving color to the world. So when she stumbles across a brochure while picking food from a Dumpster, she stops to read its ad for an art school in Chicago. Again, she imagines going there with Boy. That vision is enough to spark her to look for more treasures in the trash, "glories in the garbage."

> a dumpster behind a framing shop yields / glue & gesso, scraps of canvas & wood, / pasteboard boxes & dabs of paint to make / collages. From metal I make robot worlds / for Boy. I pretend Boy collects food / labels to paste in kaleidoscopic designs. / We sculpt new shapes from old boxes, / form new worlds from old trash. / We laugh / & surprise ourselves with joy. I lift up / like I might float away. Boy's not gone / not as long as I remember. (128)

Sissy finds a job, finally gets back in touch with Raynelle, and eventually shows her the art school brochure. Raynelle tells her that if Boy were alive, he would tell her to go. And Sissy does. She also gives herself a name, Skye. In Chicago, Skye navigates, with help, the realities of work-study and financial aid and registration. She says,

> I gather beads— / to feed my / hungry art—faceted / & luminous, string / into ropes & / I hang on my art school walls / pearly loops, haloed / rainbows of silken / light, shining (like / Boy) on black / robocoptors & velvet- / winged nightmoths / suspended by threads invisible but (like / Skye Lexie) strong / enough to hold. (147)

Sissy transforms into Skye; Boy becomes her muse; she has a future because of her art.

Without Tess

In Marcella Pixley's *Without Tess*, the main character, Lizzie, is coping with the guilt that she feels five years after her older sister, Tess, committed suicide. Unlike Skye, Cora, and Andi, Lizzie is not an artist—Tess was. Tess's journal of sketches and poems is the vehicle through which Tess expressed her disturbing view of the world; it documents her difficulties in living within the boundaries of her physical existence as she descended into madness. The journal, however, cannot save Tess in the end; her artwork cannot give her the release described by Aristotle. However, Tess's journal is ultimately the means through which her younger sister, Lizzie, comes to better understand Tess's emotional pain and move herself out of her own depression, grief, and guilt, finally achieving catharsis and a release from the pain that she has felt for the five years since the death of her sister.

As the novel opens, Lizzie is in her second year of high school—her first year was so disastrous that the guidance counselor lets her return only if she sees the school psychologist once a week. Lizzie interacts with Dr. Kaplan and goes back in time to her childhood with Tess. In those first memories, Lizzie is nine and Tess is eleven; the two girls are best friends, living in an isolated home on the water with their mother, a writer, and their father, a restorer of old boats. Tess is wild, imaginative, bold, daring; Lizzie adores her and follows her in her fantasies and into her imaginary worlds.

Gradually, it becomes clear that Tess cannot draw the line between her pretend worlds and reality. Lizzie finally realizes that there is something deeply wrong with Tess. As they pretend to be unicorns, Tess punches a hole in Lizzie's hand so that they can mingle their blood and be best friends forever. Lizzie ends up in the hospital. By the time that their parents take action after this incident, which they cannot ignore, Tess is beyond help. One night, she decides to leave this world behind. She begs Lizzie to go into the wintery water with her, saying, "I know it's all been make believe for you, but just for tonight, just for this one last time, please tell me you know the magic is real."[12] Tess turns back into the selkie (mythological sea creature) that she claims she has always been. Both girls jump into the river as Tess chants a magic spell. Lizzie holds her breath as long as she can but finally bursts through the surface of the water into the night air, but Tess does not.

Lizzie has spent the past five years holding on to Tess's journal, which she grabbed out of Tess's coffin just before it closed but has not really looked at. As she meets with Dr. Kaplan, she begins going through the journal. But looking at Tess's drawings makes Lizzie begin to realize how sick her sister was. She finds pictures of a girl with worms in her head, an army of toads, a drowning horse on which Tess has drawn her own face, the horse "gazing off into the distance somewhere, at a world unraveling" (6). She begins to realize that through working with Dr. Kaplan and the journal, she has been moving through Kübler-Ross's stages of grief—from denial that her sister will never return through anger at her sister for being sick, for dying, through the massive depression and pain that she has felt for years and, finally, to readiness for acceptance. When Lizzie shares the journal with a friend and writes her own poem, she is on her way to redemption.

LOSS OF A FRIEND

Hate List

Friendship is one of the central relationships of adolescence. According to Ryan in "The Peer Group as Context for Development of a Young Adult's Motivation and Achievement" (2001), friendships influence motivation and achievement in school, and having strong, supportive friendships with emotionally stable individuals helps teens develop socially. Students who lack such friendships are less likely to participate in class and are more likely to perform poorly in school—even more likely to drop out. A friendship can feel more important than the bond between siblings; thus, the loss of a friend can be equally devastating.

While *A Map of the Known World* and *Without Tess* focus on the movement through grief toward catharsis and, ultimately, some sense of redemption after the main character has lost a sibling, each novel shows how friends of the individual who died need to work through these same feelings. Many young adult novels deal with the struggle to work through the grief that a survivor feels when he or she has caused an accident that has left a cherished friend dead or seriously wounded.

In Jennifer Brown's *Hate List*, Valerie and Nick have been best friends as well as boyfriend–girlfriend, but it turns out that Valerie does not know Nick as well as she thought. They have spent months creating a "hate list," a list of students at their school who have hurt them, taunted them, and made their lives miserable. But then Nick takes a gun to school and opens fire on those whose names are on the list. He shoots Valerie in the leg when she attempts to stop him, in the process saving one of the girls on the hate list, Jessica. Then he turns the gun on himself.

After spending the summer recovering from the trauma (at least physically), Valerie has to return to school for her senior year knowing that, in the minds of many of her schoolmates, she is as guilty as Nick. After all, it was Valerie who started the hate list. As Valerie plods through dreary days at school, she continues to look at what she is seeing, to draw pictures of students, teachers, and administrators. During this time, she finds new insights about their inner lives. One day, Valerie's mom is late picking her up from therapy. Valerie decides to walk across the street to see if maybe her mother is shopping in the little mall there. As she explores the mall, she comes across an open door and sees a woman wearing an apron and working with fabric paint and costume gems and glitter. The woman invites her into her space, where there are a dozen easels and lots of supplies—paints, ribbons, clay, pens. Valerie asks if the woman, Bea, teaches classes. Bea says yes, but not just anybody can take a class; she teaches only people who can teach *her*. Bea somehow senses that Valerie needs to paint.

Valerie convinces her mother to let her return to Bea's place on a regular basis so that she can continue to express her roiling emotions through painting as well as drawing. It is through her art that Valerie moves forward. It is through her art that Valerie rediscovers her sense of purpose and begins to figure out who she is. She is someone who is smart, who wants to go to college, who likes school and learning, and who is interested in other people and what makes them unique.

Jessica, the girl that Valerie saved, reaches out and pulls her into a student council project to create a memorial—the two girls together begin interviewing survivors and those who lost loved ones: parents, coaches, and other students. Valerie begins to see herself in a different way, not as the monster of her earlier painting. She is able to say to her psychologist, Dr. Heiler,

> The Hate List was real. I really was angry. It wasn't a show for Nick. I mean, I wasn't as angry as he was, you know. I didn't even realize how angry he was. But I was angry, too. The bullying, the teasing, the name-calling . . . seemed so messed up and pointless and I was really pissed about it. Maybe back then a part of me was suicidal and I just didn't know it. [13]

Valerie and Jessica present the memorial at graduation. It is a "concrete bench, almost blinding in its white-grayness" (397), next to a hole into which a time capsule will be buried, filled with memories and artifacts. The name of each student in the school—including Nick's—is inscribed on that bench. Valerie says in her speech that, through the shooting, everyone at the school has gained a better understanding of reality and has had to face the fact that people hate. She tells the crowd that it is probably not possible to take hate away, even from people who have seen firsthand what hate can do. Then Jessica takes over and continues: "You can change a reality of hate by opening up to a friend. By saving an enemy. But in order to change reality, you have to be willing to listen and to learn. And to hear. To actually hear" (399–400).

Valerie takes the microphone back and confesses in front of the school that people died because the shooter—her boyfriend—and she had thought they were bad people, but she says that she and Nick did not know others' realities. At that point, Valerie and Jessica present the results of their interviews, fleshing out the reality of who the dead and wounded students were. Jessica takes Valerie's book of sketches—the sketches in which she has captured her growing understanding of the complex realities of people, including herself—and puts it into the time capsule. Valerie is now free to move forward with her life.

* * *

For all the young people whose stories are chronicled in this chapter, art is a window into the possible. Through making music, painting, dancing, taking photographs, and working in the theater, they find ways to deal with the reality of grief and, when necessary, confront guilt and move toward redemption.

NOTES

1. Kathryn Erskine, *Mockingbird*, reprint ed. (New York: Puffin, 2011), 72.
2. Stephanie Hemphill, *Sisters of Glass* (New York: Borzoi Books, 2012), 94.
3. Jen Bryant, *Pieces of Georgia* (New York: Yearling, 2007), 58.
4. Cath Crowley, *A Little Wanting Song* (New York: Knopf, 2010), 46.
5. Maria Boyd, *Will* (New York: Knopf, 2006), 34.
6. Allen Zadoff, *My Life, the Theater, and Other Tragedies* (New York: Egmont, 2011), 4.
7. Karen Hesse, *Out of the Dust* (New York: Scholastic, 1997), 127–28.
8. Conrad Wesselhoeft, *Adios, Nirvana* (Boston: Houghton Mifflin, 2010), 43.
9. Jennifer Donnelly, *Revolution* (New York: Ember, 2011), 25.
10. Lisa Ann Sandell, *Map of the Known World* (New York: Scholastic, 2009), 1.
11. Sharon Darrow, *Trash* (Cambridge, MA: Candlewick, 2006), 11.
12. Marcella Pixley, *Without Tess* (New York: Farrar, Straus and Giroux, 2011), 246.

13. Jennifer Brown, *Hate List* (New York: Little, Brown, 2010), 388.

Chapter Four

The Arts and Solace: Abandonment, Abuse, and Mental Illness

All young adults search for the answers to questions about their identities as they wonder what their futures might hold. The development of resilience and the achievement of identity are dynamic processes. Despite enormous challenges, resilient individuals thrive as they come to terms with what happens in their lives. Resilient individuals seek and find external resources to help them. Often, there is at least one major adult who provides support to the young person facing adversity, helping him or her build resilience.[1] (The role of adults in a young person's life is more fully addressed in chapter 6.)

Achieving resilience is difficult when the identity search is overshadowed by the need for escape, especially when a young person feels lost, fragile, and broken. In stories about young people searching for answers to difficult and confusing situations, such as abandonment and abuse, talented young artists can find some relief when they are practicing a piece of music on the piano or guitar, working on a drawing, changing the colors in a painting, using a camera lens to record what is too painful to watch with the naked eye, or finding the right materials to finish a sculpture. Engagement in the arts helps these young people rebound as they find a way out of their confusion and loneliness to take steps toward resiliency and identity achievement.

Whether it is the loss of the sense of self that happens when illness or some other event—such as a drastic change in economic circumstances—challenges the assumptions on which that sense of self is based, whether it is facing abuse on a personal level or abuse at the societal level, or whether it is facing destruction of any sort, a young adult who has at his or her disposal the sketchbook, the guitar, the stage, the open wall (legal for graffiti), the ballet barre, or just a safe space in which to dance has the advantage over the young adult who lacks such resources.

For example, at a party right before the start of her first year of high school, Melinda in Laurie Halse Anderson's *Speak* is the victim of date rape at the hands of a popular senior. Because she calls the police—who arrive and disband the party, arresting some of those present for underage drinking—Melinda finds herself an outcast at school with no outlet for discussing what has happened to her. So she goes mute, communicating with her family through sticky notes and becoming increasingly depressed. She begins skipping class, spending time in a makeshift shelter that she creates in a janitor's closet, and blaming herself for what happened to her, thinking that she was drunk. But she continues to attend her art class, where Mr. Freeman encourages her to express her feelings.

When Melinda learns that her former best friend, Rachel, is now dating Andy, she breaks her silence, trying to protect Rachel. While at first Rachel reacts with disdain, eventually she decides that Melinda's assessment of Andy is on target, and she drops him. Andy finds Melinda in the janitor's closet, accuses her of being jealous of Rachel, and attempts to rape her again. Melinda breaks a mirror and holds a shard up to Andy's neck, screaming loudly enough that members of the lacrosse team race to the closet and rescue her—in the process revealing Andy for what he is. After this incident—as the rest of the school learns the truth about Melinda, the party, and Andy—she is no longer ostracized. On the last day of school, Melinda stays late to finish her art project; she receives an A for the course—although she knows that she will have to attend summer school because she failed the rest of her classes.

In the following passage, Melinda examines her artwork and considers what her next steps might be:

> *My tree needs something.* I walk over to the desk and take a piece of brown paper and a finger of chalk. Mr. Freeman talks about art galleries and I practice birds—little dashes of color on paper. . . Water drips on the paper and the birds bloom in the light, their feathers expanding promise.

IT happened. There is no avoiding it, no forgetting. No running away, or flying, or burying, or hiding. . . . And I'm not going to let it kill me. I can grow.[2]

Melinda can now speak. With the help of her art, she reclaims her voice.

The young people described here show how they use the various art forms at their disposal to deal with a myriad of difficult experiences and events, both for escape when life seems too difficult to bear and for solace as a way of moving forward with their lives.

ABANDONMENT AND A MISSING PARENT

Young people who have to deal with the difficult situation of the death of one parent often have at least the surviving parent to whom to turn. Most of them—such as Georgia, Donna, Will, and Adam, as discussed in chapter 3—have at some point known what it can mean to be encouraged, nurtured, and supported by that parent. They feel the death of that parent intensely, and sometimes it is hard to connect with the surviving parent, who is also grieving. But as Donna in Jen Violi's *Putting Makeup on Dead People* imagines, her father is always behind her, a sort of "backup singer" to the song that she is making out of her life. There are young people, however, who grow up without ever having even one parent in their lives. They contend with an ache and hollowness in their hearts that they really do not know how to fill. Calle from Kim Culbertson's *Songs for a Teenage Nomad*, Jace from Michael Wenberg's *Stringz*, and Jude from Cathryn Clinton's *The Eyes of Van Gogh* exemplify how young people in such circumstances turn to the arts for solace.

Songs for a Teenage Nomad

Songs for a Teenage Nomad opens with lines from Bob Dylan's song "Mr. Tambourine Man." Calle quotes them from her song journal, in which she also writes, "Inside my dreams sits a song, way back in the shadows. Somehow, my memories begin with this song. I can't seem to put an image to it; it's a memory blurred and swirling, with no shape."[3] Calle's journal includes written memories from songs as she hears them, "like glimpses of my life as I remember it," "snapshots" as she and her mother move from town to town (3). Whenever her mother finds a man and moves in with him or gets married, they start a new life—and shortly thereafter, things fall apart. Throughout all their moves, Calle searches for the mysterious "Mr. Tambourine Man" of her memories and tries to get her mom to provide answers about the father she has never known.

With Rob, the newest man, Calle and her mother land in a new town where Calle starts high school for the first time. She is befriended by Drew, who is part of the theater crowd, and she is accepted by the drama kids because they perceive her, journal in hand, as a writer. Although she says of them, "Drama kids, they're at every school. Reading Shakespeare for fun, dressed in black, talking about famous directors. Ignoring the rest of us. I have no idea what to say to them" (13). Calle accepts their friendship and begins working with Alexa, a stage manager and set designer. After a few weeks, Calle is feeling more settled for a change.

For the drama kids, the Little Theater "makes school bearable" (27), and Calle is soon Alexa's assistant set designer. Alexa outlines her designs on the flats; Calle fills them in while they "talk about movies and music. . . . We sing to Alexa's favorite singers . . . and of one of my favorites, Jack Johnson. She doesn't laugh when I tell her his music band-aids my soul" (31). Calle says, "I sing loudly around Alexa [because] music always makes things better" (32).

Calle finds herself excited by the way that "the theater hums with a full closing-night house who wait in papery light for the start of the play" (67). She likes being backstage, watching the actors change costumes, watching them make the play come alive on the stage, and feeling good about having done her part to make that magic happen. In the theater, Calle finds solace from the constant ache of not knowing who her father is, and she begins to feel that her whole life has more of the lightness and sense of possibility that the theater set conveys.

But one day, while rooting through the pantry for real food because her mom has become a vegetarian, Calle comes across a box that she has never seen before—and inside, at the very bottom, she finds a picture of her father and learns his name: Jake Winter. This find sets Calle off on a quest to learn the truth about him and his absence from her life, a quest made more urgent when she also finds a letter from him addressed to her and realizes that her mother has been getting such letters throughout her life and has never allowed Calle to have them.

In the process of initiating her quest, she makes connections with a football player, Sam, whose family life is a mess because his mother suffers from a serious depressive disorder. Calle routinely uses music and references to help Sam understand her situation, calling up an Indigo Girls song called "Leaving," in which the speaker says that leaving is basically the only thing that she knows how to do, something that Calle deeply understands. Other characters also communicate with music. Eli, of the drama clique, has a crush on Calle, so he leaves a note in her locker saying that she should "listen to Green Day's 'Sassafras Roots'" (70). And Calle's relationship with her mother is one forged through sharing many hours of music on the road together; many of Calle's music journal entries feature her mother singing a specific title or dancing to a specific song. In these characters, Culbertson gives the reader a model of how to communicate using the language of the arts when words otherwise prove difficult to find.

When Rob, the newest husband, leaves abruptly and Calle's mom goes into a meltdown, Calle takes a phone call from Rob in which he says, "He'll only find you again" (176). This odd statement makes Calle push her mother for the truth of her father's situation. Calle learns that Jake, her father, has been in and out of jail for the whole of her life and that every time he gets out, he tracks down her mother and then calls the man with whom she is living, threatening violence. This repeated situation is why her mother's partners take off and why Calle and her mom are always on the run. But Calle also learns that her father has loved her, in his own way and from a distance, and he has tried his best to let her know that he is proud of her.

When Jake dies in an accident, Calle and her mom can stay in Andreas Bay and feel safe, building a new life there that is free. Readers do not know what Calle might become, what profession she might pursue, but it is clear that she has kept her footing because of her song journal and because she has begun to create stable friendships through her involvement in theater, which will give her the foundation that she needs as she faces the future.

Stringz

Jace, from *Stringz*, faces a double whammy. His dad was never in the picture, and, like Calle, he has moved from place to place, mostly along the California coast, as his mother is always chasing a new man, a new job, a new possibility. Jace and his mom move to Seattle three weeks into his first year of high school to live with Jace's Aunt Bernice. *Stringz* begins when Jace walks into his new high school to see a tall geeky kid being trashed by three guys. When the thugs pick up their victim's violin, Jace cannot help himself. He is African American, he is a surfer, he is a loner—but he is also a gifted cellist, and he cannot just watch a beautiful instrument being destroyed. His older brother taught him to "*always* respect"[4] a musical instrument, so he attacks the bully and tosses the violin to its owner. This incident means that Jace is off on the wrong foot, but when he shows up at orchestra class—where he finds the geeky kid, Elvis, as the concert master—he has a friend in his corner.

However, the orchestra conductor, Mr. Whitehead, does not believe that Jace really belongs, because there are not many young African American males who play the cello. Mr. Whitehead challenges him to play a C major scale; Jace starts with the scale but then jumps into the finale of a Hayden cello concerto. The conductor, embarrassed by Jace's virtuoso performance, feels the need to cut Jace down and re-marks, "An orchestra is like a basketball team. . . . You people know something about basketball, don't you?" Jace realizes that, to Mr. Whitehead, he "looked like just another useless black teenager, end of story" (37).

To escape from the turmoil inside him as a result of this disastrous first day at school, Jace takes his cello to the concert hall where the Seattle Symphony is playing and sets up shop, recalling, "The first time I pulled a bow across the strings, I was only six, but that amazing sound must have worked its way inside my soul from the first notes. Since that day, the cello's been the only thing that's never let me down" (50). He plays Bach, Beatles, jazz, even hip-hop on any street corner that he can claim, and people give him money. That evening, Dr. Aldo Majy-kowski—a former professional cellist who is retired and teaches only those individuals that he feels can make it in the world of professional music—is in the crowd that swarms around Jace as he is playing on the street. Dr. Majykowski leaves Jace a hundred-dollar bill with a busi-ness card attached saying, "Want to make a difference? Call me" (66). Jace ignores the invitation. For him, music is a way to process his loneliness and hurt—and there is a lot of it in his life. Just as Jace is feeling settled, his mother leaves town without him. Jace takes out Ruby, his cello, and plays B. B. King's blues to sort himself out, rely-ing on Ruby for compassion and solace.

Eventually, Jace connects with Elvis, the violinist in the school orchestra, and Marcy, the first-chair cellist. At first Marcy is jealous of Jace, whom her father heard that same night at the symphony, because

Marcy's dad does not even acknowledge her existence, except when she is playing the cello. But Marcy is a decent young woman who appreciates that Jace has a gift beyond her own, and she works with Elvis to talk Jace into going to see Dr. Majykowski. They tell him that there is a scholarship competition for African American and Latino cellists and they think that he is good enough to win. They give him the nickname "Stringz."

Marcy accompanies Jace on his first visit to Dr. Majykowski and even talks for him when Jace initially freezes in front of the old man. On their way back home, on the ferry that runs to Seattle from the island where the doctor lives, Jace is so excited that he may have a future in music and may not just be "baggage" all his life, he shows Marcy that the cello, too, has capabilities of which she is not aware, and he launches into a Jay-Z hip-hop number. Jace thinks,

> Most people think there's all sorts of music. But to me, there are really only two kinds: good and bad. That's all that matters, not the style and not the performer. . . . With hip-hop and rap, it's not about melody; you'd be hard pressed to whistle along with any of the songs. But the rhythms and the pulse, the pops and the way everything interacts with the words are what make it all work. Even though a cello's meant to play notes, it also does a pretty good job on rhythm, 'specially if you treat your bow more like a drumstick. I started by slapping the cello for emphasis, picking out the rhythms and cadence of "Rid or Die." (136–37)

When he stops playing, Marcy claps with joy.

Unfortunately, because they are on the ferry, Marcy and Jace cannot escape when the three bullies who Jace interrupted his first day at school show up, throwing Jace's beloved Ruby overboard. Without thinking, Jace goes after her. Though ruined, Ruby saves his life, helping him stay afloat in the frigid water. But then Jace is heartsick—he has lost his instrument. Dr. Majykowski again steps in, taking him to see Mr. Blue, a rich older patron of the arts who possesses a beautiful cello that he is willing to loan Jace as long as he is a pupil of Dr. Majykowski. Mr. Blue tries to explain why he is willing to provide this gift: "I do what I can to nurture beauty. Play beautiful music, young man, and make the world a better place because of it. That's all I ask" (169–70).

Note that up until this time, "musician" is not how Jace describes himself. Music—until Jace becomes friends with Marcy and Elvis—is something he *does* to keep the world at bay; it is not a part of his self-definition. Jace thinks of his cello playing primarily as a way to ease his heartbreak, earning a few bucks on the street in the process, but Mr. Blue gives him an alternative perspective and, with Dr. Majykowski and his new friends, a new way of viewing himself—as a musician, a potential virtuoso performer.

RESILIENCY AND ESCAPE FROM ABUSE

Abuse and mental health difficulties are ongoing situations that require strength and courage to face. Involvement in the arts can be a lifeline for young people trying to stay afloat—a shore of normalcy toward which to swim through the tumultuous seas of their daily realities.

As discussed in chapter 3, facing the death of a parent or a sibling is difficult for young adults. Yet to the extent that death is an event with associated rituals and that grieving in response to the loss is not only accepted but expected, it is possible to put the death into context and recognize that life goes on, as Andi in *Revolution* and Cora in *A Map of the Known World* finally do. For the young adults who feel trapped by the cruelties that they experience or witness in the world around them, it can be harder to move past the memory of a horrifying event. In some situations, they feel the urge to do something about societal wrongs, but they feel incapable of tackling them. In difficult ongoing circumstances, young adults can use the arts to escape; they can move themselves out of the situation, and they can use their art to give themselves a voice even when they may otherwise feel silenced.

Spite Fences

In Trudi Krisher's *Spite Fences*, set in Georgia during 1960, thirteen-year-old Maggie Pugh, like Liz in *Exposed*, sees life through a camera lens. Maggie treasures her camera and takes pictures as she walks around town. She sees some things through her camera lens that she feels she must record but cannot speak about—the insanity and inequities of the world in which she lives. Kinship is a town where there are fences, both literal and figurative, that surround the people who live there. It is a place where children are at the mercy of their parents. The rich live on the hill on the north part of town; the poor live in the east. The bathrooms and drinking fountains are labeled—whites use one; people of color use another. Blacks cannot sit at the drugstore lunch counter or check out a library book. But during the summer of 1960, things are changing. Maggie begins to chronicle the changes through the lens of her camera, a gift from her black friend Zeke.

Maggie is physically and verbally abused by her mother. Neither her mother nor her gentle, withdrawn father understands her. Maggie appreciates the camera that Zeke gave her and is "thankful for his friendship, his many kindnesses, his example of courage."[5] Maggie learns self-respect from another black man, Mr. George Hardy, her secret employer who tells her that she does splendid work cleaning his house. He also tells her that it is OK to look at things up close, even if they are painful; it is the only way that she can expect to understand them.

The kindness and courage of Zeke and George are a vivid contrast to the madness of Maggie's mama. When Maggie tries to tell her that there is no shame in her friendships, her mama says, "No daughter of mine's friend to no colored man, parading her shame for all the world to see" (224). She hurls a collection of colorful jelly glasses at Maggie, who then realizes that her mama cannot be reached by reason and that she does not want to become like her mama and live in fear of others. If she is to escape the whippings, the meanness, and the spite, she is going to have to break away. "Her lack of trust about her own voice is like a fence she cannot climb until she confronts the racism and the abuse in her family and her community" (Zitlow and Stover, 2011).[6]

Maggie supports Zeke, George, and others when they take a nonviolent stand against unfair laws and customs. One day at the drugstore, she witnesses an especially frightening event:

> Everything was out of control. . . . I held the camera to my eye. . . . The images before me swam red, filling up the lens. Trip the shutter, Maggie Pugh. What filled my lens was more than the blood gushing from my sweet friend. It was the red color of the fence, the red color of the earth on which I stood. It was red, the color of my life this summer. Cock, Trip. Red: it was the color of Kinship. (271–72)

Maggie knows that she must tell the world about the awful things happening, "memories inside the camera . . . undeveloped snapshots" (70).

Through the camera lens Maggie is able to face the evil around her and find the words to tell what is inside her. She gives Zeke the gift of words by teaching him to read. She leaves her abusive home situation and continues to use her photographs to document the racism that she has witnessed, particularly the cruel treatment by bigoted white men toward Zeke and others in Kinship. The magazine *Life* pays Maggie for her photos, which helps her leave Kinship; her friends and her photography help Maggie escape abuse and achieve resiliency.

You Don't Know Me

Fifteen-year-old John in David Klass's *You Don't Know Me* cannot escape his belief that no one knows him. He feels as much misunderstood as Maggie. John's story is presented in one long second-person monologue about the challenges that he faces with friends, dating, "anti-school," his tuba, and, most of all, his home situation. In his "up-till-now-miserable life that is not a life,"[7] there is a lack of communication with his long-suffering mother and cruel "man who is not my father" (4). His deep cynicism and sense of isolation, his pain and anger, make his long search for escape difficult.

John's home life continues to deteriorate. His mother's boyfriend becomes more abusive, and John struggles to cope because he feels that his mother, once vibrant and happy, has sold her son out by surrendering to this man. The uncomfortable, sometimes frightening feeling that John has in his home is similar to Maggie's feeling of entrapment. Both suffer from abuse and wonder if there is any escape.

John is sure that when he plays the tuba, described by him as "actually a giant frog pretending to be a tuba" (14), his band teacher, Mr. Steenwilly, is disturbed by the sounds that he makes. The only reason why he is in band is that his "anti-school" has a rule that everyone must participate in one extracurricular activity. One day after the band plays a piece written by Mr. Steenwilly, the teacher calls John into his office and asks him if everything is all right at home. He has noticed the red marks on John's arms and shoulders, as well as his sad eyes. He tells John that music was the magic portal that helped him escape the trap of spending too much time in his own head: "When I found music, John, all kinds of things opened up for me" (24). He suggests that John try playing music as if it were not a jumble of notes but a story; he also tells John that he will have a solo in a new piece that the band will start soon.

One nightmarish evening, John is beaten by his mother's drunken boyfriend, locked in the back of a truck, and taken to an unknown destination, where he is forced to load and unload televisions, which John assumes are stolen. After this event, John does not want to go to school, but he also does not want to stay in his home. He tells the reader, "You do not know me, so you can't possibly know how trapped I feel. . . . I am trapped in the worst kind of trap a fourteen-year-old boy can be trapped in—I am trapped inside my life that is not a life" (174).

John knows that when he gets to school, Mr. Steenwilly will expect significant progress on his tuba solo. What he does not expect is that there is a guest at band practice: Mr. Steenwilly's professor from the Eastman School of Music, who is there to hear the song that the band has been practicing, "The Love Song of the Bullfrog." All the students play well until it is time for John's solo. The burst of sound from the tuba is "angry and forlorn and powerful . . . a sound that has never been heard in a band room before" (201). Tears stream down John's face. "The frog is dead" (202), he says. Mr. Steenwilly dismisses the band members and calls John to his office. He understands that John needs help, but at that moment, the assistant principal drags John to the school office because of something he said earlier in the day to the algebra teacher.

John is suspended from school, and the man who is not his father takes him home and beats him with a belt. When John's mother is away, the beatings continue. One night after John comes home from— to his surprise—having had a great time at the Holiday Dance with his fellow band member Violet, he finds the man drunk. He attacks John and again beats him, punching him in the face repeatedly. Suddenly there is someone pulling the man away. It is Mr. Steenwilly. The police come, and John is rushed to the hospital, where he fades in and out of consciousness. Finally, he hears from his mother the words that let him know that she really does know him: "Don't you know who you are? You're part of me . . . all the family I have . . . the only person I can count on . . . and nothing else comes close to that" (253).

John recovers, but he is in the audience at the Winter Concert. He cannot play the tuba with his jaw wired shut and a plaster cast covering much of his face. The professor from Eastman asks John for permission to play his tuba. John agrees, though he wishes that he were onstage playing it himself. He is also surprised when Mr. Steenwilly announces that the band will play "The Love Song of the Bullfrog," written for a promising musician in the band who, unfortunately, is not able to per- form that evening but is in the hall. The piece is dedicated to John, who has come to appreciate the role of music in his life. It is "in the end, a love song" (262).

I'll Be There and *I Hadn't Meant to Tell You This*

Like Maggie, Sam, of *I'll Be There*, by Holly Goldberg Sloan, and Lena, from Jacqueline Woodson's *I Hadn't Meant to Tell You This*, have experienced abuse at the hands of a parent. Lena, from a lower-class white family, has had a fairly stable and happy home life until her mother contracts cancer and dies. Her father begins to move Lena and her sister from house to house and turns to Lena for the physical love and connection that he has lost as a result of his wife's death. Lena is befriended by Marie, an upper-class African American, after Lena's arrival at Marie's school during eighth grade. The two girls become friends because they understand each other's sense of loss; Marie's mother abandoned her and her father several years before the start of the story. As the girls become close, Lena tells Marie the secret of her father's abuse. Lena has stopped bathing, stopped washing her hair, and has let herself go to keep her dad from molesting her, but when she realizes that he is now going to turn his attentions to her younger sister, Dion, Lena makes plans to run away and lets Marie know.

Lena puts all her emotions into her drawing. She tells Marie, "When I'm drawing, it's like I go into another world or something. Nobody can bother me."[8] Lena draws on any spare scrap of paper that she can find, and it is through drawing that she eventually creates another view of reality, one in which she leaves her father's house. It is through her art that Lena makes herself visible. When she and Dion finally head out of town, Lena leaves behind a drawing for Marie that is signed, "Elena Cecilia Bright and her sister Edion Kay Bright lived here" (113). Woodson says that while she herself has little talent in the visual arts, she gives her characters opportunities to sew, play musical instruments, or, like Lena, draw, as a way of providing her readers with models of strategies that they can use to handle anger, fear, and sadness.[9]

Sam, like Lena, has an abusive father, a probable paranoid schizophrenic who trusts nobody. When Sam is in second grade, his father takes Sam and his younger brother, Riddle, and leaves home. In *I'll Be There*, Sam is close to eighteen. He has never been to school, although he managed to learn to read up to the fifth-grade level and to calculate. At this point, Sam's dad, Clarence, no longer even feeds the boys. They are left to their own devices and have mastered ways of staying out of sight during the day as well as getting by on scraps from Dumpsters behind restaurants and from small tips that they earn helping people unload their cars at the dump.

Sam and Riddle both use the arts as a way to escape this horrific day-to-day existence. Riddle draws and draws; he rescues old pencils and covers the pages of an old telephone book with intricate drawings of the insides of things. Sam carries a battered guitar with him through all the moves that Clarence abruptly makes. When Sam was five, his grandfather had taught him a few basic chords on an old four-string guitar. But Clarence had taken the boys away, plucking them out of a backyard wading pool and tossing them into his truck, never to return. It is a year later before Sam holds another guitar, "but when he did, he knew it was his salvation."[10] The boys and Clarence live for a time above the apartment of a blind blues guitar player, who teaches Sam, then eight years old, the acoustic blues. When Sam is dragged off yet again, he has a battered instrument that his mentor has given him. He plays it every day, "for hours and hours," and he becomes proficient enough to play anything he hears on a radio and "any song he hears in his head" (113).

On Sundays, the only time when it is safe to be out during the day (as young people such as Sam and Riddle are supposed to be in school during the week), Sam attends church services to listen to the music. That is where he meets Emily Bell, who is singing "I'll Be There." Sensing that Emily is unhappy about her performance, Sam seeks her out when she races from the church, and they form an immediate connection. At Emily's house, Sam, urged by her father, is given the opportunity to play a really fine instrument, and when he does, Mr. Bell is amazed. He has "never had a student as talented" (13) as Sam, and he is determined to do anything that he can to help nurture that talent. Sam "understood music, he loved music, in the most pure way that Tim Bell had ever witnessed. . . . He had made his own musical language . . . and he was doing things musically with the instrument that were completely innovative" (151).

Riddle's drawings have the same effect on people who view them. Both boys turn their experiences in the world into art. When Sam's father discovers that Sam and Riddle have been spending time with the Bells and so drags them out of town, Sam sits in the truck making "music in his head." He imagines the piece—"a stirring melody over a pulsing beat that was angry and constant. His fingers were gliding over his old guitar" (200), actually air-guitar fashion because Clarence destroyed the instrument. But tragedy prevents that symphony from being finished. Clarence gets the truck stuck on a mountainside; when he threatens to shoot the boys, Sam finally takes on his father, fighting and wounding Clarence enough so that he cannot pursue the boys farther through the difficult terrain.

There is a great deal of adventure after this point. The boys get away, but Sam is badly hurt. They survive in the woods for quite a while but eventually take off down the river in a canoe they find. Meanwhile, Clarence is found in his truck and arrested. The boys are separated when their boat goes over a waterfall, but both are rescued and they find their way back to the Bells' home.

Sam's journey there is made possible by his guitar playing. He has had a head injury and cannot even remember his name. But when he is in a bus station, trying to figure out where to go, he sees a street musician playing. He gets up the nerve to ask if he can hold the instrument—and in the act of taking it in hand, he comes back to life. He remembers his name, the Bells, the music that he played to be transported from reality into another place. He did not just make music; he became the music. He earns enough money to make it to the Bells' home, where he is reunited with Riddle and finds refuge. While it is clear that Sam will solidify his sense of self by becoming a true musician, up through the end of this beautifully crafted novel, filled with lots of love and hope in spite of Clarence's abuse, it is the cathartic power of the music that is at the center of Sam's life.

SEEKING SOLACE WHEN DEALING WITH MENTAL HEALTH ISSUES

The following stories portray the questions, frustrations, fears, hurts, and struggles that a young adult feels when a loved one suffers from some kind of mental illness or when a young person questions one's own sanity to the point of considering suicide. From the time that Clarence appears in *I'll Be There,* it is clear that he is mentally unstable, but as noted in chapter 3, this truth evolves more slowly about Tess in *Without Tess*, by Marcella Pixley. Tess's sister Lizzie gradually accepts the fact that her sister was ill, and she finally realizes that she was not responsible for her illness or her death. Lizzie's resiliency begins as she learns more about Tess through her sister's art.

The Cranes Dance

Like Lizzie, Kate, in Meg Howrey's *The Cranes Dance*, gradually becomes aware that her sister is mentally and emotionally unstable. As the older sister, Kate tries to keep things in balance while worrying about her younger sister Gwen and feeling guilty because she wonders if she could have done something more to help her. This story, told with frequent flashbacks, clearly conveys the intensity of the world of ballet. Kate is a soloist in a competitive New York City ballet company. As she struggles to maintain her standing in the company, she is haunted by the absence of her younger sister Gwen, whose potential for a brilliant career as a dancer in the same company had at one time surpassed Kate's.

But as their story begins, Gwen is back in Michigan and will not return Kate's calls or messages. Kate is hurt that her sister will not communicate with her and is frustrated that she cannot seem to get clear answers from her parents about Gwen's condition. The other members of the ballet company believe that Gwen is at home recovering from knee surgery, but the real story is that Kate had asked her father to take Gwen home because she was out of control, sometimes even delusional and paranoid. At times Kate wonders whether she made the right decision in calling her father, but she recalls being afraid that Gwen would harm herself, which Gwen actually does by trying to smash her knee through the patio screen door at home. Gwen is always on Kate's mind: her "negative space takes up so much room."[11] Still, even in her sister's absence, Kate feels close to Gwen.

Kate also feels guilty that, of the two sisters, she is the one still in New York and not Gwen, who is a truly gifted dancer. Kate recalls that even when they were young, she would coach Gwen but not necessarily on technique. "Gwen is a phenom. It's not really possible to dance as well as she dances" (90). Kate worked as hard as Gwen but could never be as good. Yet because it was obvious that Gwen needed to be made happy so that she could live up to her amazing potential, Kate always felt responsible for the task. Kate was "the stronger one, the outgoing one, the one quicker to laugh." She thought, "What was I going to do, let her fall apart?" (131).

Kate and Gwen always did their dance training together, but it is only when Gwen joins Kate and her roommate Mara in New York that Kate realizes that Gwen is teetering on the verge of mental collapse. Gwen was always extremely neat and organized, but she becomes increasingly more obsessive and repetitive about cleanliness and the placement of things. For instance, Gwen does not just wash the dishes and dry them; she repeatedly washes and dries the sink, then the kitchen floor, then pots and pans not used. Kate "knew it wasn't right. That it wasn't just eccentricity. . . . She was there and she wasn't there" (134). Kate's confusion about Gwen's behavior and her questions about Gwen's sanity lead Kate to question her own mental health. Yet at work, Gwen begins to blossom and dance with more confidence. At the same time, Kate and Mara cannot ignore Gwen's strange and frightening behavior, which leads Kate to finally call her father.

After Gwen's departure, Kate begins to have difficulties of her own. During a performance of *Swan Lake*, as Kate turns her head, she feels something in her neck imploding, and pain shoots down her right arm all the way to her hand. "It felt like someone had hit me with a wrench and then set my arm on fire" (16). To mask the pain, she uses Vicodin found in Gwen's Advil bottle. Her use of it increases, and she keeps on dancing, even though the doctor tells her that most people dealing with pain like hers would be given a neck brace and be kept more or less immobile. Kate promises that she will rest after a few more weeks, when the season is over, but she wonders if there is something wrong in her approach to dancing that is causing an injury that she might not be able to correct. She thinks,

> I could just be facing a long struggle not to get worse. The descent of the body has begun. I have passed my peak, my prime. This is . . . the physical reality that conquers all others. This is my body, and there are things happening to it that cannot be imagined away. (217)

After the curtain call of her performance of *Swan Lake*, she has tears in her eyes and thinks that she "cannot bear this love. Nor the loss of it" (217).

Kate gets to the point that she does not even know how painful her neck is anymore. Nor does she want to know. To keep on dancing, she drinks two full glasses of water and eats a banana before her first Vicodin of the day to lessen the stomach cramping. There are times when she wonders if she is becoming a drug addict, but her whole world is dance. While struggling with her neck pain, she continues to be upset that she cannot talk with Gwen or find out how she is doing.

After repeated calls home to talk to Gwen or find out more about how she is doing, Kate's mother finally tells her that Gwen is much better and "in a program, I guess you'd call it. She goes five times a week to a therapy situation" (246). Kate becomes increasingly frustrated that her mother will not tell her if there is a diagnosis, instead referring to Gwen as having a "little evaluational." Kate becomes incredibly angry and yells at her mother and then her father. She takes refuge the only way she knows—in dance.

When she is back in the theater rehearsing, Kate realizes, with every emotion exhausted, that she loves everything about being a dancer: looking up in the theater, the sound of Dvorak, the drama, being able to "turn on one foot, run, . . . glissade, and then jump into the air. . . . I lifted my arms and felt the muscles undulating down my back, and this too I loved. . . . And then it was over" (253). She wishes that her neck did not hurt and that she was not a quasi drug addict. Yet when Kate dances, even alone on the stage, she feels that "there is no other place in the world, . . . no more powerful aphrodisiac than being gorgeously, achingly, perfectly lonely in front of two thousand people" (278).

Finally, before Kate's big performance of *Midsummer Night's Dream*, Gwen, who is on the way to the therapist's office, calls Kate to wish her *merde* (a dancer's term for "break a leg") and says that up until now, she just has not wanted to have a big talk. Their mother then gets on the phone and tells Kate that Gwen is now willing to take her medication and continues to do better. They end their conversation, agreeing that after the season, when Kate is home, they will talk about whether Gwen is ready to return to New York and again live with Kate.

The news that Gwen might be able to return to New York unsettles Kate. She recalls one time when she was returning from her boyfriend's apartment and found Gwen standing on a chair with a rope around her neck. As Kate begs for her to get down, Gwen says, "You can't help me. . . . You don't know how. . . . You can't ever feel things the way I do. You are just pretending to be alive" (342). Finally, when Kate tells Gwen to go ahead and do it, saying that she will then do it, too, Gwen hands her the rope, inviting Kate to go first. Kate did not do it then but feels that she "could do it now. . . . The thought of disappearing feels so . . . easy" (343). But dance is what saves her. She decides that before she goes home, she wants to get things right in her role as Titania. Before the performance, Kate's guilt is apparent when her friend Mara asks her about Gwen. As Kate pulls out the bottle of Vicodin, she admits that the pills make her sick and she cannot sleep. She continues,

> My mouth feels like it's filled with ashes and it makes me too fucked up to even dance on them [the pills] anymore. But Gwen's got a pill that makes her feel totally fine. She's not crazy anymore. Look at what I've DONE TO MYSELF and SHE'S NOT EVEN CRAZY. (345–46)

Mara helps Kate, who is struggling to get dressed. Onstage, Kate performs Titania as Gwen would have done it. Kate thinks how she herself
"got tricked into loving dancing. But no one ever came and took the
spell away, so I had to ruin it all on my own" (347).

When Kate is back in the dressing room, she thinks about killing
herself, but there is a knock on the door. It is Bryce, a young ballerina
who adores Kate and proudly tells her that she is starting pointe. She
asks Kate to autograph a photo taken of them, and she gives Kate an
extra copy, which Kate requests that Bryce sign. After they exchange
their autographed copies, Kate notices that Bryce has written, "You are
my favorite dancer ever!" (357). Bryce tells Kate that she will see her
Friday and actually skips out of the room. There is another knock on
the door, and it is the director, Marius. He gives Kate a suggestion
about her bourrée and tells her not to be afraid to put the Kate Crane
stamp on the dance, which is what he expects her to do. She thinks that
there are countless reasons to stay alive, including what her death
would do to her family and friends and to Bryce, who adores her, but
the first crack in her resolve to end her life comes from the thought that
she needs to fix her bourrée. Marius tells Kate that he is setting *Dream*
in Amsterdam in July, and he wants her to go along to help because he
sees a place for her on the artistic staff. She accepts his offer, telling
him that she has been a mess during the season and starting to cry. She
thinks that she will do things differently in the future and "participate in
all parts of this world, not just the event, but the thing before and after.
Life, or whatever" (362).

Kate goes back to Michigan for two weeks to find Gwen dancing
with the Grand Rapids Ballet. Kate drives Gwen to ballet class and
therapy sessions and feels a great sense of pride watching Gwen dance
the role of Giselle. Gwen tells Kate that she does not know if the bad
feeling is gone. She feels fine when in class, but the rest of the time, it
is sort of like she "can't quite feel the floor" (369). At the same time,
she does not get as upset and scared as she had been in the past.

Kate leaves and goes to Amsterdam, after which she returns to New
York and to dancing. She is not sure what she is feeling, but it is
"something like feeling the floor. And that it is my privilege to feel it"
(373). As the story ends, Kate reflects on a sculpture that was a favorite
of her patron, Wendy, who has just died of cancer. Kate does not know
what it was about that piece that satisfied Wendy so much, but Kate
learned how important art was to Wendy, who loved the stories told in
art, paintings, sculpture, and dance. Kate knows that Wendy loved

ballet enough to be a donor, an appreciative member of the audience, and the one who supported her as a young ballerina. Kate thinks about art and realizes that things like the sculpture "pick up where words fail us" (365). She would like to think that dance can do that, too. The reader is left feeling that as "the Cranes dance," the sisters will find their way toward a more balanced and healthy relationship and will continue to use their particular art form to express their emotions and face what life brings.

The Eyes of Van Gogh

Kate and even Gwen, in her own way, find solace in ballet, and while dancing, each live the life of someone else in the story they portray. They ultimately find the strength to make the important decision to live. Jude—in *The Eyes of Van Gogh*, by Catheryn Clinton—also faces the decision about whether her life is worth living. She has always taken refuge in her art from the painfulness of her life. She tries to work through the increasingly intense despair that she feels by recording her reactions to Van Gogh's paintings, which she has recently discovered. Jude and her mom have moved—*a lot*. But when they arrive in a new town to take care of Jude's grandmother, whom Jude did not even know existed, Jude is hopeful that she will find a family—and maybe find the sense of "home" that she has missed for so long, as she has coped with nine schools in thirteen years. She reveals, "Pain and sadness are homeless beggars in my life . . . sleeping in any corner of my brain. . . . Sometimes, though, a trigger pulls inside me, and the pain goes off, getting bad."[12] The newness of yet another new school is one such trigger.

After the first day, Jude finds herself walking along the train tracks, looking into the lights of the freight train bearing down on her. They look like eyes, and the train seems to be saying, "Maybe it would be better if you weren't here." But as she focuses on the train, tension leaves her. She is left with a feeling of "creative energy," which makes her ready to escape into her art, where she comes alive: "I live in the pencil, the paper, the object that I see gliding from my mind to my hands. It's a way of seeing that's mine, my way of defining a world" (3–4). Jude escapes to this other world when the real one becomes too bleak to bear. Through her drawings, Jude explores questions that she has about life. As she draws a star with a tail, she tries to capture her swirling thoughts, wondering if there might actually be some timeless place "where people actually held stars in their hands" (5).

Unfortunately, when Jude and her mom, Stella, land in Ellenville, they learn that Stella's mom has had a stroke; she is paralyzed and unable to talk. But Jude is so hungry for family that she establishes a routine of going to the care home every day and talking to her grandmother, taking with her the pictures that she has drawn, and sharing all her feelings about this move.

On a happier note, Jude makes friends with a pair of cousins, Jazz and John Mark, who recognize in her a fellow practitioner of acting "small"—meaning, staying off the radar screen of anyone, teacher or student, who might take an interest in her or, worse, bully or torment her in some way. She also is fortunate to end up in an art class with Ms. Dennis, who has organized a field trip to a special exhibit of Van Gogh's portraits at the Philadelphia Art Museum. There, Jude is drawn to Van Gogh's self-portraits, especially his eyes, in which "I could see the frenetic, dispossessed cells of his mind bumping against each other. . . . I look through those eyes every day" (23). She determines that she will write her assigned art term paper on Van Gogh. Jude and Jazz look at the famous sunflower painting, and Jazz wonders why there is one brown sunflower in the corner. Jude shows her understanding of the language of painting by explaining that Van Gogh put it there because a composition needs "the unexpected." Ms. Dennis overhears the remark and pulls Jude into conversation, agreeing that the flower invites questions, "and art should leave space for that" (24).

Even while Jude is developing her first real friendships and beginning to date Todd, she feels a "desolation thing" settling on her, especially when reading about Van Gogh and studying his paintings. She describes her feeling in terms of color, saying that her sadness "was a blue, deep midnight blue. I'd successfully pushed the pain away for a while, but I knew it hadn't really left. It had just been sitting at the edge of my mind. . . . It had its turf" (45). For Jude, drawing is a way out of that pain. While learning more about Van Gogh makes Jude "think and draw" in ways that she has not done before (62), she begins to feel a sense of destiny because she finds so many parallels between her life and that of the suicidal artist. Jude tells Jazz and John Mark that she paints to fill up the "godawful hollow that comes when you finally realize that something is lost forever. . . . There's a sucking whirlpool inside where something fine used to be" (104).

When Todd breaks up with Jude and her grandmother dies, that sucking whirlpool increases in power—more so when her mother says that, yet again, she is moving, this time to be with a man named Lou, who has a house in a different town. Jude starts to worry that her life really is destined to end up like Van Gogh's: in suicide. She becomes unclear about where her thoughts—and what she has read about Van Gogh's thoughts—end, and her painting no longer works. Colors run together as she tries to draw a sweet gum tree because "they weren't strong enough. They muddled together into gray, gray, gray" (143). One day while she is painting, she finds that her hand has "a life of his own" (144). A painting that she is doing of her art classroom captures her internal state of turmoil: "I painted myself sitting in the corner of the room on Vincent's chair. I painted crows on each of my shoulders. As I painted, I could feel them pecking at my neck" (145). Assigned to paint a portrait, Jude paints her mother as having the body of a girl but the head of a woman:

> She was standing next to a giant chair, twice as big as she was. It was Van Gogh's chair, the one he painted after Gauguin abandoned him in Arles. Stella's dress was green with black swirls running through it. Her mouth was wide open, and her eyes were blank. Her arms hung by her side, her hands empty. My inner world was bleeding into my art. I couldn't keep things separate anymore. (172)

Ms. Dennis recognizes that Jude is breaking down and asks her to come and talk, but Jude feels that she will not be able to handle her teacher's kindness. She is drawn to a quote by Van Gogh, "You take death to reach a star," and plans to follow his lead. She gives away her paintings, takes aspirin and vodka to the railroad tracks, planning to just lie down and wait for the train, "with Van Gogh's eyes," to end it all. She wants to cheat fate out of giving her so much pain because "the mindache felt terminal, and I was tired of fighting it. . . . I knew why Van Gogh had done what he did. He wanted to escape his own life—the inevitability of what he saw in front of him" (208).

At the last minute, Jude cannot do it. She wants to say good-bye to the stars, but when she looks up to them, she experiences the light as coming down from above and surrounding her. She tells her friends, "It was transcendent. I was in some sort of cosmic intersection—God, that sounds so made up, but it wasn't. And this place wasn't empty; it was full, and I just knew I wasn't alone" (209). When she sees the train coming, it no longer has Van Gogh's eyes, and she knows that she wants to live. She clings to life—but in turning away from the tracks, she slips, falls down a bank, and breaks bones. After her friends and teacher find her, she is taken to the hospital. When she finally wakes up, she says that she still does not know what she will do with all the pain and sadness, but she wants to return to school, to return to the art room: "My fingers could almost feel a paintbrush in them. . . . I knew I wanted to go back to school. I wanted to finish something" (210).

Jude thus makes a choice to accept life, with all its attendant difficulties and heartbreaks, because she realizes that she can use her art to make sense of the chaos—and because she has friends who will stay by her side to help her in this effort.

THE ARTS AS AN OUTLET FOR SORROW OF ANY KIND

Perhaps Rosie, from Beth Kephart's *House of Dance*, can be viewed as a representative for all the young people mentioned in this chapter who come to value the arts for solace and escape, a way to achieve some level of resilience. Like Melinda, Rosie stumbles into an artistic outlet for her sorrow—and then is able to use it to bring joy back into the lives of people in her family who are distanced from one another. Rosie and her mom have basically just coexisted in the same house ever since Rosie's father abandoned them. Rosie's mom spends a great deal of time with her boss, a married man—leaving Rosie to fend for herself. When Rosie's grandfather, her mom's father, develops multiple myeloma and is facing death, Rosie begins spending time with him. He asks her to sort through his belongings, placing those things that matter most to him "in trust." In doing so, he introduces Rosie to many of his favorite old albums and begins to give Rosie a picture of the grandmother that she never knew, a woman who loved to sing and dance, especially to Ella Fitzgerald's "How High the Moon."

In the dialogue between Rosie and her grandfather, he describes his wife, Rosie's grandmother, dancing:

> I'd come home from the refinery, and I'd find her here, in this room, all the furniture all shoved aside and Fitzgerald on the radio, live from Birdland or the Apollo or someplace. Aideen would be dancing with the moon. Whole moon or quarter. Never mattered. She'd have the music dialed up so loud that she wouldn't have heard me come in. . . . Nothing was more sensational than Aideen when she danced. [13]

Buoyed by these images of movement, Rosie talks her way into lessons at the "House of Dance," where she enters a very different world of light, color, music, and movement. She grows determined to bring dance once more to her grandfather's home, giving him the gift of other times and places. Rosie talks her friend Nick into helping out, explaining why dance is so important: "Dancing is the opposite of dying. . . . Dancing is going somewhere without packing your bags. . . . Dancing is the thing I'm giving Granddad" (228).

For all of these young people, making art is ultimately "the opposite of dying." Even in the face of death and loss, creating music, dancing, painting, or taking photographs provides an anchor to life, which is a lesson of infinite value. In dealing with despair from especially difficult and challenging situations, making art brings solace.

In May 2001, at an International Reading Association Conference in New Orleans, author Tracy Mack, whose story in *Drawing Lessons* is a part of this book, gave a speech entitled "Lighting the Dark Places: The Longing for Beauty and the Restorative Power in Art." Her words are applicable here. For her,

> art had lit a part on the sometimes dark journey of my own childhood and adolescence. . . . It not only buoyed and sustained me through turbulent times but it actually healed me. . . . More than anything I could think of, I longed to find the beauty in this world and add some of my own to it. (Zitlow and Stover, 41)

It is clear that Melinda, whose story begins this chapter, and Rosie, whose story ends it, would understand what Tracy Mack means by the healing power of art.

NOTES

1. Nan Henderson and Mike Milstein, *Resiliency in Schools: Making It Happen for Students and Educators,* updated ed. (Thousand Oaks, CA: Corwin Press, 2002).

2. Laurie Halse Anderson, *Speak* (New York: Puffin, 2006), 197–98.

3. Kim Culbertson, *Songs for a Teenage Nomad* (Naperville, IL: Sourcebook Fire, 2010), 1.

4. Michael Wenberg, *Stringz* (Lodi, NJ: Westside Books, 2010), 17.

5. Trudy Krisher, *Spite Fences* (New York: Laurel Leaf, 1996), 90.

6. Connie Zitlow and Lois Stover, "Portrait of the Artist as a Young Adult: Who Is the Real Me?" *ALAN Review* 38, no. 2 (2011): 34.

7. David Klass, *You Don't Know Me* (New York: HarperTeen, 2001), 115.

8. Jacqueline Woodson, *I Hadn't Meant to Tell You This* (New York: Bantam Doubleday Dell, 1994), 88.

    9. Lois Thomas Stover, *Jacqueline Woodson: The Real Thing* (Lanham, MD: Scarecrow Press, 2003), 57.

  10. Holly Goldberg Sloan, *I'll Be There* (New York: Little, Brown, 2011), 112.

  11. Meg Howrey, *The Cranes Dance* (New York: Vintage Books, 2012), 32.

  12. Cathryn Clinton, *The Eyes of Van Gogh* (Cambridge, MA: Candlewick, 2012), 2.

  13. Beth Kephart, *House of Dance* (New York: HarperTeen, 2008), 137–38.

Chapter Five

Friends, Enemies, Rivals, Boyfriends, and Girlfriends

Young adults appreciate the many crucial elements of friendship. They know the importance of keeping their friendships in repair and that they will be judged by the company they keep. They know that when the adults in their lives are pushing them down paths that they do not want to follow or when there are expectations from their families and cultural contexts that they do not want to fulfill, they can turn to their friends for validation, support, and understanding. They appreciate that true friends help one another to better know themselves. One of the key roles of friends in the lives of young artists is that of understanding the artistic temperament, often because these friends are also artists. In some cases, young artists have friends who are collaborators, such as members of the same musical, dance, or theater group. There are situations when young adult artists need a friend to help them stay focused and sane—even protect them. Sometimes it is the role of the friend to push the artist to be more realistic and honest about his or her talent and other aspects of life. There are also the nonfriends—peers who discourage, taunt, and disrespect, even betray, the artist—although out of such difficult relationships unlikely friendships can sometimes form. Even when there is no true friendship between two young artists, one of them can serve as a touchstone, giving the other a way to measure levels of talent and commitment. Finally, there is the roller coaster of relationships that turn romantic when young people involved in the arts work out what it means to be a boyfriend, a girlfriend, or a significant other through one's artistic endeavors.

FRIENDS AS SYMPATHIZERS

Young adult authors seem to understand the importance of providing artistic protagonists with a support system of peers, which often includes other artists who understand the vision, drive, and commitment of the artist. Thus, as described in chapter 4, Jace from *Stringz* blossoms as a musician and begins to think of himself as an artist when he is befriended by Elvis and Marcy, who show him what it takes to be a musician. They understand the importance of having a good teacher, practicing, and being part of an ensemble. Because Jace is talented enough to recognize others' talent, he respects what Elvis and Marcy have to say. When they tell him that he has a chance to win a prestigious award for minority string players, he believes them and pursues it.

Good Enough

In the funny and poignant *Good Enough*, by Paula Yoo, Patti, a talented violinist, struggles to be the perfect Korean American daughter. Still, in spite of all the time that she is supposed to spend with her Korean church youth group, on SAT practice tests, and on college applications to "HarvardYalePrinceton," Patti spends a lot of time thinking about the "cute trumpet guy" Ben Wheeler, whom she meets at all-state orchestra auditions. Patti develops a crush on Ben, but their relationship develops into a platonic one based on their genuine respect for each other's musical abilities.

Patti begins to think that she has a chance to make music her profession, so with Ben's support and without her parents' permission, she applies to Juilliard. Ben also pushes Patti to explore new genres musically. When they get together to jam, with Ben on guitar (his first musical love), Patti realizes that she is the more advanced musician, but he is much better at improvising. Patti closes her eyes and really listens to what Ben is playing. As she relaxes into the moment, she plays just one long sustained note and thinks, "A rhythm builds between us, and without planning it, I take over the chords and Ben plays the melody, improvising a new variation. The pressure not to make any mistakes disappears. I love this! I want to jam forever!"[1]

Learning to really hear and feel the music serves Patti well in several important contexts. On the basis of her Juilliard admission CD, Patti is invited to audition live for a spot at that prestigious arts institution. Imagining herself jamming with Ben, she plays with passion and feeling, earning a highly unusual verbal response of pleasure from the judges. At the all-day rehearsal for state orchestra, where Patti is assistant concert master, the conductor—frustrated by the other first violins—asks Patti to play the passage because she is the only one keeping the tempo. Patti does so well that the conductor has her play the solo passage, usually reserved for the concert master. Patti has to sight-read and again moves into the zone of improvisation, hearing Ben's voice telling her just to play.

> I plunge ahead with the solo, my fingers stumbling as I play very unfamiliar notes. But . . . when I miss one note, I quickly improvise a harmony to make up for it. I stop worrying about wrong notes and start having fun. The music comes alive. My bow sweeps across the strings with a flourish. (299)

The conductor is impressed, and the concert master tells Patti that she plays the music in ways that he does not, even though he plays the notes with more technical proficiency.

Patti is admitted to Juilliard, which causes a crisis of sorts with her parents, who feel that music is too risky a career option and who want Patti to attend one of the Ivy League colleges. Yet, they finally listen when she says that she wants to consider all options. She decides to go to Yale, which has a special music program for serious musicians who want to pursue a liberal arts degree. While Patti and Ben go their separate ways after high school, Patti's life as a musician has been enriched, and her understanding of what it means to make music has been changed by her friendship with the "cute trumpet guy."

The Opposite of Invisible and *My Not-So-Still Life*

In two interconnected novels, *The Opposite of Invisible* and *My Not-So-Still Life*, Liz Gallagher writes about visual artists who lean on each other for emotional and artistic counsel. Sixteen-year-old Alice, who develops an interest in glassblowing, is at the center of *The Opposite of Invisible*. She is invisible at school except to her best guy friend, Jewel, a photographer, who is "the opposite of invisible" in terms of how he presents himself. During their long walks through Seattle, they make fun of the typical high school "populars" and their activities. When popular Simon notices Alice and they begin dating, her relationship with Jewel is compromised. For comfort, Jewel turns to Vanessa, known for her punk look and talent as both painter and sculptor. Alice breaks up with Simon, and her relationship with Jewel develops from best friends/almost siblings into something romantic and deeper.

Alice chooses Jewel, not knowing if their friendship will become something more, because she gains clarity recognizing that Jewel is the guy who can help her best develop her artistic sense of self. It is Jewel who convinces Alice to try glassblowing, somehow recognizing before she does that she needs to find a medium of her own. On a trip to the Seattle Art Museum, Alice is therefore drawn to an exhibit of Dale Chihuly, amazed at the clarity of his color. She thinks, "Looking at them [the artist's glass creations] I realize there's a whole world I want to step into. A place away from Vanessa and away from perfect couples, and away from school. Even away from Jewel maybe. Toward . . . just me."[2] By the end of the novel, Alice has made new friends and is seeing the world as a glassblower. She wants to create a series of different-colored globes, with "colors swirling . . . shapes that pulse, glide, and fade. I can see glass, heating and cooling" (145). It is clear that glassblowing is Alice's future.

Vanessa is at the center of *My Not-So-Still Life*, which continues the story from the first novel. She is devastated when Jewel and Alice connect romantically, but she begins working at an art supply store, experimenting with graffiti art, and dating an older guy. She is known as being "out there," showing her artistic nature in her hair colors, wild clothes, and makeup. Her friend Nick, Jewel's partner in working on graphic stories, is Vanessa's hair stylist, who understands when she says, "It's not enough to make the art. You have to be the artist."[3] Their friend Holly, a talented musician, understands the commitment necessary to be an artist, as Vanessa explains:

> Holly practices cello from six until eight every night, even Friday and Saturday. Even on days when she's got organized practice after school and has already played for two hours. Practice makes perfect, and Holly's driven; she doesn't want to accept less than perfect when it comes to her music. (19)

Interestingly, while Alice and Vanessa are rivals for Jewel's romantic attention, they admire each other as artists. Alice turns away from painting to glassblowing because she recognizes that Vanessa has a level of skill, talent, and commitment as a visual artist that Alice cannot match. Vanessa admires Alice as a person and as an artist. After Jewel breaks up with Vanessa to pursue Alice romantically, Vanessa gives Alice a tiny beautiful sculpture that she has made of a dove, a peace offering in keeping with the Picasso "Dove Girl" print that she knows, from Jewel, is so important to Alice. When these young people go on Friday night "Art Walks," they talk about their art, as well as artists from DuChamp to Pollock, encouraging one another in their individual artistic pursuits, going to their shows and concerts, giving each other art-based presents, and accepting one another as artists.

Another Way to Dance and *A Time for Dancing*

When the young ballerinas in *Another Way to Dance*, by Martha Southgate, and *A Time for Dancing*, by Davida Wills Hurwin, need comfort, they depend on others who know the competitive world of ballet. Vicki, from *Another Way to Dance*, a novel set in the early seventies, is a fourteen-year-old African American who fell in love with dance at age eight, when she saw *Don Quixote* with Baryshnikov in the principal role. Six years later, she wins a place in a prestigious summer program of the School of American Ballet in New York City. If she does well, she could be invited to join the yearlong corps program.

At the ballet school, Vicki meets Stacey, the only other black girl in the program, who has a short-cropped Afro and wears big hoop earrings. For the first time, Vicki has someone to talk with about "sticking out" in the world of ballet, about the difficulties of being black when one of the principles of the corps de ballet is "absolute visual harmony."[4] Vicki can feel herself getting better as a result of the summer intensive training, but she begins to realize that she still does not have that ineffable quality necessary to make it to the next level. The girls are friends with Debbie, a white girl, whom they appreciate as being the best in the class. Vicki compares her physical presence and movements with Debbie's and recognizes that they do not measure up. Stacey introduces Vicki to the Alvin Ailey Dancers and talks about "another way to dance." As a result of her friendship with Stacey, Vicki faces the disappointment when not selected for the year-round program, knowing that she has options and can still enjoy the feeling of flying that ballet gives her.

In *A Time for Dancing*, the relationship between Sam and Juliana, "Jules," is a much deeper one than that between Vicki and Stacey. For more than half their lives, Sam and Jules have been dance partners and best friends. But in their senior year, Jules gets sick. By the time that she realizes that she has far more than the normal pain that dancers feel, the diffuse histiocytic lymphoma causing that pain is probably incurable. The girls realize that, individually, they must figure out how to use their dancing to remain connected while figuring out how to face the reality that Jules will probably die. In alternating chapters, the two girls convey how their friendship and their art are challenged but ultimately give them strength. As Jules says, even when she is dying,

> dance was more than a thing I did. It was my definition and my strength. It could reach out and bring me back to myself. It made me real and whole and strong. No one could take it or keep me from it. And no one, except for another dancer, could understand how it felt. [5]

Their teacher asks Sam and Jules to dance a duet at their final show. Choreographed before Jules was diagnosed and became so ill, the dance mirrors how the two became friends as little girls and grew up together. As they dance it together one last time, they infuse it with the poignancy and sadness of their current circumstances, as Sam describes:

> We danced the little girls' games, and Jules mimed taking a ribbon from my hair, in play, and throwing it up to the sky. As I watched it come down, I turned to her smiling, innocent, and she was looking at me, knowing something I didn't yet understand. Our game continued but now it was broken, and as we danced our growing up, growing apart, growing older, I couldn't tell where the music stopped and we began. The end came—years later, walking our separate ways, seeing each other, recognizing and reaching out, wanting to know if there was still a connection. We touched and, in the last moment, looked up. The imaginary ribbon was floating down again. Jules pointed to it, and on the final note, I reached up and grabbed it. (203–4)

It is through this dance that the girls realize that Sam will be left alone in this physical world, but Jules will be with her: "Dancing. And free" (257).

FRIENDS AND OTHERS AS COLLABORATORS

Sometimes young artists are fortunate enough to have friends and fellow artists with whom to collaborate in the making of their art, as Sam and Jules do. Perhaps not surprising, there seem to be more novels about young musicians who are friends and collaborators than there are about collaboration among young people in other artistic arenas. While dance and theater require many people to make a performance happen, usually the young dancer or thespian is being directed or choreographed by an adult who creates the artistic vision of the dance or the play.

Audition

In perfecting a performance, collaboration between dancer and choreographer is important, as portrayed in Stasia Ward Kehoe's *Audition*, as Sara conveys what it is like to work with Remington, a slightly older young man who becomes her boyfriend. Sara becomes a muse to Remington, as he watches her movements while she is falling asleep, sprawling in the bed, waking up, and testing the floor with a toe. She in turn delights in the way that her actions become part of the creation of the dance. Sara also describes the way that she and two other ballerinas have to be totally in sync to do a particular dance. Even after she breaks up with Rem, she has to collaborate with him as they perform their parts in a children's ballet *The Three Bears*. But ultimately, Sara describes the dancer as being primarily responsible for herself and her own skill. Without input into the overall vision for the production, she does what the ballet master or the choreographer directs her to do.

Visual artists and photographers tend to work alone, not like the company of a corps de ballet. While there are solo musical performers and while good musicians must practice alone with their instruments, as Patti and Ben show in *Good Enough*, it is possible for musicians to come together to create music without a director, improvising and building off one another in ways that are more difficult in other artistic venues. Jonathan from *Adios, Nirvana*, by Conrad Wesselhoeft, needs his "thicks" to rescue him when he attempts suicide, and, in the end, he needs them to push open the door to his dead brother Telly's room and bring back to life his guitars and the music the brothers used to make together. His friends orchestrate his public performance at the end of the school year, which gives Jonathan the closure that he needs after

Telly's death. The most important part of the collaboration among Jody, Giselle, and Vivian in Rosanne Parry's *Second Fiddle* occurs when they make a last-minute substitution for their contest piece and play Jody's new composition "Canon for Three Friends," a piece that not only defines their friendship but also impresses the contest judges. Throughout their experiences, they are devoted to one another and to their music, becoming better musicians as a result of their collaboration and shared commitment.

Harmonic Feedback and *Amplified*

When friends are also artistic collaborators, they can together bring to fruition a bigger artistic vision than what they can accomplish individually. The commonalities about this process are described in *Harmonic Feedback* and *Amplified*, two novels by Tara Kelly. In *Harmonic Feedback*, Drea (Andrea), who plays guitar and works with a synthesizer, describes what it is like to play with friends Justin and Naomi:

> Justin began with a chord progression that instantly connected with me. My fingertips buzzed with anticipation, and I heard a billion different guitar melodies over the top. Maybe a gentle synth—bell-like without the piercing edge. Then he played a fast, erratic melody with his right hand. Every note made me shiver, each one building into something even more amazing. . . . I guessed at Justin's tempo, setting it around 100bpm, and fished around for some drum samples. Most of the time I'd start with a loop that felt right—couldn't explain why. Then I'd EQ the sound so it fit the tone of the song and add more drum samples from there.[6]

As Naomi adds lyrics, Drea picks up a twelve-string acoustic and says, "Layering the guitar chords on top of the piano gave the song a dreamy atmosphere. But Justin's melody and Naomi's lyrics took the song to a place I could never go on my own" (11).

In *Amplified*, Kelly describes the collaboration among a larger group of rock musicians. Jasmine, the narrator and new guitarist for the band, explains what happens in rehearsal:

> When Veta's riff kicked in, my focus shifted to her vocal melody. Songs always put images in my head, kind of like watching a music video. . . . The chorus made me feel reckless, like I was kissing some guy I barely knew. Back of his car. 2 a.m. Cold leather seat against my skin. The kind of scene that called for a glass slide. . . . I put the slide

over my pinkie and went from one note to the next, keeping the lick sparse and mindful of Veta's vocals. It added a nice bluesy edge and gave the song more personality. [7]

The musicians agree that they have found the right combination to make the song really rock. None of them could have created this version of the song working in isolation. For friends who are artistic collaborators, making art together works because of their friendship and respect for one another.

Hidden Voices

The three friends who support one another in Pat Lowery Collins's *Hidden Voices: The Orphan Musicians of Venice* live in the Ospedale della Pietà, an orphanage renowned in the early eighteenth century for its extraordinary musical program. The talented girls work with Father Antonio Vivaldi, who, during his early career, taught the girls and composed pieces for them to perform. Luisa, almost fourteen years old, has a remarkable soprano voice and is different from the other girls because she has a mother, a wealthy duke's mistress, who sometimes comes to visit. Anetta is fifteen and has the ear and touch for the viola d'amore. The dreamy, gleeful Rosalba plays all the instruments well but is especially skilled with the cello and oboe. Each chapter of the story is a first-person narrative by one of the three friends. Part of Father Vivaldi's responsibility at the orphanage is to write solo parts for a girl deemed ready to be chosen by a duke, who will request an interview. If the duke is pleased when he hears her perform while hidden behind a grille, he will take her as his wife. The girls know that what a nurse tells Anetta is true: "It's the ones who play and sing who have a chance at something better than the life [she] leads." [8]

When it is carnival time, Rosalba, longing for romance, slips away from her friends and the orphanage to flirt with a wig maker's assistant. To her surprise, he brutally rapes her and then runs away. Anetta and Luisa are worried the next morning when they discover that Rosalba is missing and there is no word about where she is or what happened to her. As a runaway, Rosalba is not allowed to return to the orphanage. She is rescued by street musicians, who realize that she is too refined to be from the neighborhood. They force her to perform with them, even when she becomes large with child. But Father Vivaldi, who cannot forget Rosalba and her desire to see Europe, seeks her out and gives her the name of a friend in Vienna who may be able to book her as an oboist in other cities to help her build a career away from the Ospedale.

Meanwhile, many at the orphanage become sick from a mysterious malady. Some do not survive. Anetta is devastated when Luisa develops a high fever, which turns her throat scarlet and leaves her too weak to sing, and is sent to the country to recover. Luisa misses her friends and making music but is surprised by how much she enjoys the quiet and beauty away from the city. She soon falls in love with a country boy. Anetta feels a constant ache without her two friends and writes long letters to Luisa, who sends back short letters asking if there has been any word about Rosalba. Luisa and Anetta share a bond in their concern and feeling of helplessness about their missing friend.

When Luisa is well enough to return to the orphanage, she learns that a duke had requested to meet Anetta after being impressed with her playing, although he did not choose her to become his wife, considering her too bold when she dared to ask him questions. Anetta knows that she wants to stay and teach at the Ospedale, not be someone's wife. One night when she is alone in the choir loft practicing a difficult new concerto on her viola, she hears something downstairs and realizes that it is the creaking sound of the wheel, a device where mothers leave their babies in hopes that the orphanage will find and care for them. On it is a girl wrapped in finely sewn clothes, with Rosalba's feather mask from the carnival hidden inside. Anetta calls out Rosalba's name "so she will know for certain that her precious child has been discovered by her loyal friend" (321). Anetta names the baby "Rosa."

Rosalba, though successful in her new life as a performer, continues to draw strength from her memories of the deep friendship that she shared with the other girls. Luisa learns that when she was young, her mother had taken her to the Ospedale because she had operatic aspirations for her. Luisa is surprised when Anetta confesses that the love she feels for her is as strong as that of a man for a woman. Luisa responds that she cannot reciprocate but tells Anetta that friends they will continue to be "because we share too much" (334).

The young women of *Hidden Voices* reflect that deep-seated sense of understanding that comes from sharing a deeply held love for music, dance, or art that gives them purpose. That love of art, that shared commitment, gives young artists a connection that transcends time and space—even death, as is true for dancers Jules and Sam.

OTHER KINDS OF COLLABORATIONS

Graffiti Moon

Sometimes young artists collaborate across artistic media using their different skills. In *Graffiti Moon*, Cath Crowley alternates chapters narrated by Lucy, a blossoming glassblower, and Ed, a graffiti artist who works with his poet friend Leo, who writes captions for Ed's work. Ed uses the tag "Shadow," and Leo just signs himself "Poet." Throughout much of the book, while Lucy and Ed have a nighttime adventure after her high school graduation, Lucy does not know that Ed is "Shadow," whom she has long wanted to meet because his work speaks so deeply to her.

Ed paints with his eyes constantly on the lookout for cops because he often paints on walls that have not been designated free for graffiti. He says that when he paints, all the tangled thoughts and emotions in his head "scream" from his hand and onto the brick wall, where he empties himself: "Tonight I'm doing this bird that's been in my head. . . . He's a little yellow guy living on sweet green grass. Belly to clouds, legs facing the same direction. He could be sleeping. He could be dead."[9] Captioning Ed's drawing of the bird, Leo makes up a font of letters "drifting and curling" in which he writes "Peace" in Ed's sky. Ed notes that the two friends see things differently: Leo sees peace; Ed sees his own future and hopes that the bird is just sleeping rather than dead.

THE AUDIENCE AS COLLABORATORS

In *Graffiti Moon*, Cath Crowley introduces yet another kind of collaboration—that between the artist and the audience, viewer, or a listener, who may be a friend but is more likely more distant from the artist. Ed's work as Shadow, who Lucy thinks of as a stranger, inspires her imagination. She has seen Shadow's piece of a night sky filled with birds flying across it: "Their feathers glow. Moon birds trapped on brick. They're not dirtied by the world; from here they look more beautiful than the real ones flying around them. I imagine being good enough to blow glass birds that look like that" (73). She imagines an installation of hundreds of such moon-colored birds, dangling from the ceiling, being lit from below, and she itches to get started on a work of her own.

Ed shows Lucy a wall that "Shadow" painted after breaking up with his girlfriend: a picture of a ghost in jar. Lucy says that Shadow must feel like that ghost: stuck, without air, with the lid on tight. Ed thinks that she is right—the lid is on so tight that "there's nothing that can open that jar but smashing" (142). He points out that there are air holes in the drawing, and Lucy says that it is the worst part, noting that Shadow's paintings are never hopeful. Ed finds this interesting because after he paints, he feels a high and relief. He wonders if that is hope (143). But he tells Lucy that maybe Shadow cannot feel hope.

Lucy gives Ed a different view of himself, saying that Shadow makes stuff better just by painting. She tells him a story about waiting for a bus and seeing a picture by Shadow of a bug across the road: "This bug looked at me with eyes that said, 'Can you believe this? I've been waiting here for half an hour'" (144). Lucy says, "A guy who paints like this is doing something. He's not sitting around" (144). For Lucy, that bug brought a smile to her face and lightened her mood. That one comment from Lucy as viewer, who still does not know that Ed is Shadow, makes Ed understand that he is able to touch his audience, to give it something unique. As a result, he decides that he wants to try reaching for a different kind of future, one beyond dead-end jobs and graffiti art.

Struts and Frets

Sammy, from *Struts and Frets*, by Jon Skovon, describes the importance of the audience to a musician, saying that when a performance went well,

> I felt like I was ripping open my chest to the audience, showing them everything I had inside. I felt like they knew me, understood me, each and every one of them, and I had nothing to hide. I felt drunk and amazed. This is why I did it. This was why it was all worth it. [10]

At one point, when Sam's band is opening for a well-known regional band, he gets nervous, and his throat tightens up. He explains that a man from the audience hands him a soda, and, in that moment, he has a new appreciation for the role of the audience:

> Right up until that moment, I guess I always thought of a performer's relationship to an audience almost like it was a conflict, like they were just waiting to expose me for the wannabe poser that I was. . . . But in

that moment . . . I realized they just wanted to hear some good music and hoped I could provide it. They were just looking for a little of that reach-to-the-moon magic. (285)

DJ Rising

For Marley, of *DJ Rising*, by Love Maia, playing to the audience on any given night is crucial to his success with his chosen "instrument": the turntable. As an artist, Marley says that he does not just want to get people dancing.

> I want to be the one who makes people think and surprises them and shows them something new and takes them on a journey and gets them moving on the dance floor to tunes they used to hate but that I've made beautiful by pulling sounds, switching beats, adding samples. [11]

Whether the young artist is collaborating with others in the same artistic medium, across artistic genres, or with the audience, one important aspect of these books is showing students that all artists need to develop the skills necessary for cooperation, for reaching out to others through their art, to really develop their talents and hone their artistic skills.

FRIENDS AS ENCOURAGERS, FOCUSERS, AND PROTECTORS

Sometimes it is important for young artists to have friends who are *not* artists, who can help them be grounded, help them with their school work, help them stay organized, or help them get gigs and go public with their art. Tiffany, a gifted athlete involved in many sports, is that kind of friend for Georgia of *Pieces of Georgia*, by Jen Bryant. She accepts Georgia's quiet nature, and she listens without judging when Georgia describes how her mother's parents cut her mom and dad off because the former did not like her mother's artistic pursuits and father's working-class background. Tiffany gives titles to Georgia's sketches and tells her that "someday you'll be famous and I can say / I knew you when you were just getting started / and I named all your pictures." [12]

In Denise Vega's *Rock On*, the main character, Ori, is a young man whose longtime friend is Alli, a girl who helps push Ori to develop as a musician and who serves as a liaison between Ori and his older brother

Del. Alli's job is to encourage and be sympathetic as well as to help Ori navigate his first serious romance, by giving him insights into how girls sometimes view the world differently than guys do. Alli first heard Ori sing when he was twelve. She tells him, "I didn't know you could sing. Wow!"[13] This is new information to Ori. She tells him that he should take lessons, "then you can be lead guitarist and singer for your band" (42). Having a band was, at that point, something that Ori had not thought about. "All because of Alli," Ori finds himself singing and loving the way that his voice and guitar work together so that, as the novel opens, he is auditioning bass players for his newly formed rock group.

In *DJ Rising*, Marley, too, needs his friends to give him a vision of his possible future and the confidence and feedback necessary to make that vision a reality. After Marley's first real gig, Scuzz tells him that he was "so creative" and "so smooooooth." Scuzz then tells other students at their school that Marley

> played these Isley Brothers tunes and then blended them into Notorious
> B.I.G. and Ice Cube. . . . The transitions came out real cool cuz Biggie
> and Cube used Isley Brothers tunes for melodies. . . . Like you're
> hearing this Isley Brothers tune you've never heard before . . . and
> you're just like, damn, is that where that melody came from? (47)

Scuzz lets Marley know that he has achieved what he hoped to create: "Marley was going for this classic old-school hip-hop vibe with a dash of R & B sexy sprinkled on top" (47). Scuzz states Marley's unarticulated dreams: "Marley's on a whole other level. This is what he's meant to do with his life, you know what I'm sayin'?" (100). Scuzz and another friend, Charlie, are instrumental in getting Marley his big breaks and in publicizing his success so that he gets opportunities to play private parties. When Marley becomes better known, he knows that Scuzz and Charlie will help keep him grounded.

Jersey Tomatoes Are the Best

In the case of *Jersey Tomatoes Are the Best*, by Maria Padian, Henry (Henriette) and Eva are Jersey girls who have been best friends forever in spite of their different interests. Henry is a teen tennis star who looks like a model and has a wicked serve. Eva is a prima ballerina with the stage mother from hell. They are each accepted to their dream camps for the summer, in two different states. Probably because Henry is not a dancer, it is with Henry that Eva can let down her guard, be playful, and just enjoy the moment. It is Henry whom Eva calls when she is feeling intense pressure to perform and to lose weight to conform to the stereotypical ballerina look. Eva knows that Henry will do anything for her—Henry actually convinces her boyfriend from tennis camp to sneak out of the compound and race by car to see Eva, who is hospitalized, almost dead from anorexia.

Henry, unlike Eva's mother, is not concerned that it might be the end of Eva's dancing career, because she cares about her friend as a whole person. Because she is not a dancer, Henry is the friend that Eva first lets back into her life when she is recovering from her battle with anorexia. Eva admits to Henry that she is enjoying dancing without a mirror, without an audience, and just for herself. Eva's mother is not likely to appreciate that Eva feels that her successes "burden her. Deep down, she doesn't believe she's worthy of the praise heaped on her,"[14] but Henry understands and accepts Eva for who she is, without pressuring her to be more.

Interestingly, it often seems to be the case that the nonartist friend, who serves as a kind of cheerleader or manager, is the opposite sex from the actual artist. In *Rock On* and *Struts and Frets*, male musicians are pushed and encouraged by female friends, and in *Rival*, by Sara Bennett Wealer, Matt nurtures and often protects Katherine, a budding opera singer. In *The Eyes of Van Gogh*, John Mark literally saves Jude after she slips and breaks a variety of bones during her near-suicide attempt. And in *Instructions for a Broken Heart*, by Kim Culbertson, while it is Clarissa who gives Jessa the "instructions" that she is to follow during her Italy tour, it is Tyler, traveling with Jessa and known for his stage-manager qualities, who ensures that she follows those instructions, gives her a shoulder on which to cry, and pushes her to move beyond her broken heart.

FRIENDS AS LIE DETECTORS AND TOUCHSTONES

Dramarama

Truly good friends tell the truth, even when that truth is hard to hear. When two young people are involved in similar artistic endeavors, they often function as touchstones against which they can each measure their levels of artistic talent and commitment. E. Lockhart's *Dramarama* provides a great example of the importance of friends who tell the truth and act as touchstones, as she chronicles the experiences of Sarah, who renames herself Sadye during an intensive summer theater camp. Sarah lives in a bland, characterless town and feels alive only when she is dancing at Miss Delilah's School of Dance, where she takes lessons four times a week and stays after class to hear the teachers' stories about the theater.

Sarah's outlook changes when Demi comes to school—a gay black male who loves the theater as much as Sarah—and the two become a team. Demi plays at being straight and being invisible. His hanging out with Sarah helps keep up the illusion that he is not gay. The two audition for a summer program at a high-powered drama camp featuring classes with Broadway choreographers and directors. They are both accepted—Sadye on the strength of her dancing and Demi for his singing and acting skill. At orientation, the head director tells the campers that they all have talent but the teachers will help them develop their physical instruments: "voice, the breath, the body. We give you techniques for self-expression and transformation."[15] He continues, "To become someone else, you must let go of yourself, and to do that, you must be humble" (83). Because of their talent and inherent competition, it is hard for the campers to accept the teachers' emphasis that theater "is a collective effort, a community endeavor" (83).

Of the four musicals and one play to be produced at the camp, Sadye, with no acting experience, is cast only as Peter Quince, a man, in *Midsummer Night's Dream*, and as a Hot Box dancer in *Guys and Dolls*, which is directed by the most experienced Broadway director on the staff. Sadye begins to realize that her talents do not compare to those of her friends, especially Nanette, who, after only five rehearsals and without any training, is dancing better than she is. Sadye also learns the harsh truth that she cannot really sing, when the director identifies her as the alto who is singing flat. Furthermore, Sadye challenges the judgment of her directors. She thinks that it is unfair when she is late to the first acting class and the director makes everyone lie on their backs for fifty-five minutes thinking about what is important. But Demi says that the director is teaching them, through this exercise, that "it doesn't matter if the cast lists went up or your landlord kicked you out, or your wife left you, or whatever; a professional actor shows up on time and doesn't let personal life get in the way" (147). Demi thinks that this exercise is "amazing" because no other teacher ever made him think for a whole hour. He tells Sadye, "You have to trust your director, trust your acting teacher. He's the one who can see the whole picture. He was showing us we had to trust his vision" (148). Sadye finds this truth—on top of those about her real level of talent— hard to take, but because it comes from Demi, her best friend, she cannot ignore it.

Part of the reason why Sadye begins to accept her lack of star potential is that she is keenly aware that Demi is really starting to shine in the camp environment, where he can be himself, not hiding his gayness or his talent. Because she is kind and smart, she comforts him when he gives his heart to another boy for the first time, only to have it trounced. Sadye really believes in Demi's future and protects him. But she is angry to learn that he applied to, and has been accepted to attend, a boarding school for the academic year without telling her. The two of them are on a dorm roof (where campers are forbidden to be), talking about next year, and Demi is drinking a beer. When a counselor discovers them, Sadye says that she bought it. In a tape recording in which Demi and Sadye describe their summer experiences, she says that she saved Demi

> because a friendship, a real friendship, should survive all the stuff that comes with it. . . . Demi Howard is my best friend, so it's okay to tell a lie to keep him in school; it's good to make a sacrifice. . . . You can't only do things because you know you'll get a return on it later. You have to do them out of generosity. (287)

Sadye leaves the camp with new information about herself, gradually realizing that she could be a director. She recalls when the director for the Shakespeare play in which she had a part had a strange vision for the actors playing trees and rocks. Sadye complained,

> The concept doesn't work . . . because *Midsummer* is not really an ensemble play. We're not *all* supposed to be one with the fairy forest— lovers, sprites, mechanicals. We're supposed to be contrasting elements and counterpoint story lines. It's confusing this way, with everyone trying to channel the spirit of magic and not being sure what their speeches even mean. (172)

Sadye tries to be a good sport and reason with the director, who then takes her aside, tells her that she has strength and leadership potential— and asks her to please use those for the good of the production. Sadye returns home with the realization that she is bossy and outspoken, that she is physically strong and even imposing, that she can be kind, but that she is not afraid to ask questions. With the awareness that there is a place for her offstage, if not on, she gets an internship assisting the assistant artistic director for the New York Theater Workshop, which Demi hopes will be the beginning of Sadye's professional involvement in the world of the theater, which she loves so much.

The Jewel and the Key

In *The Jewel and the Key*, by Louise Spiegler, Addie, like Sadye, has dreams of becoming an actress, although she prefers straight drama to musical theater. She, too, is in high school and has been entranced by the theater for a long time.

> Since she was eleven or twelve she'd been reading her way through the skinny Penguin editions of plays, eventually tackling the big, bound collections: Shakespeare, Shaw, Ibsen, Williams, Wilson. She loved them all. The words jumped off the pages. She could hear how the dialogue should sound, imagine how a scene should look onstage. [16]

When the novel opens, Addie is a normal seventeen-year-old living in Seattle, coping with Algebra II, trying to keep her best friend, Whaley Price, who lives with the family, from enlisting in the army, and dreaming of getting a starring role in the high school production of *Peer Gynt*. Then an earthquake hits the town, damaging her father's bookstore/home and revealing a previously unknown closet filled with costumes and artifacts from the old Jewel Theater. Addie becomes curious about the Jewel, and she and Whaley become determined to help its owner achieve historic landmark status and then renovate the building to its former glory.

A handcrafted magical silver mirror from the stash of artifacts takes Addie back to 1917, when the Jewel was at the height of its popularity as a venue for serious theater. There she meets Reg, a member of the Jewel's acting company who wants to enlist in World War I. As Addie travels back and forth in time, she becomes involved in antiwar protesting in both centuries and, watching Reg onstage, comes to realize that she does not really have the acting ability to be a professional. But she is given opportunities to organize and help with the production at the Jewel, which make her see that she has both the vision and the skill to become a director.

The novel is part mystery, as Addie and the people in the contemporary story try to find out about the Jewel's past, and part romance, as

Addie falls in love with Reg. It is also part historical fiction based on Spiegler's research about the "Wobblies"—the Industrial Workers of the World—and their antiwar stance. And it is part coming-of-age, as Addie, in both periods, has to rely on her friends and mentors to create a new vision of herself, her skills, and her future.

When Addie watches Reg as Macbeth, she becomes aware of what it means to be an actor. She is transfixed:

> She watched him stare at the ghostly procession of kings in mounting horror as they wafted by him. . . . He spoke the Elizabethan poetry with such familiarity that it sounded like natural speech. . . . It sent chills down her spine. . . . A truth hit her: Reg was an actor. A *real* actor. And she . . . she was good. But she would never be *that* good. (170)

It is clear, nevertheless, that the theater is where Addie belongs. When she is in the Jewel of 1917, her heart beats faster, and it is "like a jolt of caffeine: the stage lights, the smell of sawdust, the voices projecting against the back walls" (259). Her imagination is ignited just by the empty physical space: no sets, no costumes, no backdrops.

Meg Turner, the Jewel's 1917 director, senses something in Addie and asks if she wants to watch Meg and some other actors fooling around with a possible project—which turns out to be *Peer Gynt*, considered very modern and shocking in that era. As Addie watches, she tells Meg, "They're too elegant. I mean, it's not a royal palace. It's the hall of the troll king—more like the monkey house at the zoo. So that music's too pretty. Hettie and Andrew are dancing too well" (263). Meg tells her to interrupt the actors and let them know her thoughts, giving her a chance to direct. Addie stumbles a bit as she begins but then gathers momentum; she explains how Peer, as a human, knows that while the trolls see their behavior as high class and elegant, it is really not. Peer, she says, should join in the revelry but then "mug to the audience to show he knows how obscene it all is, but then be sort of seduced by it too" (266). She gives direction to the piano player to play more wildly, and she shows the actress playing the troll princess how to dance like a princess but then as a troll. Peter now sees her for what she is. Addie sees the stage swirling with dancers, ringing with stamping feet, and she conveys that vision to the actors. Meg tells her that she has a job if she wants one and that, if she works hard, she could end up sitting in Meg's director's chair.

After the rehearsal disbands, Addie and Reg have a conversation in which Addie tells Reg, "I'm a . . . director!" She says the words softly, tasting them in her mouth. Then, more firmly, she adds, "That's what I am" (74). Addie has to use those directorial skills in both time frames to save the people she loves. In 1917, she organizes an improvised drama when she and Reg are hustling a union worker out of town who has escaped prison, using the costumes and props at hand to convince the police officer who has chased them that they are different characters than the one he wants. In the present time, she helps orchestrate the grand reopening of her father's bookstore and helps organize the movement to restore the Jewel, where she can see herself in the future. The magic mirror, now cracked and no longer magical, is in her pocket as she gives her notes to her future actors and directs her future cast.

Audition and *Bunheads*

For Addie, like Sadye, having friends against whom to measure herself as an actress and having friends who help her see where her true talents lie is an invaluable gift. While it appears that Sadye and Addie will ultimately find their way to becoming theater professionals, young adults sometimes come to realize that what they thought they wanted for themselves as artists is actually not desirable. Comparing themselves with friends is one way that young artists can arrive at such a decision point. In both *Audition*, by Stasia Ward Kehoe, and *Bunheads*, by Sophie Flack, a young female dancer comes to realize that she does in fact have the talent to succeed as a professional but does not have the single-mindedness to make the commitment necessary for that talent to flourish. Sara from *Audition* lives with doubt about her commitment, waffling between her desire to dance like Bonnie, one of the lead dancers at the school, and her desire to be home with her parents.

Sara also compares herself to Lisette, who is the star of the studio. Ultimately, Sara recognizes that Lisette is driven in a way that she herself is just not:

> Lisette practices / Alone / Before and after / The teacher and the rest of us / Fill the room / With our lesserness. . . . / Ballet / Is her one and only / Uncomplicated lover, / Best friend.[17]

After comparing herself in terms of talent and commitment to her friends, Sara decides to return home; she has "stopped wanting a life without words beyond / Fat romances to fill the moments / Between dances" (455). After their last performance of the season, which is Sara's last performance with the company, she says,

I know, / For Lisette, for Rem, this stage is a paradise found; / For Bonnie, an altar at which she sacrifices. / The curtain closed, the work lights come up. / Stagehands sweep. / Dancers rush to change into their next costumes. / In my head, I choreograph a poem / About reverence. (458)

Without Lisette and Bonnie with whom to talk, to compare herself, and to reflect on what it means to be a dancer, Sara could not have arrived at this new, somewhat scary, though exciting, point in her life. Hannah, the nineteen-year-old main character in *Bunheads*, has actually made it in the world of dance but is not sure that she has the drive to move to the next level of her profession. As a member of the corps de ballet of a prestigious New York company, Hannah makes her living as a dancer and is working to become a soloist and, perhaps, the featured ballerina. Again, as a result of her friendship with the other women in the corps and the chance to compare herself to them on a daily basis—combined with a developing relationship with Jake, a college student—Hannah comes to new insights about what she wants from life.

Because Hannah is the understudy for a dancer who lands wrong in the middle of a performance, she has to go onstage, without warming up, in a costume too small for her, without makeup, and not really well rehearsed. Nevertheless, Hannah is ecstatic:

> I'm buzzing with adrenaline. . . . Suddenly I forget that I'm not wearing stage makeup and that I wasn't even warmed up. I lose myself in the music, even though my heart is pounding so loudly I swear the audience can hear it. The rush is incredible. *This is why I love my job.*[18]

The audience responds with great enthusiasm. Her fellow dancers tell her that she was brilliant and they always knew that she had it in her to be successful.

Hannah gets noticed in a review for her mix of "innocence and impulsiveness," for her "contagious energy"; her dancing is described as spontaneous and her feet precise (69). For a time after this performance, Hannah says that there is nothing she can imagine better than being onstage and dancing with her friends and fellow artists. Doing yet another performance of *Nutcracker*, Hannah describes what it is like to be onstage such that she cannot imagine giving it up:

> I run into the snow, with my feet pointed in front of me, and tour jete in unison with the girls alongside me. Imagine that I'm a snowflake falling

from the sky: I am brushed by the wind, and swoop this way and that. I
cross paths with other snowflakes; I smile at Bea, and she smiles back.
Even though we've performed this part over a hundred times, there's
always something magical about the snow and the music, about dancing
with your friends. (93)

The pressure increases for Hannah when Annabelle, a ballet mistress,
tells Hannah that she has gained weight and that she must lose it in her
breasts. The costumers can make Hannah a special undergarment that
will bind her bosom, making her silhouette once more that of a classic
ballerina. Hannah begins to compare herself to Zoe, often a competitor,
who started in the corp at the same time and whose privileged background makes her an unlikely friend. But Hannah says at one point,
"I'll always be grateful for the way Zoe befriended me in those first
weeks at [the Manhattan Ballet Academy]. I might have died of loneliness without her" (159). Their friendship is based on a long list of
shared experiences.

But Zoe has no interest in life beyond dance. Hannah knows that
after her success in the solo, she is on the way to being promoted, but
she knows, as her colleague Bea tells her, that she will have to be more
like Zoe, which means, "You can either have a life, or you can dance.
You can't have it both ways" (279). Hannah does not want to choose,
but Bea tells her what she does not want to hear—that she *has* to
choose.

Hannah's relationship with Jacob is also a touchstone for her as she
wrestles with her decision. Jake asks her what she might do if she left
ballet, something that she had not considered before meeting him, going to museums and coffee shops with him, and having wonderful
conversations with him about books. She tells him, "I'm envious of all
you're able to explore and learn. And I want that. I want to learn
Italian, too, but for real, and I want to have the time to go see really
amazing art. And I want to get to know my parents" (285). But she also
says, "The idea of having a life *terrifies* me" (285).

Nevertheless, Hannah does choose to leave ballet, telling her director, "Thank you for this adventure, but it's time for me to go explore
something else" (290). Hannah is scared and crying as she leaves his
office; however, she says, "But I was also free" (290). It turns out that
the entire novel is really the entrance essay that she writes as part of her
application to attend New York University and study creative writing.
Hannah would not have had the courage to imagine this future without

Zoe and Bea, unlikely friends who became friends because of sharing most of their waking hours together. Once she becomes a creative writing student, Hannah doubts how much contact she will have with them, but they played an important role in the person she becomes.

Curveball: The Year I Lost My Grip

In Jordan Sonneblick's *Curveball: The Year I Lost My Grip*, Pete finds an unlikely friend who is, at first, his partner for a class project. Later, as they spend time together, this young woman becomes someone who pushes him to be honest about his circumstances and his abilities, and over time, she also becomes his girlfriend. As the novel opens, Pete has no idea that he even needs a new friend. Pete Friedman is a "sports guy,"[19] and his focus has always been on baseball, a passion that he shares with his best friend, AJ. But at the end of eighth grade, Pete's elbow explodes, and the subsequent surgery to repair the cartilage that broke loose inside his elbow joint leaves him unable to play baseball in high school. After being a successful pitcher, he finds it difficult to accept this fact, and he cannot bring himself to tell AJ, who thinks that once Pete completes therapy, they will be playing together again.

As his ninth-grade year unfolds, Pete is surprised that it is not AJ but a girl who becomes his closest friend, his touchstone—a girl who is the super-hot star of the girl's dance team and a photographer. Pete never thought of himself as an artist or a photographer and did not expect photography to take the place of baseball as his focus. Yet he knows some things about photography because his seventy-eight-year-old grandfather is a professional photographer and Pete has long enjoyed going on photo shoots and spending time in the darkroom with him. But something is happening to his grandfather, who seems at times frozen in place, just staring blankly. The first time that Pete notices it is when they are on the top of a mountain waiting to get the perfect shot of an eagle. Grampa completely misses the shot and, to Pete's surprise, soon gives him all his expensive camera gear, saying, "This is all yours now. I'm done" (41).

On the first day of ninth grade, Pete goes to "Introduction to Photography" because his mother had insisted he register for it. The teacher begins the class by asking questions, and after Pete surprises her with his detailed answers, he is quickly asked to move to "Advanced Photographic Techniques." Soon Angelika Stone, also from the introduction class, enters the room. The teacher, Mr. Marsh, assigns

Pete and Angelika, the only first-year students in the class, to be partners for the first class assignment—to do a photographic portrait of
another person in which they develop a concept and think about what
they want the world to see through their lens.

Because Angelika wants to know more about Pete to help her develop a concept for her portrait of him, she talks to AJ to get ideas. Pete is
surprised to learn from Angelika that AJ told her that Pete is training
really hard to get back into condition for spring and that AJ gave her
Pete's "incredibly special baseball" (105) from the best game that he
and AJ ever played together. When Pete holds the baseball again, a
huge lump forms in his throat, and in his mind, he is back on the field
with AJ. When he comes back to reality, he is crying, and he sees that
Angelika has been clicking away.

As they continue to progress with their project, Pete and Angelika
find themselves attracted to each other. But Pete is nevertheless sad. He
continues to notice how his grandfather is changing and seems to black
out at times. One day when Grampa falls, he calls Pete for help but
insists that he not tell his mother. When Pete talks about the incident
with Angelika, she suggests that Grampa sounds like her grandmother,
who had Alzheimer's disease, and she tells Pete that he must tell his
mother what happened. But Pete knows that his grandfather has never
let anyone make decisions for him, so he puts off deciding what to do.

Pete and Angelika are given the task of taking photographs of sports
events for the school newspaper. As they work together in the school
photo lab editing their shots, they follow a comfortable routine, as
Angelika makes technical comments that help Pete begin to recognize
when he has a really good shot. Pete increasingly realizes that he *is* a
photographer and that taking photos is becoming a part of his core
identity. But he still struggles with worries about his grandfather and
the realization that the damage to his own arm means that he cannot
return to baseball. He also starts to consider the ethics involved in
photographic decision making. In class, Pete and Angelika learn about
the photographic style of Henri Cartier-Bresson, a well-known photographer in the 1930s. The class members debate whether persons being
photographed have a right to withhold permission for the use of the
photographs taken of them, a debate that hits close to home because,
while Angelika is excited about the shots that she has taken of Pete, he
is not sure that he wants his classmates to view images that show him
upset, although he realizes that the pictures do capture some kind of
truth, showing his feelings about baseball. Yet, Pete recognizes the

truth of a quote by Cartier-Bresson that the teacher has posted on the board: "We photographers deal in things which are continually vanishing, and when they have vanished there is no contrivance on earth which can make them come back again. We cannot develop and print a memory" (204). Angelika realizes what baseball means to Pete, and she encourages him to be honest with AJ about his injury, saying that she is not sure that she can be Pete's girlfriend if he is not honest. Pete tells her that he has tried to tell AJ but feels that he just will not listen.

At Thanksgiving, when Pete sees that Grampa does not even recognize the camera equipment that had been his, Pete begins to talk to him about his memories. Pete finally asks Grampa if he is OK being alone; he tells Pete that it is getting harder but that he wants to be the one who determines when to make other arrangements. Finally, after Grampa gets lost driving in a snowstorm, barefoot and looking for a shoe store, he calls Pete because he does not know where he is or who he is. Grampa then is moved to an assisted living facility.

As Pete is adjusting to the changes in Grampa's life, he is trying to adjust to his own changed physical condition. As baseball season approaches, Pete encourages AJ to try out for the baseball team. At this point, AJ admits that he realized months before that Pete could not play, but he was waiting for Pete to acknowledge this painful truth for himself. As the season unfolds, instead of playing, Pete goes to every game and takes photos of AJ, as his grandfather had done for him. By their junior year, AJ is the athletic star of the school, his accomplishments captured on film by Pete. Often, AJ goes with Pete to visit his grandfather.

One day during a visit, Grampa thinks that Pete is his own father rather than his grandson. Pete has a special gift wrapped for his grandfather. It is a picture of an eagle soaring, lit from below by the early morning rays of the sun. Grampa tells Pete that the picture is perfect, and Pete tells Grampa that it happened because he did just what Grampa had always taught him to do. Thus, moments later, when Grampa tells a nurse that he had taken the shot, Pete does not correct his grandfather but instead leaves the room in tears. When Pete goes to the parking lot, Angelika, AJ, and his girlfriend are waiting for Pete because they realized he might need some support. When he flashes back to his Grampa claiming that he had been the photographer of the eagle's portrait, Pete realizes, "In a bigger sense, that picture was [Grampa's] all along. He took me to the mountain, he gave me the tools, he gave me the love. I just put myself in the right place, at the right time, and got the shot" (285).

Pete, the photographer, will preserve the memories of his beloved Grampa and special times with his friends. Grampa's legacy lives on in Pete, who is finally able to accept his identity because of the friends who force him to confront the truth about himself and his injury and, at the same time, help him appreciate his artistic gifts.

UNLIKELY FRIENDS—AND FRIENDS (NOT!)

Many of the stories from previous chapters include young people who are surprised that an unlikely friend becomes the one who supports them. In *Map of the Known World*, by Lisa Ann Sandell, it is not Rachel, Cora's best friend for ten years, but Helena who supports Cora when she most needs it. In art class, Cora watches Helena, a sophomore whose easel is next to hers, draw broad strokes across her paper to create heavy and thick lines with her dainty hands. When Helena notices Cora watching, she tells her "it's therapeutic."[20] Cora thinks that maybe she should try it. Later, at a school dance, when Rachel sees Cora dancing with Damian, who survived the accident that killed Cora's brother, Rachel tells her that she cannot believe that she would dance with "that waster, in front of *everybody*" (140). They have a nasty exchange that makes it very clear that Rachel's goal of becoming more popular is threatened if her friend associates with Damian. Tears roll down Cora's face as she sprints down the corridor and then hears Helena streaking toward her, asking if she is okay.

After another upsetting scene, when Cora watches her parents argue about what to do with her dead brother Nate's things, she starts to dial Rachel's phone number but instead calls Helena, asking if she would like to go to the mall. At the mall, they see Rachel with Elizabeth, "another Nasties hanger-on" like Rachel. They exchange a few words. When they leave, they hear Elizabeth refer to Cora as a freak, saying that she cannot believe that Rachel was ever friends with Cora. Helena whispers to Cora, "Ugh, I can't believe you were ever friends with her" (191). Cora wonders if she and Rachel have grown out of each other, grown out of their friendship, even though she realizes that she knows how to be a friend because of her history with Rachel. Helena's friendship is crucial in the next phase of Cora's life, as they work together to stage the art show that includes Nate's work and as Helena encourages

Cora both in her artistic endeavors and in her efforts to reconnect with her parents.

Paradise

"Paradise," given that nickname because he is currently living in Paradise, Texas, shows up at a rehearsal of the Waylon Slider band in response to an ad calling for lead singers to audition for that spot. The novel *Paradise*, by Jill Alexander, begins as the band members know that they need someone really good, someone who can take Waylon's songs and make them reach an audience, someone with pizzazz and presence. Paradise seems to fit the bill—but there is immediate tension between the handsome newcomer and Waylon. Waylon is firmly rooted in a Southern country rock tradition, with some elements of gospel at the edges, a result of his weekly performance with his father's band at a local church in the tiny town where the band members live. Paradise is from a well-to-do Colombian farming family but is also descended from "royalty" in the accordion world; his grandfather is known as the "Accordion King," and Paradise feels that his roots are in the music called *vallenato*, or Colombian cowboy songs. When Paradise enters the airplane hangar where the band is rehearsing, the band members are desperate because they only have a short time to get ready to perform at the big Texapalooza music festival. The various band members have different reasons for wanting to play there. Waylon longs to earn his father's approval, while Paisley, the fifteen-year-old narrator of the book and the group's drummer, just wants to break out of town. Paradise has answered the call for a singer, but what he really wants is a venue in which to play his accordion.

When Paradise says that he is ready to sing, Paisley counts everyone in and says, "At first, Paradise pulled and pushed the accordion just on the downbeats—almost like an accent. Then he seemed to settle into the bluesy groove of Waylon's song. . . . His fingers began to race across the buttons as he pumped the accordion."[21] The band realizes that in addition to his obvious facility on the accordion—though not a sound that the band members think they want—the new guy can really sing, making Waylon's lyrics his own. Stuck with no other options, the band agrees to the terms that Paradise lays out—he will sing, but he will also play his instrument.

As the band continues to rehearse, getting ready for the festival, Paradise begins to bring out the musical best in many of the members.

There is a strong love story line as Paisley and Paradise connect, but they connect first as musicians. Paradise recognizes the way in which rhythm is an essential element of Paisley's being. He teaches her about Colombian drums, by playing recordings of various drums in action. He gives her a *caja*, a little drum. When she has it in hand, Paradise tells her to play barehanded, asking for more meringue. Paisley takes the drum and starts softly, "keeping it simple in two-four time, drawing the sound out instead of beating it in. There was a physical connection. Immediately. I could feel the beat all over" (117).

But Paradise has the most significant effect on Waylon. Paradise seems to recognize that Waylon needs to be center stage—something that Waylon does not know about himself—and so Paradise begins a somewhat surreptitious campaign to turn Waylon into the lead singer of the group. At a campfire one night, Paradise tricks Waylon into singing, by starting a song and pretending that he does not know how the rest goes. He hums it until Waylon pops in with some words. As Waylon goes on, Paradise drops back, and Paisley explains that

> Paradise had gotten him to sing without Waylon ever thinking about it. . . . Kind of twangy, but honest and authentic sounding. We'd all assumed Waylon couldn't sing, but he could. He just needed for someone to believe in him, and Paradise did. (145)

The more Paradise backs off, the stronger Waylon moves forward. "Paradise—always more interested in the accordion than singing—was pulling the lead vocals out of him. Paradise was giving Waylon his band" (170).

At the Texapalooza show, Waylon really finds his voice as band leader. He lets Paisley get the crowd wound up with her little *caja*. Then Waylon appears on the side of the stage and holds Paradise back "until the crowd reached a fevered fist-pumping, hand-clapping, foot-stomping crescendo. . . . He was running the show on pure feel" (219). Then Paradise does something that they have never practiced—he gives up center stage and steps to the side as "Waylon tore into the old Strat. It was like Waylon was plugged into the wall. Playing like a man possessed. He bent the blues out of every string, every fret" (219). The band members respond, and they take second place at the festival.

There is tragedy at the end of the novel. Paradise dies in a small plane crash flying off to an accordion gig that he has been offered as a result of the Texapalooza performance. The book really belongs to

Paisley, as she works through her grief and returns to drumming. But Waylon's story is also important because through the collaboration with Paradise, a truly unlikely friend, Waylon shows his father that he is in fact a musician to contend with.

These unlikely friendships are a reminder that just as a young adult artist can never be certain from which direction the support will come, teachers cannot always know what book might appeal to a given reader or have the most impact. Thus, it is useful to maintain a vibrant classroom library, talk to students about their reading interests, and share responses with them about books. Also, teachers need to be open to nurturing the young artists in their classrooms through any appropriate avenue. They should be willing to use arts-based teaching strategies to help reach the musicians, actors, dancers, painters, or graffiti artists in classrooms, as well as introduce young people like Cora or Waylon, who do not perceive themselves to be "center stage" artists, to new understandings of themselves.

PEERS WHO DISCOURAGE AND DISRESPECT

Paradise in some ways has a generous soul. He is a natural at being center stage, but he is happy to foster Waylon's development as a singer and then turn the limelight over to him. But often, competition among young artists is as difficult to overcome as the mental and physical challenges that the artist faces in honing his or her craft. Hannah and Zoe from *Bunheads* are friends but also competitors. Hannah is always aware that Zoe spends more hours at the theater, takes more master classes, and rehearses on her own, which Hannah understands is what leads to Zoe's selection as a soloist; nevertheless, she cannot help but be jealous and resentful.

Young artists are not always appreciated by their less artistic peers. In *Jersey Tomatoes Are the Best,* Eva has been teased for years because of her passion for dance—and because her mother keeps her out of normal activities, such as gym class, for fear of a career-ending injury. Eva says that her friend Henry does not get that you have to

> play up the things they mock, like sliding into leg splits at inappropriate moments, or wearing eccentric styles of dress. Then they start to think you're in on the joke. They think you like them, and they like you, and they never realize they're mean little bastards who lacerate your feelings every day. (74–75)

And when Eva is accepted to her elite summer dance program, which all participants know can lead to being selected for the corps de ballet, she describes the tensions in that rarified world, telling Henry, "Some of these girls would slit my Achilles tendons if they thought it would give them a leg up on me. They are intense, focused, killer ballerinas" (109).

Vicki, from *Another Way to Dance*, too has to cope with racist attitudes on the part of both her teacher and other students. Vicki overhears other girls talk about how she and Stacey were probably accepted to the prestigious summer dance program in New York (where they meet) because of affirmative action. Vicki begins to think that no matter how good Stacey and she are, people will only ever think they got in "just because [they're] black" (128). Vicki acknowledges the difficulties of being black:

> I'd look at myself in the mirror with all the other girls and I was always the first thing I saw. My own dark skin, my fuzzy hair, my long brown legs. I started feeling like I just stuck out so much. And then one of our teachers, Mrs. Gore, was always talking about how ballet, especially the corps work, was based on an "absolute visual harmony" and then looking quickly at me and away. (16)

Mrs. Gore approves when Vicki straightens her hair, although Vicki cannot win. Her mother, who lived through the Martin Luther King years, cannot accept the thought of changing appearances to look more "white" just to be successful in the ballet world.

Take a Bow

Take a Bow, by Elizabeth Eulberg, is the story of Emme, Sophie, Carter, and Ethan, who are students at the New York City High School of the Creative and Performing Arts (CPA), where it is expected that all students are talented and that fame is their goal. Each chapter is narrated by one of the four, who all seem to be friends that are supportive of one another. But their narratives make it clear that competition can destroy friendships when an individual's future success is on the line and a seeming lifelong friend is in reality *not* a friend.

The four artists begin their stories as they audition to be accepted as students at CPA. Carter Harrison feels like his whole life has been an audition. He is an actor who has performed in commercials, movies, and soap operas. As a child star, he was a big box-office draw by the time that he was ten years old, and auditions came to him without effort. Thus, it was a surprise to his actress mother when he made the decision to go to high school. He stays on television to appease her, but for himself he goes to school, and the paparazzi wait outside when he arrives.

Sophie is a singer who wants to be a star pupil in the vocal music program at CPA. Part of her "Plan to Superstardom" is to have a Grammy before she is twenty. Ethan hears a song and can play it instantly on the piano or guitar. Emme is Sophie's friend, songwriter, and accompanist and has always been in Sophie's shadow. The students' time is filled with extra classes, studios, concerts, and the pressures of constant competition because each semester they must audition to maintain their places at CPA. Of the 10,000 who initially audition, 634 enter as freshmen; by senior year, only 513 are left, and they wonder who will be invited to perform for an assembly and, later, in the Senior Showcase. Emme feels fortunate that when she auditions, she is part of a band called "Teenage Kicks" with Ethan and two other students: Jack, the drummer, and Ben, who along with Emme plays the guitar. Ethan writes original songs for the band and is thought of as one of the best music students at CPA. He does not grandstand but does command attention with a charisma that is palpable when he is onstage as the band's soloist.

Sophie does not become the star that everyone thought she would, but she is determined to try Broadway and search for record contracts, a decision that Emme, as her friend, does not think is wise. Sophie has been Carter's girlfriend for two years because she wants the publicity that comes from dating a star, and she gets upset when her name and photographs are not included in the gossip columns next to his. With homework, rehearsals, school performances, and band gigs, Emme's time is limited. She feels the pull between spending time with Sophie and rehearsing with the band, but she always finds time for Sophie and continues to write songs for her. Usually, when Emme accompanies Sophie's auditions, she improvises to enhance Sophie's voice. Emme is surprised when Sophie asks her to write out the accompaniment part for a different person, Amanda, to practice so that she can play for Sophie's next audition. Emme tries to hide her hurt, but she remembers that she has always been a part of Sophie's plan. When she agrees to do it, Sophie calls Emme "the greatest friend ever,"[22] but Ethan, Jack, Ben, and even Carter, as Sophie's boyfriend, see how Sophie uses Emme and is really *not* her friend.

Carter thought that going to high school would give him a sense of who he is, but he feels as though being a student is just another role that he is playing. He is aware that he is not the best actor, and Shakespeare is his nemesis, yet he is often chosen as the lead for productions at CPA because "Carter Harrison" still sells tickets and the school always needs funding. Sophie is so obsessed with being the biggest star of CPA that Carter feels that he is also "playing the role of Understanding Boyfriend . . . and it's getting in the way of their relationship" (46). When the friends wait for the announcement of the names of the ten students chosen to perform at an assembly, which will be the first test to see who are the lead contenders for the Senior Showcase, Sophie is nervous not only about making the list of performers but also because she wants to be chosen as either the first or last to perform. Instead, it is announced that she will be the third performer, singing "an original song by Amanda Jones" (48). Carter thinks to himself that the song was written by Emme, not Amanda. The list continues with Ethan, Ben, Jack, and Emme chosen to be the second-to-last act, performing an original song by Ethan. The showcase will close with Carter Harrison. When they are excused, Jack confronts Sophie, who acts like she did not hear that it was Amanda, not Emme, given credit for the song. Emme says that it was probably a mistake, and she continues to believe that Sophie is her friend.

Carter has noticed the friendship that Ethan, Ben, Jack, and Emme share. But even more than their friendship, "it's the passion for what they're doing" that Carter envies. "It's clear that each one of them loves playing music . . . It's what they want to do" (62). At one point, Carter decides to reveal his feelings to Emme. He tells her that he hates acting and wants to draw and paint. He does not feel that he has the desire or depth to do more adult roles. His art is the only thing that he feels belongs to him, but he has not shown it to anybody because "it feels too personal" (70). He also tells Emme that when he sees her onstage with the guys, she seems happy in ways that he does not see when she is performing with Sophie. Carter feels like Emme is the first one who has really listened to him, and he tells her that he is done pretending. He surprises everyone when he announces that he will be dropping out of CPA to study drawing.

Emme continues to think of Sophie as her best friend and does not admit that Sophie deceives her and uses her as a personal composer. Sophie certainly does not think of Emme as a vocalist. But when Sophie finds out that the director of the school has asked Emme to compose a song and sing it for a solo audition to determine who will get into the Senior Showcase, Sophie is determined to "put a crack in Emme's perfect world. To put me on top again. . . . I can't let her get one that belongs to me" (150). The others see through Sophie's various efforts to push down Emme, but Emme continues to have a hard time believing that Sophie is not really her friend.

One day when Emme is practicing with Sophie, who leaves the room briefly and misses a call on her phone, Emme sees on its screen a text exchange between Sophie and Amanda. In it are Sophie's words about Emme: "Can't believe I have to spend an hour kissing up 2 her. . . . Gah, she's here. Barf!" (179). The text makes it clear how Sophie really feels about Emme, who runs out of the room sobbing uncontrollably. Ethan is there to comfort her; as Emme tells him what happened, she thinks back to everything that she has done for Sophie. She has no doubt that they were close friends once, but she realizes that she has not wanted to believe how things have changed since their arrival at CPA. She realizes that she has hung on to something that was not there for a long time. Emme tells Ethan, "I kept making excuses for Sophie even though I knew she was using me. I let her do it because I was too scared. I needed to hide behind her. But maybe this is the push I need to finally stand center stage" (182). Because Sophie thinks that Emme would never let her down, Sophie is surprised when Emme tells her that she has learned a lot about friendship lately and will not be accompanying her in the showcase auditions. Emme adds that although she cannot stop Sophie from using the song that she wrote, she will not provide her with the written accompaniment, and if she is truly her friend, she will sing another song.

Sophie is desperate because she is sure that if Emme does not accompany her, she will not get into the final Senior Showcase, the talent scouts will not discover her, and she will not get a record contract. "No record, no Grammy. This is it. Doesn't she see she is ruining my last chance? . . . Emme was the only part of my Plan that was working" (189). She pleads with Emme to change her mind and accompany her, but Emme stands firm. The day of their final audition, Sophie tries one more time, telling Emme that it is laughable that she thinks that she can waltz in and become a singer.

> Here's the thing you need to realize: A bad singer can ruin a good song, but a good singer can made any song better. So let's be clear on who's been doing who a favor all these years—it's me, the voice. But I guess

we're both about ready to get that proof when you fall flat on your face. So really, good luck. (193)

Emme replies by saying that she had come to the auditions with the intention of accompanying Sophie because she did not want the possibility of ruining Sophie's chances for success on her conscience. But after hearing Sophie's words, Emme instead thanks Sophie for being honest for once and walks into the audition room by herself. When Emme comes out with a big smile on her face, she races past Sophie to Ethan, who picks her up, and Ben and Jack are also there to congratulate her because her solo went so well.

When the lineup for the final Senior Showcase is announced, Ethan is nervous because he wants Emme to get in so badly and there is only one spot left. Before, that spot had been Carter's, but with Carter out of the picture, it could belong to anybody. Everyone is surprised when it is announced that there will be *two* songs in the final featured spot: the band, with an original song by Ethan, and then Emme, who will end with her own song. Sophie accuses Emme of ruining her life. Ethan tells Sophie to quit blaming Emme for her own failures, and Sophie begins berating him. In a calm voice, Emme tells Sophie not to dare talk to Ethan like that. "He's been a true friend to me, unlike you" (197). Emme goes on, finding her voice:

> I can't believe it has taken me this long to see what you're really like. Since you feel the need to air dirty laundry in front of everybody. . . . Guess what. When I write songs for you, I have to limit the melody to ten notes because those are the only notes you can hit well. You don't have good range, which is what your problem is. I've known that for years, but I've hidden it. That's why you only shine when you sing *my* songs, because I've been trying to help you . . . by disguising your biggest flaw. Well, one of your flaws. You can't blame me for your lack of range. You can't blame me for you not getting into the showcase. You always want things to be all about you. Anytime I come to you with a problem, you don't want to hear it, unless it has to do with you. (198)

Emme runs to a practice room sobbing, and again it is Ethan who is there to comfort her.

When it is time for the Senior Showcase, the students performing are nervous because they will be facing hundreds of administrators, talent scouts, and prestigious alumni. The band with Ethan, Jack, Ben, and Emme has become a tight, cohesive unit, and Ethan feels that when he has the guys at his back, he has the courage to be a "front man." Emme is so tense that she cannot eat. As she begins to sing, her voice is quivering and soft but becomes louder and stronger, and her performance shows what she can do in both singing and composition. College auditions are the next thing that they face, and each one has to "go it alone" (226).

By the time they are ready to graduate, the group knows that Ben will go to Oberlin, Jack will go to CalArts in Los Angeles, and Ethan and Emme will both stay in Manhattan—Emme at Julliard and Ethan at the Manhattan School of Music—but they plan to write songs together. Sophie cannot wait for the ridiculous graduation ceremony to be over because she decides that CPA does not *deserve* to showcase her talent. Carter, no longer a student at CPA, is happy to be working with a tutor to prepare his portfolio for art school. He thinks about how Sophie was never happy unless she was the star, in contrast to Emme, who was "happily strumming in the background" (240). Carter tells Sophie that she will never be happy if she is interested in only the spotlight, spending her whole life chasing fame. He shares what he has learned the hard way: "Fame and money aren't worth it if you have nothing else in your life" (241).

As the story ends, it is not clear if Sophie has really learned much about being happy, being successful, or how to be a friend. Ironically, probably because Sophie ended up not really being a friend to her, Emme knows what it means to be surrounded by true friends, and she is on her way to artistic success.

Rival

Rival, by Sara Bennett Wealer, is another story in which the pressures of performance and competition lead to a change in the friendship between two high school vocalists. In fact, they were the only two freshmen who made it into Honors Choir, and they continue to be its leading voices. Each section of their story begins with a musical term that sets the stage for what is to follow, such as "Dissonance: a harsh sounding of notes that produces a feeling of tension and unrest."[23] The story alternates between events that occurred during their junior and senior years, with each chapter narrated by either Kathryn or Brooke. Kathryn is the leading soprano in the choir, and Brooke is a popular alto.

Brooke, who loves singing, is known in the high school as Queen B. But she is torn between her choir friends and her status with the popular "A listers" led by cruel and powerful Chloe, who refers to choir members as "music freaks." When they lived in New York, Brooke's mother sang Cabaret; now she is a public relations director for the biggest bank in town. Brooke's twin brothers, students at the University of Minnesota, call Brooke, who is a tall and statuesque young woman, "Amazon or Brookehilde" (32). Her father lives in New York with his partner Jake, a famous actor. Brooke longs for her father, who first put her on the "stage," in New York at a party, and had her sing.

By contrast, Kathryn is a tiny, beautiful soprano who, for part of their junior year, is Brooke's best friend. Kathryn's father (who recently lost his job) and her mother worry about whether they will have enough money in a college savings account for her. During their senior year, Kathryn and Brooke are invited to perform at an important musical competition, the fiftieth-anniversary Blackmore Young Artists' Festival, where first-place winners receive a check for $25,000 and often end up at a prestigious school, such as Juilliard or Peabody. Kathryn and Brooke are both under great pressure to succeed. For Kathryn, winning would mean that she would not have to drain her parents' bank account. For Brooke, who wants to prove that she can be successful to impress her father, winning would be her ticket out of Minnesota. She decides that it is her time to win. She must keep Kathryn in her place—and she is willing to risk their friendship to do so.

Brooke is probably the only person who knows that Kathryn cannot swim. When the choir has a pool party at Brooke's house, she tries at first to keep her brothers out of the way and sober while the party is going on. But when they see Kathryn sitting by herself away from the pool, they decide that everyone should join in a volleyball game, and Brooke agrees. She aims every serve right at Kathryn, before turning the game into dodge ball. Kathryn is pulled under water and struggles until her friend Matt pulls her out, as she gags and coughs up water. Thoroughly embarrassed and humiliated, she goes to Brooke's room to change and there recalls when she and Brooke enjoyed spending time together for part of their junior year. On one of those occasions, Kathryn saw a picture of Brooke's dad on a tropical beach with his partner, the famous actor Jake Jaspers, who, for publicity purposes, is often photographed with a woman.

The reader follows Kathryn and Brooke's memories of how that friendship was first forged and then how it deteriorated in part because of the schemes of Chloe, who had become jealous of the fact that Kathryn and Brooke shared such a passion for music. Chloe decided that she should get to know Kathryn and give her a false sense of belonging. Later, when Chloe, another girl, Dina, and Kathryn were having a good time at the mall, Kathryn innocently let slip, as part of their conversation, the information about Brooke's dad and Jake. Chloe then posted online this information that she had promised to keep confidential and let Brooke think that Kathryn has done the posting. At a party after homecoming, Brooke and Kathryn had a verbal exchange that was bitter and vicious and ended with Brooke slugging Kathryn in her left eye. Brooke made it clear that she would destroy Kathryn, and she does, posting on YouTube pictures of her fist flying into Kathryn's face, who looks small and awkward next to Brooke. The harassment begins—Kathryn's locker is egged, and during the weekend, she fields hang-up calls and obscene instant messages. At school, Alex, who had taken her to homecoming, asks her to leave him alone. Someone has been giving him notes with "an uncanny imitation" of her handwriting. Although Kathryn does not think that she deserves all that is happening, she does realize all the mistakes that she has made, including

> believing Chloe when she said she would keep Brooke's secret; believing my newfound popularity was real and not an illusion that would shatter as soon as Brooke decided to end our friendship with her fist. . . . I'd betrayed Brooke, and I'd betrayed my parents, who'd gotten a call just days earlier from the school counselor, concerned about how badly my midquarter grades had fallen. (236)

From that point on, Kathryn walks with her head down, keeps moving, does not make eye contact, buries herself in her schoolwork and her music, and spends time with her friend Matt. Chloe has been successful in her effort to pull Brooke and Kathryn apart. Kathryn is an outcast, and Brooke is still Queen B.

Kathryn's avoidance of Brooke and Chloe continues their senior year, a time described by the musical term "Stretto: the overlapping of the same theme or motif by two voices a few beats apart" (89). Both Brooke and Kathryn feel the pressure to prepare for the Blackmore competition. Kathryn is concerned about learning all the music that her teacher has given her. Brooke is upset that her father is away from New York, working on an opera, and she cannot go to the city to get special help. At her lesson, Brooke's vocal teacher notices that she sounds hoarse and so sends her to an ear, nose, and throat specialist because it

is obvious that she is abusing her voice. She hopes that it is not polyps
or nodes. As Brooke walks by a practice room, she hears Kathryn
practicing but having trouble with a difficult part. Then she hears soft
crying. Brooke thinks, "I should be happy she's upset. But what I really
feel is a tired kind of sympathy" (123). Brooke leaves Kathryn alone
and thinks about how they have "been enemies for a year now. How do
you fix something like that? And do I even want to after all that happened?" (194). Brooke recalls how, after she punched Kathryn, people
got the message: "If they wanted to be friends with me then they
couldn't be friends with her. . . . They made her into a complete and
total leper" (256). Brooke realizes that she has liked the power and
sometimes even enjoyed punishing Kathryn; more than anything else,
the past year has been painful, and Brooke realizes that she is tired of
hating Kathryn.

The stage is set for the last section of the story, with the term
"Resolution: the changing of a dissonant pitch to create a group of
tones that are harmonious to the ear" (297). Kathryn is exhausted, but
she manages to pass her anatomy test, write an A-plus English paper,
and sing so well in her solo at regional competition that the Honors
Choir earns the top score and will go to the state competition in the
spring. Her mother surprises her with a beautiful midnight-blue gown
that she has made for the Blackmore competition. At the competition,
Kathryn knows that her parents and Matt are in the audience to hear
her. Before it is her turn to perform, she takes a break from going over
last-minute exercises to listen to Brooke, who seems quite confident.
To Kathryn, Brooke's "singing seems so advanced: beyond Honors
Choir, beyond our rivalry, beyond even the Blackmore . . . instead of
being intimidated by her, I am calm. Ready" (313). When Kathryn
sings, her love of the music takes over. She realizes that she is singing
because she can: "not for money, not for recognition, not for revenge.
But simply because it is wonderful" (314).

Both girls are named to the final ten vocalists for the last round of
the competition. Brooke will sing first, Kathryn second to last. They
see each other before performing. When Brooke takes the opportunity
to ask Kathryn if Chloe and Dina were the only two people that she told
about her dad and Jake, Kathryn assures her that was the case. Brooke
believes her. They wish each other good luck. Kathryn is named as the
third-place winner and given a check for $5,000. She is surprised that
along with the sting of failure, she feels relief and a "whole new set of
possibilities" that she will explore and "make happen": "the ones that I

choose instead of waiting for someone—or something—to do it for me" (324–25). She sees fear on Brooke's face until Brooke's name is announced as the winner. Brooke makes it down the line of winners to Kathryn, "leans in for the hug," and Kathryn thinks that the long story is not about the two of them anymore. "That story is over. It's time to start a new one—a story all my own" (327).

EXPLORING ROMANCE AND GENDER ROLES

The story of Brooke and Kathryn, with the scheming, controlling Chloe, is one of unlikely friendship, competition, rivalry, and, ultimately, growth and maturity as the two young vocalists each come to a new understanding of what music means to her and of the possibilities that life holds. In the process, they—particularly Kathryn with her friend Matt—also begin to have some new insights into the depth and complexity that characterize a quality romantic partner. Not surprising, many novels that feature young adult artists center on how they use their art to explore both romance and gender roles and how they come together because of their shared commitment to the arts.

In *Sisters of Glass*, by Stephanie Hemphill, Maria and Luca come together and eventually marry because they understand the depth of the importance that their art—in this case, glassblowing—has in their lives. When Maria asks Luca what he would do if he could not blow glass, he responds,

> I have never considered it. / To make glass to me at this point / Is to breathe. Whatever else I did / Would be inconsequential.[24]

In response, Maria tells him that her father says that he would have been adrift, "like a sailor without a compass" (95) if he could not blow glass, and thus Luca knows that she truly understands him. As they work together to produce beautiful glass in this historical novel set in Venice, Italy, their respect blossoms into affection.

Many stories that young adult authors write show how young people work through relationship issues by their engagement in their art. Not surprising, because theatrical productions are so often about the negotiations of relationships, there are a number of books about teens involved in play rehearsals that show this negotiation in process. In *Instructions for a Broken Heart*, by Kim Culbertson, in *The Sweet, Terrible, Glorious Year I Truly, Completely Lost It*, by Lisa Shanahan, and in *The Flip Side*, by Andrew Matthews, among others, readers meet young adults who are sorting out their feelings toward the opposite sex through their artistic endeavors—and, often, they are figuring out something about who they are, in the process of working through their relationship issues.

Instructions for a Broken Heart

Culbertson's sweet and poignant story about Jessa, who met and fell in love with Sean as they participated in various high school Drama Club productions, describes a fairly conventional relationship, its demise, and Jessa's ultimate return to equilibrium. Trouble begins when Jessa walks into the costume shop and finds Sean entangled with another girl, only days before the Drama Club is supposed to be leaving for a spring break trip to Italy. So, not only is she alone for what she had expected to be a romantic excursion through cities about which she has long dreamed, but she also has to see Sean and Natalie entwined every day. Her friend Carissa, who is not going on the tour, sends her off on the trip with twenty envelopes, each with a reason why Jessa should be glad to be rid of Sean and with "instructions" for healing her broken heart. Tyler, who is also on the trip, has a directive from Carissa to make sure that Jessa follows the instructions. Because of the writing assignments she is given from her teachers, Carissa's advice, Tyler's shoulder on which she often cries, the caring presence of her drama teacher and the book he has her read (Joyce's *Portrait of the Artist as a Young Man*), and conversations with a cute Italian boy and Dylan Thomas (another young man on the trip), Jessa returns home with a much better understanding of herself, the nature of friendship, and love.

Jessa's drama teacher, Mr. Campbell, gives her *Portrait of the Artist as Young Man*, telling her that it had "kind of changed my life . . . in the way that some books can change what you know about yourself. For better or worse, when you look at the world through an artist's eyes, it's nice to know you aren't alone."[25] This teacher shows Jessa that she is an artist at the core. In Joyce's book, Jessa comes across the passage "A day of dappled seaborne clouds" as she reads about Stephen (188). She thinks,

> In the book, Stephen had realized that words, the sheer beauty of them, could alter the *glowing sensible world*, turn it into a *prism of language*. . . . She preferred the words, the music, to dust-covered reality.

She saw the world the way Stephen did—in all its crazy, beautiful disorder. (188–89)

Jessa finishes *Portrait*, and Stephen's words settle into her heart, "I will not serve that in which I no longer believe. . . . I will try to express myself in some mode of life or art as freely as I can and as wholly as I can" (249). The quote forces Jessa to think about "the holes in herself, the patchy places that didn't seem formed yet" (249), and she realizes that she has to think about what she wants, not just what school personnel and other people want for her future. She will have to figure out how to "express herself in her friendship with Carissa" and deal with Sean in "a whole way," to figure out how she really feels about him, the whole him, not "just the cheating part" (250).

Jessa manages to find a way to use her love of words and her theatrical sensibilities to put things to rest. She digs a hole in the Italian soil, into which she intends to scream all that was not good about her and Sean and their relationship with each other. In a final monologue, presented to the whole group traveling together, she tells everyone about this action while directing her full focus to Sean:

> Now I can bring home a heart full of the light patches. . . . I will take home your final Hamlet monologue on the dark stage when you cried closing night and it wasn't really acting, you cried because you felt . . . the way I feel every day of my life, every second, the way the words, the light and dark, the spotlight in your face made you Hamlet for that brief hiccup of a moment, made you a poet, an artist at your core. . . . We are over. . . . But we are not blank. We were a beautiful building made of stone, crumbled now and covered in vines. But not blank. Not forgotten. We are a history. We are beauty out of ruin. (277)

It is through the language of the theater that Jessa is able to think about what has happened with Sean and what she is learning about herself, and it is through using the tools of the actress that she is able to bring closure to this difficult breakup.

The Sweet, Terrible, Glorious Year I Truly, Completely Lost It

In some ways Australian Gemma, of Lisa Shanahan's *The Sweet, Terrible, Glorious Year I Truly, Completely Lost It*, is the opposite of Jessa, who uses drama as a way to come to terms with her breakup with Sean. It is through working together on a production of *The Tempest* that Gemma gains the courage to reach across barriers of class to connect with a classmate. Raven De Head is the delinquent of Gemma's year 9 class; he gets suspended a lot, but he is also very cute. When he sees Gemma reading *The Tempest* and learns that she is thinking of trying out, he reminds her that in the past, when asked to speak in public, she vomited from the pressure. He challenges her to tell him why the play is so great. Raven ends up quoting the play to her, which surprises her, and when he asks her why she thought that he would not know Shakespeare, she turns red, realizing that she has bought into the theory "that the only reason people like him got into trouble at school was because they were too stupid to do anything else."[26]

Gemma agrees to prepare for auditions with Raven. As they continue to rehearse over the next few weeks, getting ready for tryouts, Gemma is aware that their peers, also preparing, view Raven as a sort of leper; they are polite but keep their distance. She is disgusted to realize that she feels the same way, especially after seeing him in the context of his family members, who are definitely not the sort of people that she is used to spending time with. She thinks,

> As Raven and I rehearsed, I found myself wanting to stand far away from him. I wanted to keep a distance between us. I wanted it to protect me. Because even as I despised the way most people treated Raven, I still wanted to be saved from their snide condescension. (91)

It becomes increasingly clear, however, that Raven has a deep understanding of the play and its themes—and that he is aware of what Gemma is feeling.

Raven wants to try out for Ferdinand, as he and Gemma have been rehearsing. At auditions, however, Raven is asked to read for Caliban, and Gemma watches, transfixed:

> Everyone else performed Caliban as if he were merely naughty. But Raven's Caliban was transparent with hunger. When he spoke, his skin was only a thin membrane round all the pulses drumming greedily in his body. I could see how he could haunt Miranda. As I watched, I felt scared. Scared like the little child who was staring at the bathwater swirling down the plughole—that whirling, grasping dark hole that gobbled and sucked whatever it was given and was never full. (172)

But she knows that he is embarrassed when he gets to the end: "It was like he had revealed something of himself he hadn't planned to, and now he wished he could snatch it back" (172). When Raven is actually cast as Caliban, against Gemma as Miranda, Raven loses it. Mrs. Langton, the director, explains why she gave him this role: "You can give me a Caliban that isn't a stereotype and I truly believe the other roles won't stretch you in the same way" (178).

Raven ultimately decides to do Caliban, but as Gemma listens to the words that Prospero throws at him—ugly, savage, destructive words—she finds that she hates Prospero, pities Caliban rather than feeling scorn for him, and even despises Miranda. Mrs. Langton tells Gemma that she is seeing Miranda through the eyes of the characters surrounding her, instead of considering how Miranda would see herself. To help Gemma overcome this obstacle, she has her do a written form of "Hot Seat." Gemma is to keep a journal of everything about Miranda's life from her own perspective, including scenes that are not actually in the play. She asks, "What was it like for Miranda to grow up with Caliban? Explore her hope of finding in him a true friend" (234).

As Gemma writes, she begins to understand how Caliban's betrayal, his attempt to rape Miranda, has "curdled her compassion" (237). She finds things to admire about Miranda and sees with Miranda's eyes the men who come to the island: "When I see them, when I see so many of them, so much mankind, I cannot help but be filled with amazement, with hope and terror, that such people, such glorious beings, can be contained by my same fragile skin and bone" (238). This insight infuses understanding behind her lines when she speaks Miranda's famous "O brave new world / That has such people in it" (238). Mrs. Langton is no longer exasperated, and even Raven thaws somewhat, coming to better understand Caliban through Miranda's eyes.

Finally, it is opening night, and the play is a success. When closing night arrives, Shanahan captures what it is like, the "fierce joy, stabbing regret and an intense longing to do it again" (249) and how Gemma feels: "happier than I had ever been—in love with everyone onstage because we had worked together to conjure something out of nothing" (250). In particular, she is feeling love for Raven.

But Gemma gets a bit tipsy, refuses to kiss Raven at the cast party, and is ambushed by the boy who played Ferdinand, who tries to kiss her, which Raven sees. So he calls his brothers, who collect him as they are on their way to blow up a new statue of the town founder. One brother loses an eye; Raven is seriously wounded; and one brother is killed. Raven wallows in grief because his brother died when he pushed himself in front of Raven to protect him from the blast. Gemma is distraught because all anyone in town can see is that the "De Head boys have gotten what's coming to them" (270). The townspeople do not see how the father will not leave the morgue, how the mother walks to the hospital every day to sit with Raven, how Raven is so sick with grief and guilt that he wants to die.

It is at her sister's wedding, when the bride hesitates just a bit when the minister asks if she will take the groom to be her husband, when Gemma finally opens up. She begins a speech of "I do's," saying that she will take Brian to be her brother-in-law, Debbie to be her sister, his parents to be her in-laws, her own parents to be her parents, and "to every person I've ever loved or hated and to those people I'll want to love or hate: I do. I'll love you, as best as I can, from this day forward" (289). Her speech is enough to get the bride unfrozen. When Raven shows up at the reception, Gemma goes to him because "even though this life scares me, I still want to fly" (295). There is no indication that either Gemma or Raven will pursue a career in the theater; it is not even clear that they will try out for other school plays. What is clear is that, through their immersion in Shakespeare's world and their characters, these two young people have come to a deeper understanding of self and each other, and their view of the larger world will never be the same.

The Flip Side

Like Gemma and Raven, Rob and Milena in Andrew Matthew's *The Flip Side*, both fifteen years old and also Australian, learn a great deal about themselves through their exploration of the parts that they are assigned in the Shakespeare play *As You Like It*. Their English teacher asks them to read the parts of Orlando and Rosalind, respectively, as their class studies the comedy. But then one of their classmates says that, in keeping with the spirit of the period in which the bard wrote, Rob and Milena should exchange roles. Then something interesting happens: they are each fabulous in their cross-gendered performances. When Milena agrees to go out with Rob, they talk candidly about the fact that they enjoyed dressing up as the opposite sex, and they wonder what this means about them. At the same time, Robert's longtime best friend, Kevin, comes out to Rob. All these experiences help Rob understand that all people have complex personalities. He has to figure out who he really wants to be and how he can honor his "flip side" while holding true to himself. He thinks,

In fact there's a whole load of different people inside you, like a collection of masks. You change your mask according to the situation you find yourself in. Sorting out which one is really you is practically impossible, because the person it's hardest to be honest with is yourself. And here's the spooky bit: maybe when you take all the masks off you're not anybody; maybe you're as blank as the white stuff inside a glue stick.[27]

Rob is quite articulate about how his acting as Rosalind and talking with Milena are mind expanding. Shakespeare started him thinking about things that he had not thought about before. "Nothing was as cut and dried as I'd assumed" (16–17). Rob appreciates the fact that taking on a very different role can be quite liberating.

It is only through taking on these parts and trying to live them that the two teens really understand the play—and thus can begin to use the play to understand themselves. The problem is that they are not experienced actors and, in some ways, can lose the boundary between self and other. As Rob puts it,

All of a sudden I felt something leap from my subconscious mind and take over, and Rosalind was me. Robert went missing in action and left Rosalind in charge, and boy, did she ever enjoy herself! . . . Rosalind was confident, feisty, sharp-tongued—everything that Robert wasn't. (30)

Being Rosalind gives Robert the confidence to ask Milena out, and he wants to talk to Kevin, his best friend, about all these runaway feelings. Meanwhile, Kevin has been "sorting some stuff out" and says, "Ever feel your entire life is a lie, Rob? Nobody says who they really are, everything's fake and you just go along with it, pretend its OK. You end up lying just like everybody else because you're frightened someone's going to find out the truth" (47). Robert is not quite sure how to respond to Kevin, but he can empathize with the underlying sentiment of feeling that there are layers of "self" to one's identity.

A classmate has decided to have a cross-dressing party, expanding on the discussion of gender roles in English class. Rob and Milena decide to go together: Rob in a girl's outfit that Milena helped him buy, with Milena done over as a male. When they get back to Rob's house, it turns out his father sees Rob, as a girl, kissing Milena, as a boy. And his dad is very upset. Milena also decides that she needs to take a break because she realizes that she cannot handle the confusion that the cross-dressing causes. Rob finally wins her back, by again taking on a new role, that of old-fashioned preppy boy. Milena asks if this means, "No more Rosalind?" Rob responds,

> Rosalind's still here, Milena. She's me. I don't need a costume to be her. I mean, take away the costumes and what have you got? . . . You've got a boy and girl—basic fact that can't be changed without expensive surgery. The rest is open to negotiation. Clothes don't make us what we are, we do! (145)

Milena is open to further conversation, further exploration. It is not clear whether she and Rob will stay together, but for the present, they have a partner in self-discovery because each of them was willing to take the risk that the vehicle *As You Like It* provided them. Rob ends the novel by saying, "I'm going to leave you with this thought: gay, straight, both, neither, any way you cut it you're in for a bumpy ride. Hold on tight and whatever you do, don't lose yourself, because you're all you've got" (147).

BOYFRIENDS/GIRLFRIENDS AND THEIR ROLES

At the end of *The Flip Side*, Rob and Milena have become, at least for the present, a couple, which is true for Gemma and Raven at the end of their story as well. But in these novels, the focus is on how the young people use their involvement in the arts to figure out something about the nature of a romantic relationship and begin to find their way into a new identity as a part of a couple. In other novels, if the romantic relationship is already established or developed as a parallel story line to that of the artistic struggles of the ones who are artists, the boy-friends or girlfriends function more often as cheerleaders and protectors who support the artists and buoy them in their artistic expression. Thus, TC from *My Most Excellent Year: A Novel of Love, Mary Poppins, and Fenway Park* is always in the audience for Ale, clapping for her as she performs, just as Andy claps for Augie's productions.

Yet, in Joan Bauer's *Thwonk*—a story in which the two main char-acters happen to have the same names as those in *Curveball*—one of the important lessons that AJ, a gifted photographer, learns is that she cannot be involved with someone who does not truly appreciate how much her art means to her. She has been infatuated with Pete, but when Cupid makes her wish of gaining Pete's attention and affection come true, AJ realizes that he will not give her the space to pursue her photographs, nor does he value her efforts, and she finally asks Cupid for a kind of "do-over" so that she can connect with someone who appreciates her artist self.

North of Beautiful

Justina Chen Headley's *North of Beautiful* provides a strong portrait of how an author develops this kind of parallel story line, with the nonartist member of the relationship nurturing the other's artistic self as each supports the other's overarching sense of identity while together sorting out what it means to be a couple. Actually, when the novel opens, high school junior Terra is dating Erik. With a tall, graceful body, long blond hair, and lovely eyes, Terra is beautiful. She works part-time at an art gallery, where she develops flyers for upcoming shows, partly in exchange for working space in which to make intricate collages. But Terra does not consider herself beautiful, nor does she see herself as an artist. One side of her face is covered with a huge port wine stain roughly the shape of Bhutan; she keeps it covered with layers of make-up, and few people at school even know about the mark—and she never allows Erik to see it. She seems to be in the unlucky 10 percent of the population who do not respond to countless treatments and surgeries, a fact that her father never tires of pointing out to her, telling her that she is ugly and will always be so. He, too, denigrates her artwork. Thus, Terra thinks of what she does as a hobby, a craft, rather than as art. But when she crashes her car into another vehicle, she and her mom meet the driver and passenger of the other car—Jacob, a somewhat odd and Goth Chinese boy, and his mother, Norah, who forms a strong bond with Terra's mother. Jacob almost immediately understands Terra's feelings of being different.

Over winter break, while spending time with Jacob—who asks questions about her art, who challenges her to be honest in it, and who pushes her to look at the narrative she is telling herself—Terra comes to realize that she has "settled" for Erik because of the "real risk that nobody else would want" her.[28] When Terra's brother Merc sends her two plane tickets to China, where he is working, and asks her to bring her mother to visit, Jacob's mother Norah, a coffee buyer with lots of travel experience, springs into action, saying that she has been planning a trip to that country with Jacob, to take him back to the orphanage from which she adopted him. Thus, the four of them end up in China together. During a walk in Shanghai's Yu Garden, Terra finds herself engaged in a deep conversation with Jacob about the nature of beauty. As Terra is trying to define beauty, Jacob listens, unlike Erik. He responds with another point that shows he has been listening closely, saying that gardens such as the one in which they are standing are not truly beautiful, in his mind, because they are too orchestrated.

The art gallery where Terra works is run by three older women, artists themselves, who want Terra to put her collages in one of their shows. Terra confesses to Jacob that she does not want to do so because she is afraid that her dad—and others—will laugh at her efforts. Jacob pushes her to take that risk, reminding her that many great artists drew laughter, from Monet to Pollock. He says, "When you think about it, the artists who make people stop and think, who push the form, who make you uncomfortable, who are laughable, those are the ones who get remembered" (153). Terra says that Jacob, unlike Erik, is able to see "through the protective layers of my denial, down to my core" (109). Headley beautifully uses Terra's making of collages as a metaphor for the way that she comes to see herself as a collage comprising all the experiences, good and bad, that have brought her and Jacob together.

Terra learns over the course of the novel that in a true relationship, each partner has to accept the other. Through their long conversations, shared explorations of China, and adventures geocaching (a real-world adventure game in which players use their GPS navigation systems or smartphones to locate hidden containers), Terra comes to appreciate the gift of Jacob's ability to mirror back to her what she really wants from life. As a result, Terra is able to open up as an artist and create something truly beautiful, which a professional artist buys, giving her a new name for what she does: pentimenti. Terra learns that pentimenti, which comes from the Latin meaning "to repent" and "correct," is the technique that she has used to build up her "Land of Beauty," a collage in which she has captured her personal odyssey in a quest for understanding beauty and the beauty of her inner self. After she finishes it, she is able to say that it is "time to explore a new subject" (363). She is able to walk into school with her hair swept back off her face in a high ponytail, the port wine stain visible, and stand proudly in front of Jacob, showing her vulnerability but also saying that, in geocache language, she is a "cache" now called "Terra Firma," a nice play on her name and the idea that her identity is now firm. The story ends with the two of them looking at each other full in the face, obscuring nothing from each other.

TWO ARTISTS TOGETHER

Headley shows us the importance of the nonartist as a significant other who pushes the artist to be more honest as an artist and in life. Romantic relationships between two artists can be easier in some ways than that between an artist and nonartist in that there is no competition: the nonartist has an easy time serving as cheerleader, and the artist can appreciate being pulled out of the isolation that artists frequently inhabit.

In some ways, having a romantic partner who understands the need to create—the compulsion to express one's inner landscape through music or art, dance, or photography—makes for a more complex and richer relationship. When two individuals who are both artists are interested in each other romantically, the fact that they have a shared investment in the world of art can bring them closer together. As boyfriend or girlfriend, each serves to encourage, applaud, and push the other artistically. Jewel and Alice of *The Opposite of Invisible* attend each other's art shows, spend time together at art museums, and comment on each other's work. They attend to each other's critiques and suggestions because they trust each other's artistic judgment. In *The Latent Powers of Dylan Fontaine*, by April Lurie, as Dylan and Angie push each other artistically, Dylan's painting and guitar playing become stronger, while Angie's filmmaking becomes more honest.

Zero

In Tom Leveen's story *Zero,* set in Phoenix, two artists begin their romantic relationship soon after they meet. Amanda Walsh, who goes by the nickname "Zero," is a seventeen-year-old artist working on a landscape of Camelback Mountain. Each chapter of her story begins with a quote from Salvador Dalí, her hero. Someday she hopes to go to "St. Petersburg, Florida, to visit (or move into) the Salvador Dalí museum."[29] Zero's bedroom is filled with her artwork, which even covers the ceiling, but she feels like "a massive sucking black hole of a failure" (1). She is facing an uncertain future after high school graduation. Although she was accepted at the Art Institute of Chicago, which she has dreamed of attending since being in Mr. Hilmer's junior high art classes, her portfolio was not good enough to earn the merit scholarship, which went to someone more talented. Her dad has a school savings account for her, but it contains enough to cover community college and maybe a year at an in-state university. One evening, to escape the almost constant din of her parents' screaming at each other, Zero goes to a punk dive where she hears a no-name band, Gothic Rainbow, that is surprisingly good. She is struck by the drummer's "priceless sapphire" eyes, and her fingers ache for her paints "to capture those eyes forever" (13). Their gazes meet, and she freezes. After the concert, she sits at the bar and talks to the drummer, Mike, and they exchange phone numbers.

Mike calls, and they plan to meet the next evening at the Hole in the Wall Café. Once there, as Zero is waiting for Mike, she looks at the artwork on the walls and wonders if she would ever have the nerve to exhibit a piece there and maybe even sell it. When he arrives, they talk about her art and his band and agree to meet again the following Friday, when his band will be the opening act for a more popular group. Zero tells Mike that she is enrolled in the community college for fall classes, and Mike encourages her to take a summer course after she tells him about not getting the scholarship, because her work lacked "technical excellence" (52). Even before they begin dating, Mike is already pushing Zero artistically.

Zero does sign up for an art class and meets Mike on Friday night at a place called Damage Control. After Gothic Rainbow's gig, Mike and Zero talk, and Mike asks her when he can see her artwork. He even wants to know what her real name is. He tells her about his dad, who was "a typical rock star . . . drinking, drugs, the whole nine" (97), whose band never made it past one album. Zero learns that Mike's band, Gothic Rainbow, has sent twelve demos to record companies but has had no offers for recording gigs. Their evening ends with a hug, not a kiss, but they plan to meet Tuesday evening.

On Monday, she finds her studio classroom, where the instructor introduces herself as *Doctor* Deborah Salinger. She picks up her clipboard and scans the roll. "Miss Amanda Walsh. Tell us, what *is* art?" (81). Zero's halting definition does not please Dr. Salinger, who says that by the end of class she hopes that everyone will be able to answer the question more effectively. Zero thinks, "The lady bugs me, but I can't stop my pulse from picking up. I'm back where I'm supposed to be, in a studio, getting ready to create" (82). Dr. Salinger grabs Zero's hat, puts it on her desk, and sketches a still life while bragging about her accomplishments and talking about her summer tryst. Zero notices that the sketch is good. As much as the instructor's personality bothers her, Zero thinks, "I need to know more if I'm going to have any chance of putting together a solid new portfolio this fall" (84).

Zero and Mike continue to see each other, and they survive meeting each other's families, each realizing, in the process, that both of them are coping with dysfunctional home lives. Mike convinces Zero to show him her work, which he tells her that he likes a great deal—he also admits that he is torn about her desire to put together a stronger portfolio and ultimately leave town for Chicago. Zero continues to work on her painting; she also patches up her relationship with her best friend, Jenn, whose sexual overtures frightened Zero. She tells Jenn that she is in love for the first time in her life and it is with Mike. He asks Zero to bring her art stuff to the Hole in the Wall; the band likes it and asks her to design flyers for their next show, which she does. She is delighted to be talking with Mike about art and creating it *for* him. Her posters are so good that she becomes Gothic Rainbow's "resident artist" (154), and the band continues to be offered better venues and become more and more popular.

In the meantime, Zero goes to class, where Dr. Salinger asks her if she sees a future for herself in art. Zero says that sometimes she does. She admits taking the class because her boyfriend suggested it, but she notes that it probably will not transfer to the school of the Art Institute of Chicago, where she really wants to be. Dr. Salinger tells her that she is using her tools and talent, her eyes and hands, but she needs to use her mind and heart. She agrees to work with Zero on her technique if she does her work. Dr. Salinger admits that there is nothing in the community college that will offer Zero what she is looking for, but she says that she will work with Zero individually to help her build her portfolio. Dr. Salinger even asks her about her nickname "Zero" and tells her to get rid of it because she is "worth more than that" (175). Zero thanks her and, before leaving, registers for fall classes, including a painting class with Dr. Salinger, plus Spanish, math, and English. Zero is so excited that she actually gets brave enough to take a painting to Hole in the Wall and (hesitantly) introduce herself as "Amanda Walsh." Eli, the owner, tells her to trust him; it will sell.

Zero's romantic relationship with Mike continues. Mike's band gets amazing news that it has won a gig at Damage Control, the most important venue in town, and the band members ask Zero to design the gig flyer and make hundreds of copies. At home she is energized and

begins designing it. To Zero, "this is like . . . a commissioned piece. It's
work for someone else" (203), and she works carefully. By the time
that she has finished the canvas, she knows that this piece will go into
her portfolio, and she takes a picture of it to add to those that she is
showing Dr. Salinger.

At the band's big show, Zero sees her flyer, and "it stands out from
the others like one of Mike's beautiful blue-green eyes—the color I
used as a backdrop behind the cymbal (or record) reflecting the guys'
faces" (243). The band's forty minutes onstage are a huge success, and
Zero thinks, "Damage is a living canvas, painted with impossible im-
pasto, thick and complex. My fingers twitch for a charcoal pencil,
something, anything. There is no paper, no canvas, no surface large
enough to contain what I want to paint" (252). She sees the crowd
grabbing her flyers as they exit the club. Mike tells her that the band is
leaving the next day for Los Angeles and might be on the road for three
months. She is tempted when he asks her to go along with them, but she
wonders about her art. At home, she finds the biggest canvas that she
has, and she reaches for her acrylics and gels. After spending a few
hours preparing, she paints and is amazed at the result:

> It's a pair of eyes. Mike's, of course, I've gotten the emerald-sapphire
> mixture just right, and the high gloss shines almost as well as the real
> thing. . . . I did it. Captured the right color, the right feeling, the—
> There's something else there too . . . a reflection. . . . It's me, reaching
> toward the eye, out of the canvas, as if I am a painting, right now, and
> the artist in the pupil is the real thing. This reflection is reaching out
> with a paint brush; it's me, painting my own image in Mike's eyes.
> (281)

She recalls her junior teacher Mr. Hilmer telling the class that artists'
self-portraits are their best work. It is her first intentional self-portrait,
and she thinks that she knows what she has been seeing in Mike's eyes
this whole time.

To Zero's surprise, Eli at Hole in the Wall Café calls her with the
news that he owes her money because her painting of Camelback
Mountain sold to a couple moving to California. She thinks, "Someone
is paying me for my painting. I did it. I'm an *artist*" (284–85). As she
heads out the door, her mother asks her if she wants to talk to her dad
before he leaves for a few weeks to go to a facility to get dried out. "I
should thank you," he says. "You called me out good and proper, kid.
That took guts. I appreciate it, Z."

"Amanda." / Dad blinks. "What's that?" / "Could you start calling me Amanda?" / Dad half-smiles. "If you want." / "I kinda do." / "You got it. Amanda." (286)

When he asks if he could get a hug from her, she wraps her arms around him as he tells her he is sorry. He will see her in a few weeks. Amanda no longer feels like she is "Zero." She drives quickly in a thunderstorm to the bus station where Mike is boarding to go to Los Angeles. As he embraces her, she tells him about her dad getting help, about selling her painting, and she says that as much as she wants to go with him, she cannot right now: "My art—I have to try again. I have to do this" (291).

As Mike's bus pulls away, Amanda recalls how her mother asked her what she wanted for her eighteenth birthday. She will tell her that she wants round-trip tickets for Florida to visit the Salvador Dalí museum and she wants her parents to go with her. She thinks that they might not get who and what Dalí is all about, but that will be OK because they will understand her, and that is enough. As Amanda drives away from the bus station, a storm ends. The book ends with Salvador Dalí's words: "I am about to begin. . . . I begin. . . . We have begun!" (294).

* * *

In many stories already mentioned, two young people first become acquainted because they are artists who work together and encourage each other in their artistic endeavors, as is true for Zero/Amanda and Mike. Eventually, their friendship develops into a romantic relationship. For instance, in *Take a Bow*, Ethan and Emme are talented musicians who spend a great deal of time together in the composition program at the New York City High School of the Creative and Performing Arts, and through their involvement in Ethan's band, their friendship and support of each other gradually turn to something more.

This plotline also plays out in the story *A Map of the Known World*, when it is Damian who shows Cora her brother Nate's art, something that she did not know existed. Cora realizes that she had more in common with Nate than she imagined. It is the two artists, Damian and Cora, who come together to find a way to complete Nate's sculpture and honor his life. In the course of working on the sculpture, Cora realizes that she is attracted to the handsome, brooding Damian. He is the one that she can talk to about Nate and about not telling her parents that she forged her mother's signature on the application to the art program in London. In *Curveball: The Year I Lost My Grip*, it is first the work that Pete and Angelika do together as two talented photographers that brings them together. They are paired to do each other's portraits and are given the assignment to take pictures of sports events for the school newspaper. At one point, Pete realizes that he and Angie are bonding, "not just flirty-bonding, but really talking about life stuff" (141).

In *Irises,* by Francisco X. Stork, Marcos and Mary seem to be very different people, but both are artists and are brought together by the art teacher, Mr. Gomez. Mary, the pastor's daughter, is at first concerned about Marcos's past until she learns more about the circumstances of his life. He is honest about why he joined a gang and the reason why he must paint a mural on a wall outside the community center. He admires Mary's art and asks her for advice about his drawing. She is surprised that she trusts Marcos; she even agrees to help him with the mural. Their friendship grows as she learns that he endured a beating when he chose to leave the gang. She realizes, "She had been wrong about him. Yes, he had been in a gang, but his heart was good. He liked her, she knew, and she was proud of that. She looked inside herself and saw that she liked him too."[30]

In *Graffiti Moon*—Australian author Cath Crowley's beautifully written novel in verse—Lucy and Ed, a glassblower and a graffiti artist, get to know each other through their art. They also fall in love, in part, because of what they learn about the other as they talk about and view each other's work. In chapters alternating between the thoughts of Lucy and Ed, readers follow these two young people and their friends through one night that changes their senses of who they are—and the courses of their lives. Lucy has just graduated from high school, and she wants to spend the night following her graduation searching the city for Shadow, the graffiti artist whose work, sprayed all over her world, tugs at her heartstrings and pulls at her mind.

Lucy and Ed both use art as a metaphor for their thoughts and feelings. Lucy tells her friend Jazz how she thinks love should feel, by describing a drawing that she loves by Michael Zavros of a horse that is falling from the sky, unable to turn itself over, not knowing why it is in this predicament. Lucy continues,

> The picture is called *Till the Heart Caves In*, and that title tears me open. I love the horse, how real it is; I love the fine lines of its legs and head. But that's not why some nights I can't stop staring at the picture. I

can't say exactly why. Only, it's got something to do with how love should be. (67)

Ed loves the way that Lucy looks at his work, as Shadow, and talks about it. He thinks,

> Feels like art's the only thing I ever figured out. Words, school, I never got the whole picture. . . . The pieces I paint come out of my head right. No spell check required. I paint to get the thoughts in me out. I paint so it gets quiet under my skin. (75–76)

As the night goes on, Lucy and Ed use their talk about their art to learn about each other. Ed takes Lucy to see a wall that he did of himself, "standing in a thin night" in which everything is slender, slivered. Lucy takes out charcoal and adds tangles around him. She tells him about her portfolio project, *The Fleet of Memory*, part boat, part bottle, part creature: "They're what I imagine memories would look like. . . . Some of the bottles are memory itself. . . . You know how sometimes a moment isn't a word in your head, it's a smell or a sound or a shape?" Ed thinks, "This night will be a bird flapping on a wall" (121). Lucy says that some bottles are clear glass—representing things that we do not remember. Some are filled with things—like ships in bottles but instead with images from her childhood.

In the end, when Lucy finds out that Ed *is* Shadow and tells him that he should not have lied, he says that he knows this now, and he uses Vermeer as an analogy, telling her about the Vermeer painting with the scales, which says to him that you have to weigh what you are doing against what you want in the end. When Lucy then smiles at him, he thinks of "wall after wall after wall. Green mazes wandering and two people wandering through them. Doorways that lead somewhere good. Skies the exact kind of blue I've been looking for" (255). At the end of their story, it appears that Ed and Lucy have a real future individually as artists but also together, as a couple, because of the way that they respect and understand the importance of each other's artistic endeavors, value each other's artistic vision, and care about each other's development as an artist.

CONCLUSION

The friendships and romantic relationships of young adult artists serve to push their development as artists in myriad ways. The novels discussed in this chapter show young adult artists the importance of having peers who accept their identities as artists and who care about how their talent and skill can be nurtured and sustained. But it is often the relationships with adults—teachers, parents, and mentors—that provide the bedrock for a young person's developing sense of identity as an artist and as a unique individual. These relationships are the subject of the next chapter.

NOTES

1. Paula Yoo, *Good Enough* (New York: HarperTeen, 2008), 148.

2. Liz Gallagher, *The Opposite of Invisible* (New York: Wendy Lamb Books, 2008), 18–19.

3. Liz Gallagher, *My Not-So-Still Life* (New York: Ember, 2012), 2.

4. Martha Southgate, *Another Way to Dance* (New York: Laurel Leaf, 1998), 16.

5. Davida Willis Hurwin, *A Time for Dancing* (New York: Little Brown Books for Young Readers, 2009), 205.

6. Tara Kelly, *Harmonic Feedback* (New York: Holt, 2010), 110.

7. Tara Kelly, *Amplified* (New York: Holt, 2011), 79.

8. Pat Lowery Collins, *Hidden Voices: The Orphan Musicians of Venice* (Cambridge, MA: Candlewick Press, 2009), 193.

9. Cath Crowley, *Graffiti Moon* (New York: Horizon, 2012), 3.

10. Jon Skovon, *Struts and Frets* (New York: Amulet Books, 2009), 259.

11. Love Maia, *DJ Rising* (New York: Little, Brown Books for Young Readers, 2013), 69.

12. Jennifer Bryant, *Pieces of Georgia* (New York: Yearling, 2007), 153.

13. Denise Vega, *Rock On: A Story of Guitars, Gigs, Girls and a Brother (Not Necessarily in That Order)* (New York: Little, Brown Books for Young Readers, 2013), 42.

14. Maria Padian, *Jersey Tomatoes Are the Best* (New York: Knopf, 2011), 286.

15. E. Lockhart, *Dramarama* (New York: Hyperion, 2007), 82.

16. Louise Spiegler, *The Jewel and the Key* (Boston: Clarion, 2011), 23.

17. Stasia Ward Kehoe, *Audition* (New York: Viking, 2011), 150–51.

18. Sophie Flack, *Bunheads* (New York: Little, Brown, 2011), 55.

19. Jordan Sonneblick, *Curveball: The Year I Lost My Grip* (New York: Scholastic, 2012), 91.

20. Lisa Ann Sandell, *Map of the Known World* (New York: Scholastic, 2009), 54.

21. Jill Alexander, *Paradise* (New York: Feiwel and Friends, 2011), 29.

22. Elizabeth Eulberg, *Take a Bow* (New York: Point, 2012), 33.

23. Sara Bennett Wealer, *Rival* (New York: HarperCollins, 2011), 1.

24. Stephanie Hemphill, *Sisters of Glass* (New York: Borzoi Books, 2012), 24.

25. Kim Culbertson, *Instructions for a Broken Heart* (Naperville, IL: Sourcebook Fire, 2011), 164.

26. Lisa Shanahan, *The Sweet, Terrible, Glorious Year I Truly, Completely Lost It* (New York: Delacorte, 2008), 24.

27. Andrew Matthews, *The Flip Side* (New York: Laurel Leaf, 2005), 2.

28. Justina Chen Headley, *North of Beautiful* (New York: Little, Brown, 2010), 229.

29. Tom Leveen, *Zero* (New York: Random House, 2012), 7.

30. Francisco Stork, *Irises* (New York: Scholastic, 2012), 282.

Chapter Six

Parents, Teachers, and Other Mentors: Adults as Positive and Negative Influences on Young Artists

The crucial, even life-changing, role of a teacher in a young person's life is shown in what happened to Junior in *The Absolutely True Diary of a Part-Time Indian.* Besides drawing and playing basketball, Junior likes shapes, such as isosceles triangles. He is excited about starting high school and is looking forward to geometry class. But when Mr. P passes out the books and Junior looks inside the front cover, he sees his mother's name inside and realizes that the book is at least thirty years older than he is. His anger grows as he realizes, "My school and tribe are so poor and sad that we have to study from the same dang books our parents studied from. . . . That old, old, old, *decrepit* geometry book hit my heart with the force of a nuclear bomb."[1] He throws the book, but he does not mean for it to hit Mr. P in the face and break his nose.

During Junior's suspension from school, he is surprised when Mr. P visits and tells him that he forgives him. Mr. P tells Junior about teaching his older sister, who wanted to write, comparing her to a shining star that faded year by year. He says that he does not want that same thing to happen to Junior, who is "the smartest kid in the school." "And I don't want you to fail. I don't want you to fade away. You deserve better. . . . You deserve the world" (40). Mr. P tells Junior that he will have to leave the reservation, that Junior was right to throw the book at him.

> I deserved to get smashed in the face for what I've done to Indians. . . .
> The only thing you kids are being taught is how to give up. . . . You
> threw that book in my face because somewhere inside you refuse to
> give up. . . . You're going to find more and more hope the farther and
> farther you walk away from this sad, sad, sad, reservation. (42–43)

After Mr. P leaves, Junior sits on the porch for a long time and thinks about his life. He makes the decision to leave the reservation and go to a high school in the nearest town, and that decision shapes the rest of his life.

When an adult understands a young person and cares about his or her future, the impact can be powerful, as Junior's story illustrates. The adult can be a teacher, another adult, and certainly a parent. The portrayals of teachers and other adult mentors—who provide the various kinds of support that young artists need to continue their artistic development—show specific ways to recognize talent: to help young people think about art, their future, and what it means to have an artistic vision. Authors of young adult novels that feature developing artists provide an array of possible parenting styles and depict, with insight and authenticity, how various interactions affect their relationships. These stories provide examples of how to respond to young people's art, music, and dance performances, in ways that can have a powerful effect. The authors also offer insight into the special tensions and connections that exist between parents who are artists and young people who are trying to forge independent identities.

MANIPULATIVE, OVERBEARING, OR DISTANT PARENTS

Eva in *Jersey Tomatoes Are the Best* is a talented dancer with the ability, drive, and stage presence to be successful in the very competitive ballet field. But when she is hospitalized with anorexia and cannot dance, she answers her best friend Henry's question about how much she misses her art: "There's a hole the size of the Grand Canyon in my chest. There's this big, black void where my heart used to beat. There is nothing inside me. I am . . . nothing. Empty, without dance."[2] What is sad about Eva's situation is that her mother, Rhonda, is, at least in part, responsible for Eva's illness because she is pushy, demanding, and so controlling that Eva no longer feels the joy of dance. Rhonda even lets out all the air from the tires of the director of *Coppelia* when Eva is not given the lead. Eva is horrified and tells Henry that she feels like she is "living with Michael Corleone's female alter ego, capable of unspeakable acts of retribution behind a cool façade" (50). What is especially sad is that the part did not even mean a great deal to Eva, but she cannot tell her mother that.

Eva's illness becomes evident when she breaks her leg because her bones have become so fragile, but Rhonda is not willing to give up her dream. Eva is aware of how much her dancing has meant to her mother. "You'd think I *died*, the way she's carrying on. . . . [She] can't accept that I'm out, and she has nothing to brag about" (206). At the end of the novel, while it is clear that Eva understands herself better and is re-creating a more healthy relationship with dance, it is not clear whether Rhonda has changed.

Eva's mother is a prime example of a manipulative parent—the antithesis of what aspiring young artists need in terms of parental support. She is a vivid contrast to Augie's father in *My Most Excellent Year: A Novel of Love, Mary Poppins, and Fenway Park*, who has encouraged Augie to be himself since, at age two, he became mesmerized by Ethel Merman's "I Got the Sun in the Morning" and sang it incessantly. When Augie asks for reassurance that his father is not disappointed that he does not have a manly, football-loving son, his dad tells him, "I got exactly who I wanted."[3] As a result of coming-of-age in a supportive environment, Augie has the confidence to pursue his love of musical theater, to test his wings as a choreographer, and to have an openly gay relationship.

Some young artists use their involvement in the arts as a way of escaping difficult relationships with parents who are emotionally distant and discouraging, such as Jace from *Stringz*, Jude from *The Eyes of Van Gogh*, and Demi and Sadye from *Dramarama*. Maggie from *Spite Fences*, Sam from *I'll Be There*, Sissy and Boy from *Trash*, Lena from *I Hadn't Meant to Tell You This*, and Terra from *North of Beautiful* are all young artists who use their art to make sense of abusive parents/foster parents. In these stories, the relationship between the young artist and the parent defines the environment in which the young person is searching for identity.

In *Struts and Frets*, Jen5, an artist and the girlfriend of the main character, Sammy, a musician, goes by Jen5 to distinguish herself from the four other Jennifers in her class. Sammy says that when Jen5 paints for an assignment, the results are full of energy. But when she paints for herself, the energy is still evident: "But these were darker, more private. It was Jen5 without the sarcasm. Without the shield. I wondered if she realized that the vulnerability she had such a hard time showing in real life was on every canvas."[4] As a result of her talent, Jen5 is given a private show at a local coffee shop. Mrs. Russell, Jen5's mom, objects to the grungy-looking kids and the cigarette smoke. When Jen5 says that two of her paintings have already sold, Mrs. Russell's only reply is that Jen should charge more. She says, "Really Jennifer, I hope this artist phase of yours is over soon. You're so much better than this" (195), and she walks out without even looking at Jen's work.

Mrs. Russell resembles parents in *Rival, Revolution, Map of the Known World, Zero*, and *The Cranes Dance*, who distance themselves from their artist daughters in various ways. The chilly environment is part of the background in which the young artist lives and works. These parents are one-dimensional in that what readers know about them is only what the young person reveals. Brooke from *Rival* longs for her absent father, who was the first to encourage her to sing. But as a high school student who is under great pressure to prepare for an important competition, she rarely hears from him. Brook's mother, who focuses on her demanding job, supports Brooke financially but has limited time to spend with her and does not understand Brooke's anxiety and loneliness. One result of Brooke's distance from her parents is that she pushes herself to be the best operatic singer in hopes that they will acknowledge her success but also to create a sense of identity separate from her family.

In *Revolution*, Andi's father has left the family but demands that Andi accompany him to Paris to work on her final school assignment. At times, it seems that he might begin to understand her, but their relationship remains strained, and Andi realizes that it will always be hard for them to be together. Andi's mother is an artist whose grief and mental illness mean that she also is distant and lost emotionally to Andi. In *Irises*, Kate and Mary's mother, who was attentive before the tragic accident, is left in a vegetative state; their strict father dies soon after the story begins; and the girls are left alone to make decisions about their future and that of their mother. In *A Map of the Known World*, since her brother Nate's death, Cora's parents are physically present but emotionally distant. Her grieving father rarely speaks to Cora and escapes to his den with a drink instead of joining Cora and her mother for dinner. Cora's overly protective mother does not understand Cora's grief or need to escape. She expects Cora to follow her strict rules and is angry when Cora becomes friends with Damian, who survived the automobile accident in which Nate was killed.

Zero's parents, of *Zero*, are also physically present, but their frequent fights resulting from her father's drinking leave Zero feeling very much alone, as if she lives in a war zone. When Zero does have verbal exchanges with her parents, they are brief and frustrating for all three of them. Kate in *The Cranes Dance* is also frustrated when trying to talk with her parents, who are both physically and emotionally distant. Kate feels that neither of them understands that she does not share their push toward perfectionism. As the oldest of three siblings, Kate feels that her parents focus on her brother's successful tennis career, ignore the seriousness of her sister Gwen's mental illness, and take her own achievements for granted. Regardless of how frustrating it is for the young people in the aforementioned titles to cope with their less-than-ideal parental relationships, these situations are merely the backdrop to the plot and to character development. But sometimes, the parent–child relationship is more central to the story, and the young adult's involvement in the arts becomes the means through which that relationship develops.

Bitter Melon

The mother in Cara Chow's *Bitter Melon* is a contrast to the parents who distance themselves from their daughters. Instead, the dysfunctional mother–daughter relationship is central to the plot. Frances, a high school senior, uses her involvement in the art of public speaking as a way to work through how she feels about her mother and how to figure out who she wants to be, independent of her mother's aspirations. The novel opens with her mother saying, "Fei Ting, you are my reason for living. . . . You give me a purpose for my suffering."[5] Her mother's suffering seems to be at the core of her identity because she was abandoned by her father and then by her husband. Frances says that her mother "hates God for abandoning us, for letting life be so unfair" (9). Frances's mother expects her to get straight As in school, go to Berkeley and become a doctor, and then take care of her for the rest of her life. She criticizes Frances mercilessly, constantly compares her to her cousin Theresa, keeps her from dating and having any kind of social life or involvement in extracurricular activities, and never lets her forget that her mother works multiple jobs to pay for tuition at a private girls' school.

Through a computer mix-up, Frances is put into speech class instead of calculus, but she fails to correct the problem because she is fascinated by the teacher, Ms. Taylor, and what she says to the class about language:

> Language is what separates humans from animals. Language gives us the ability not only to talk about the present but to reflect on the past and plan for the future. . . . [We] can create and recreate our identities and our cultures. Through language we can exchange ideas. In so doing, we discover what is true for us and we can speak those truths. (23)

Frances wonders about the plural of "truths." When she writes her first speech, she begins toying with the new idea of multiple possibilities. Ms. Taylor tells her that her speech has a lot of potential and that it would be a "waste of talent" not to continue in speech, which is the first time that a teacher has looked at Frances as an individual with unique possibilities.

Frances thus begins a year of subterfuge, taking speech against her mother's wishes and then deciding to compete in forensics competitions as a way to set herself apart from the other Chinese American students applying to the most elite schools. In the process of coaching, Ms. Taylor challenges Frances to think about whether she really wants to be a doctor and to think about schools other than Berkeley. But Frances says that it is the only school prestigious enough for her mom and within commuter distance. Ms. Taylor suggests Scripps, which Frances cannot afford and is too far away. But Ms. Taylor tells her about scholarships and loans and says, "Far away is a great opportunity to develop your sense of identity and independence" (63).

It is hard for Frances to get out of her mother's clutches. She always picks out the best parts of food for Frances, including the biggest pieces of bitter melon, which Frances does not even like. She says, "The cook has added sugar to this dish, but no sweetness can dull the bitter taste that lingers on the tongue, tainting everything else you eat" (42). When Frances complains, her mother sums up her whole philosophy of life: "If you eat bitterness all the time, you will get used to it. Then you will like it" (42). She constantly tells Frances, "You have what you have only because I choose to give it to you" (85). Frances's mother is an example of an authoritarian parent who—as Baumrind characterizes in "The Influence of Parenting Style on Adolescent Competence and Substance Use" (1991)—shows little warmth but high control. The resulting effect on the child's development tends to be that the young person constantly feels a sense of guilt, often leading to depression.

Fortunately for Frances, as is the case for many other young people, her art form—speech—gives her a way to be strong and fearless. When competing, she states, "I am assuming a different persona, somebody stronger and more confident" (101). Theresa, her cousin, notices, saying, "You look taller now, brighter somehow. It made me think that maybe I had made a mistake by not taking any risks" (144). Through her speeches, Frances processes her changing sense of self and the relationship with her mother, who makes diatribes against her selfishness, attempts to blame Frances for things that go amiss, and even beats Frances with one of her speech trophies. Gradually, Frances realizes she had become

> the rope in a game of tug-of-war between Ms. Taylor's thinking and my mother's. One offered me words, while the other gave me things. Then I started to speak. I saw the effect I had on people who listened. Over time, I also saw the effect my mother had on me when she spoke. The former made me feel bigger, whereas the latter made me feel smaller. I realized that Ms. Taylor was right, that words are more powerful than things precisely because they are abstract. . . . They can also be an invisible sword, spiritual mustard gas . . . a cloaking device. . . . Once I realized this, I didn't want to let my mother make me smaller anymore. . . . In spite of her efforts to crush me, I have to believe that my truth matters. (227)

Frances is accepted at Scripps and given a number of scholarships, but her mother closes out their joint bank account, takes the plane ticket from Frances's backpack, and destroys it. Frances decides that it is time to truly speak the truth to anyone she can. The final confrontation comes when Frances demands her money back. Her mother, defeated, pulls out her checkbook and says,

> "Everything I did, I did for you."
> "No," I say, "you did it for yourself."
> Mom looks at me, her eyes wide with confusion. "Aren't the two the same?" (303)

Frances leaves home, goes to Scripps, cuts ties with her mother, and does well, but she misses her mom. When her mother reaches out to her by sending her ten one-hundred dollar bills for Chinese New Year, extending a cultural tradition, Frances accepts the peace offering. She realizes that just as she has learned the use of words to give voice to her sense of self, her mother has learned, from her own difficult background, to use money as a voice. Frances knows that her mother "cannot take me back to where I was a year ago" (309), and because Frances is confident that she will finish her college education and forge her own path to the future, she calls her mother. Frances has transformed who she is and how she relates to her mother.

Carmen's mother in Jessica Martinez's *Virtuosity* is another example of a manipulative mother whose career in opera ended after unsuccessful throat surgery. She is determined that Carmen will win the prestigious Guarneri competition, even choosing her gowns, giving her antianxiety drugs, and paying the judges to be sure that Carmen's competitor is not chosen. Carmen finally asserts herself by performing without the drugs, not showing up for the finals, and revealing her mother's bribe. She and Frances are role models for young artists who feel stifled by overbearing parents. Their example shows that it is possible to use the arts as a pathway to find a voice and the strength to take charge of one's own destiny.

SUPPORTIVE PARENTS

Parents Doing the Best They Can

Sometimes authors give young artists parents who exist one-dimensionally as supporters of their offspring. Even if encouragement from their parents is just part of the plot, it makes the young artists' achievements more possible. In both *The Opposite of Invisible* and *My Not-So-Still Life*, Alice, Jewel, and Vanessa all have parents who come to their art shows, ask about their work, and encourage their children. In *Rock On*, Ori's parents give his band practice space in their garage. In *Audition*, Sara's parents support her desire to move to New Jersey and test out the world of professional dance, although they also tell her that she can come home at any point if she decides that ballet is not her future. When she wants to return to Vermont, they arrive with brochures for colleges and a willingness to help her rethink her future. In *Leap*, Natalie decides that she no longer wants to be part of the school dance team, because she wants another way to dance. She then has the opportunity to take part in a modern dance show in a neighboring city, and her mother helps her figure out how to get there and what to do about housing—and both her parents bring their partners to her performance.

In *Curveball: The Year I Lost My Grip*, Pete's relationship with his parents is another example of family support, even though it is not fully explored. During the course of the story, Pete worries about his grandfather's declining health but does not discuss it with his parents. It is not until Grampa is hospitalized that Pete's parents tell him that they made a deliberate decision to try to keep Pete from knowing how bad Grampa was getting. His dad says, "I know, buddy. He's your favorite person. And we felt, that after all you'd been through with your arm, and starting high school on top of that . . . you didn't need any additional stress."[6] Pete's mother explains that his dad's working overtime was to save money for when Grampa could not live alone anymore. "But we should have told you a long time ago that this was going on. . . . We thought we were doing what was best for everyone" (268). Parents like Pete's are doing the best that they can to be supportive, and their children come to realize this important fact.

Some parents are less clearly supportive, but they do what they can, given their difficult circumstances, to support their artistic sons and daughters, and such a relationship becomes more important to the texture of the novel. In Kim Culbertson's *Songs for a Teenage Nomad*, the mother–daughter relationship and its difficulties are integral parts of the plot and central to Calle's development. Culbertson consciously thinks about such relationships:

> As for the parents, I mostly wanted to create real worlds around these kids. I . . . have so many students who have wonderful parents, and I've had many students with really broken parents. . . . And I have to say that it's rare I've met a parent who doesn't love their kid. Even when they are royally messing everything up, the love is mostly there. In *Songs,* Alyson really loves Calle and thinks she's protecting her. She makes some questionable choices as a parent but I think her intentions are really in the right place. I think my hope is to create full, rich characters in the adults in my stories who have whole lives. What I've noticed as a teacher is that the health of a parent mostly rests on the health of that person as an individual. Bad parenting, I've noticed, is a by-product of being a broken person. I think most people hope to be good parents, but stuff gets in the way. . . . I once had a mother in my office, clearly high on drugs, sobbing, "I just want to be a good mother" . . . but had so much broken stuff messing it up.[7]

Although Alyson has spent Calle's lifetime fleeing Calle's criminal and abusive father, running from job to job, boyfriend to husband, and town to town, she has taught Calle a love of music and a way of using it to capture her emotions and reflect on them. Calle has fond memories of singing with her mother and watching her mother sing and dance. She has a song journal in which she tracks not just lyrics that speak to her, but her reflections on the circumstances of hearing specific titles and the memories surrounding those listening experiences; she keeps the journal as a way to keep herself grounded and, ultimately, as a way to connect with new people.

Junior's parents in Sherman Alexie's *The Absolutely True Diary of a Part-Time Indian* do not oppose Junior's decision to leave the reservation to attend a nearby high school, yet their support is limited by their circumstances. Junior thinks,

> But it isn't weird that my parents so quickly agreed with my plans. They want a better life for my sister and me. My sister is running away to get lost, but I am running away because I want to find s*omething*. And my parents love me so much that they want to help me. Yeah, Dad is a drunk and Mom is an ex-drunk, but they don't want their kids to be drunks. (46)

Junior's dad reminds him that it will be hard to get him to the school because there is no school bus that he can ride. But the first day of school, Junior's dad, with his breath smelling "like mouth wash and lime vodka" (54), drives him the twenty-two miles to Reardan. Some days there is not enough gas, or the car breaks down, so Junior walks, if he cannot hitchhike a ride. Still, Junior knows that his dad, in spite of all his shortcomings, will continue to try to support his pursuit of a better life.

Actively Supportive Parents

Sister Mischief

In Laura Goode's *Sister Mischief*, Esme's father and Rowie's mother take more active and important roles by providing advice and comfort to these two girls as they sort through their developing sexual relationship and take action against their high school's policies Their principal tries to ban hip-hop and rap music that "incites violence," and he demands that all students sign a statement of support for this ban. The girls, members of a hip-hop band, decide that if the administration refuses to let them start a student group to listen to and talk about the music, they will draw all kinds of attention to the situation. While they are good students and active in other school activities, their musical life together is central to their identities and to their friendship. Esme, the narrator, asks how she can possibly give up rhyming:

> To me, hip-hop is a reflection of your surroundings, and an instrument of change. And if that's true, it can't belong only to black people, or to white people, or to brown or green or blue people. . . . I like to think that all subversive people are, or should be, welcome, because busting rhythm and poetry loose is the only way anyone with hip-hop pumping in their veins can feel free. We're getting free. . . . If we're being really honest with ourselves here, we rap exactly because a lot of people think we shouldn't.[8]

Rowie's mom is supportive and reads them a poem that reminds them of the importance of early friends, of the love between women and how magical that is. She listens and participates in the group's conversation and discussions of issues, such as the use of "whore" and "bitch" in their lyrics. The girls agree that the language used to describe women is "messed up," but they wonder whether, "if enough women rappers break through, it's something [they] can reclaim" (116). Yet, they are not sure if participating in the debate by using language that still reflects violence against women is really a good idea. They spin out a whole list of alternatives. Rowie's mom says, "It is good to question. To demand to know" (198).

When Rowie breaks up with Esme, Esme is outed without her consent, and kids at school view her like she is a "leper." She finally confides in her dad, who says that he was always a little worried, given Rowie's desire to keep things private, that she would never be able to love Esme the way that she deserves to be loved. When she lashes out at him, he understands that she is really angry with her mother (who abandoned them when Esme was little) and with Rowie. He tells Esme that he finds her beautiful, amazing, and wonderful:

> No one with half a brain would ever be anything but proud and lucky to love you. Rowie's not ashamed of you. She's afraid of herself. . . . You deserve to be loved for exactly who you are, and . . . I promise—that you are going to come out of all this even more beautiful and amazing than you went into it, . . . Esme. You are an artist. Use all the ugliness

you're feeling to make something beautiful. Don't you know that you're
the most amazing artist I've ever met? (255–56)

He is very wise and tells her that she was brave to fall in love. He
suggests that she write: "something, only you can make people consider. It's about moving people. . . . Try to *make* something out of all this,
and it won't fix everything, but I can promise you will start to feel
better" (257).

Esme's father is also supportive of the girls' efforts to push back
against school policy. The girls stage a takeover of the school assembly
and deliver their message to the entire community. The principal is
forced to agree to allow them to have a club devoted to discussion of
hip-hop, rap, and other music, but he does suspend them for a few days
and charges them with writing a mission statement for the group 4H
(Hip-Hop for Heteros and Homos). They write a statement that is a
powerful call for acceptance for student voices, calling for a space,
through the investigation of hip-hop and sexuality, where people can
really explore ideas of importance:

> Queerness, as we understand it, represents a refusal to confirm to roles
> prescribed to us by others and a belief that we are all equal as intercon-
> nected agents of love: each in our own way, whether we love women,
> men, or both, we are all queer, either because of our own orientation or
> because of the orientation of someone we love. We reclaim a word that
> once expressed hatred to express support for and solidarity with our
> GLBT brothers and sisters. (359)

Esme and Rowie and the other members of "Sister Mischief" are strong
young women who are able to work through a lot of issues on both a
personal level and a community level and who, by the end of the novel,
are clearly comfortable with who they are. They are confident and
strong because their parents believe in them and actively stand with
them throughout their struggles and triumphs.

Parents Who Grow in Understanding

In some novels about young adult artists, the ways that the parents
change and grow in understanding of their young adult is part of the
plot and is important to thematic development of the novel overall. In
such cases, one of the reasons for the note of hope on which the novel
ends is that the parent or parents have come to a better appreciation for

the role of art in their adolescent's life. Paula Yoo's family in *Good Enough* contrasts effectively with Frances and her mother from *Bitter Melon* in this regard.

Good Enough

The novels *Good Enough* and *Bitter Melon* are both written by Asian American writers reflecting on Asian American family dynamics. In some ways, Patti's parents and Frances's mother are portrayed as having an authoritarian parenting style. But researcher Ruth Chao, who works with Asian American families, says that such interactions cannot always be so interpreted (see her 1994 article "Beyond Parental Control and Authoritarian Parenting Style: Understanding Chinese Parenting through the Cultural Notion of Training"). She would argue that Patti's parents more clearly reflect the concept *chiao shun*, an emphasis on training the child in the virtue of obedience. On the surface, Patti's parents, with their high expectations and strict rules and regulations, may seem to be distant and cold. While it is true that Patti struggles to create a sense of self as she pushes against these expectations, she never doubts their love for her. When Patti's SAT scores do not hit the desired 2200 mark and she studies even harder, her mother makes her special Korean treats and urges her to take study breaks to nourish her brain.

When Patti is struggling with a newly introduced math concept in her AP calculus course, her dad tutors her. Patti realizes that her dad really enjoys mathematical and computer science challenges. Patti eventually does understand what her father is saying, and, unlike Frances's mother, he rewards Patti with a genuine smile and a "Good! You got it!"[9] When Patti protests that it took her an hour to do so, her dad counters with a story about when, back in Korea, he had to go to a *hagwon*, a private school after regular school ended for the day. Yet, the first time that he took the college entrance exam, he failed, which made his mother cry. He was left with the shame that he brought on his family, even though he passed the exam the second time. Patti is astonished to realize that Korean families take education as a "life or death situation," and she begins to wonder whether he pursued a career in computers because he was good at it or because numbers and computers make him happy. She wonders if there is a difference. "Even though my dad is helping me find the answer to this one [math] question, there

are now suddenly many more questions that I don't know the answers
to" (115).

Patti learns that her parents usually do not smile when she is performing, because they are afraid that she will make a mistake and feel
bad. She learns that they are not against her pursuit of music as a career
but are just genuinely worried about her ability to support herself. She
notices how difficult life is for her parents because they speak fluent
English but with a heavy Korean accent, and she begins to feel frustrated on their behalf. She comes to the awareness that success and happi-
ness mean the same thing for them. While she does not share this
belief, this understanding helps her accept their version of support.

When her acceptance to Juilliard arrives and her parents are worried
that Patti will go there, she is able to explain how happy she is when
she plays her violin. Her parents listen to her and, after a concert, tell
her they *saw* how happy she was while playing. They go out for ice
cream to celebrate, letting her know that they will support whatever her
decision is regarding college.

Paradise

In Jill Alexander's *Paradise*, Paisley's relationship with her parents
evolves as she and they develop a better understanding of each other.
Paisley's life is different from Patti's. She lives in a small rural town in
Texas, and while she is smart and takes AP classes, her parents do not
exert the kinds of pressures that Patti's parents do. In fact, what they
want is for Paisley to stay close to home and settle into small-town life.
They recognize that Paisley has talent as a drummer, but they do not
have any sense at all that a girl can become a professional percussion-
ist. Because they do not really approve of her music, Paisley hides her
involvement in the band in which she plays. But she is not happy about
doing so, because she really wants her mom and dad's approval. When
she sneaks off to perform a gig in a cantina known by Paradise's
family, she says,

> I wanted my dad to hear me play, watch every stick spinning, bass kick,
> and roll. I wanted to see him circle his finger in the air like he does
> when his young pitchers nail their first curveball. . . . And I wanted my
> mother there. . . . If for no other reason than to show her that I could do
> this. . . . Without them, drumming felt as hollow as a blown bottle
> rocket. Nothing left after the big boom except a sour, burning smell
> lingering in the air. [10]

Thus, when Paisley is sneaking away to go to the city for the day to play in the big Texapalooza band competition, trying to fulfill her dream of "living large," she finds that she cannot do it—and she heads back home because part of "living large" means having her parents' blessing and living in the open. "Everything had worked just like I planned. Except for the nagging, creeping feeling that I was leaving something behind. . . . What I left wasn't something I could carry. It was the thing that carried me" (196).

Paisley learns that her mother gave up her dreams to marry her father but does not regret her decision. So Paisley tells her parents about her dreams and how playing in the Texapalooza in Austin can help her achieve them. Her parents, like Patti's, listen. Her mom says that she wishes Paisley had told her sooner about the showcase and had given her a chance. "But I can't sprout wings and take you there" (206). The phrase about sprouting wings gives Paisley an idea. She suggests that her mom ask her brother for a ride to Austin in his private plane, and then go with her. Afterward, Paisley's parents comfort and support her as she copes with the tragedy of losing band member and boyfriend Paradise; Paisley and her sister support their mom as she attempts to begin a catering business; and Paisley's parents begin to encourage her in pursuing her dream. As the novel ends, Paisley calls the guys in the band to meet her at the hangar, and she sets out

> for the hangar. For the drums. For whatever the future held. Texapalooza wasn't the dream come true; it was the dream taking off. A rhythm I couldn't escape hung in the air. I heard a heartbeat I'd never forget. It would always be with me. I set my stride to the pulse in my memory and pushed on. Wide-open. (246)

Everyone in the family grows in insight and confidence as a result of Paisley's adventures.

The Other Half of Me

Sixteen-year-old Jenny Fitzgerald of *The Other Half of Me*, like Paisley, has felt misunderstood by her parents, indeed like the odd person out in Team Fitz. The rest of the Fitzgerald clan is athletic; they are coordinated lovers of team sports who delight in family volleyball night. But Jenny's impulse is to duck and run when she sees a ball coming, and her parents and siblings do not appreciate how participating in a family obstacle course race makes her feel ungainly, nor do they value what she does enjoy doing. She is a painter and has always seen the world in terms of colors and light; she thinks about events in terms of famous works of art. She has turned her closet into a tiny art studio and does janitorial chores at a gallery/studio complex in exchange for studio time. Although she is trying desperately to complete several paintings in hopes of having one accepted at a professional gallery show, she feels even more like an outsider when her parents ask her to leave the studio and her art in progress to be part of her twin sisters' and brother's events.

In Jenny's mind, she is so different because her mother conceived her with the help of Donor 142 six months before meeting her husband, who adopted Jenny as soon as he married Jenny's mom. Tate, Jenny's boyfriend, encourages Jenny to search for possible half siblings conceived from the same donor sperm. It turns out that two gay rights activist attorneys from New York City used the same donor sperm to have their daughter Alexa within just a few months of Jenny's conception. The girls begin e-mailing and calling each other; they feel an immediate connection and are alike in many ways, except that Alexa is impulsive while Jenny is careful and thoughtful. Alexa decides to visit Jenny, which does not sit well with Jenny's father, who did not know about their correspondence. But Alexa is gregarious and funny in ways that Jenny is not, and she soon wins over Jenny's family—especially as she, too, is a varsity athlete and not at all artistic.

During Alexa's visit, Jenny is forced to confront her understanding of the meaning of "family," but so are her parents. In particular, her dad is finally able to tell her how scared he has been that she would somehow always think of him as "less than" because he is not her birth father. He even confesses that he does not know how to respond to her artwork because, as a nonartist, his praise might not seem believable. But Jenny feels loved and valued when he tells her that four of her watercolors, which she had framed for him and which she thinks he stuffed into a closet, are actually hanging in his office, where his clients find them soothing. She is able to explain her desire to find a "missing part" of herself, and her dad is able to tell her that she is actually more like him in terms of personality and worldview than any of his biological children. When Jenny learns that her whole family has conspired to create a real studio in the attic and plan a party to celebrate her acceptance into the art show, she knows that she is where she belongs. As she stands in front of her painting at the art show, she thinks,

Tate once commented that my paintings are filled with circles, and I guess he's right. Now I realize the spheres are like family, everything joined together in teams. Maybe the point or art—and of everything—is that you can't predict the outcome, that the crazy upheaval of it is all part of life.[11]

The stories of Jenny, Paisley, and Patti all provide hope for parents and young artists that, with some courage and openness based on genuine love and affection, bridges between parent and child can be built that lead everyone to new understanding. This developing understanding of the importance of the child's art to the sense of self allows the parent to figure out ways to provide active support for the child's artistic endeavors that will smooth the way for the young person in the future—and will ensure that the parent–child relationship stays intact.

Parents Who Are Artists

The relationship between a young adult artist and a parent who is also an artist can be complicated by their shared interest in the arts. In some cases, the older artist wants the younger artist to take over a family tradition. In others, the young person may fear the comparison with the artistic parent. In yet other situations, the two parties learn about each other through viewing the other's art. The young adult novels that portray these relationships cover the whole spectrum and offer insights into the positive elements of such shared artistic gifts as well as the difficulties and tensions that can be present.

Silk Umbrellas

Silk Umbrellas, by Carolyn Marsden, takes place in northern Thailand. Eleven-year-old Noi and her older sister Ting help their grandmother Kun Ya as she paints silk umbrellas to sell to tourists. Then Ting has to go to work in a radio factory to help earn money for the family, and Noi begins to realize how such a daily routine would sap her soul. When her grandmother becomes ill, when the rains prevent her father from working as a bricklayer, and when her mother's recent batch of mosquito netting is no longer needed by the person whom she supplied, Noi realizes that it is time to show her gift for painting, which she has learned from her beloved Kun Ya.

When Noi was young and Kun Ya asked her to mix paints, Noi, unlike her sister, enjoyed the colors and textures of the paints. While her sister is content to wash brushes and do other menial tasks, Noi "longed to paint. Sometimes Kun Ya let her paint simple things like leaves. Noi's whole body came alive with the shades of green. Her hands felt magical when she guided the brush." [12] When Kun Ya asks Noi to paint a butterfly, Noi says that she does not know how, but Kun Ya says, "You've watched me for years, Noi. Now try yourself" (6). Noi is nervous and is trembling as she brings her brush close to the umbrella. Kun Ya tells her that the trembling is good because it gives life to the butterfly on the silk: "Let the movement spread to your whole body, not just your fingers. Paint with all of you. Become the butterfly."

> In an instant, Noi understood what Kun Ya meant. She sensed the butterflies hovering in the thick shade of the banana leaves, the fluttering out into the sunshine. The flit of the butterflies moved into her, then out into the brush, so the paint seemed to lay itself down. (6)

And Kun Ya is very pleased.

In many ways, Kun Ya is a natural teacher. She tells Noi, "We must be still for a moment, Noi, and listen to the umbrella. Look at its color and the way the light touches it. Know the story it wants you to tell before you begin" (48). Kun Ya starts an umbrella but asks Noi to finish it, telling her, "It's time for you to go further." Kun Ya intuitively understands Vygotsky's (1962) notion of scaffolding, outlined in the classic *Thought and Language* of providing structured guidance with lots of modeling, which eventually leads Noi to be able to paint on her own. Kun Ya teaches Noi to really "see." One morning, she holds out a mangosteen, telling Noi to just look at it. "Noi sat back and studied the mangosteen. Then, when she no longer heard the rain crashing on the roof or felt her own body or saw Kun Ya's thin hand, when only the round fruit existed, she reached for the paintbrush" (81). Noi mixes "red and more and more blue, red again, then black" to get the color just right, and then Kun Ya tells her that "to make the fruit round, watch how the light falls on it. The purple here . . . has a touch of white. . . . And here it casts a shadow, and the shadow runs up into the skin" (81–82). As she works, Noi becomes increasingly aware of the diversity of shades in the skin. But when she is done, she is concerned that the fruit she has painted does not look at all like the real fruit. Kun Ya reassures her, "Of course they look nothing alike, Noi. This . . . is only a mangosteen. While this . . . is the mangosteen plus you" (83).

Thus, the first time that Noi approaches a blank umbrella, she knows just what to do.

> She took an umbrella of a soft brown color. She closed her eyes and listened for the scene as Kun Ya had taught her. She saw Kun Ya holding a stick of sugar cane out to an elephant. . . . How could the umbrella have asked her to paint something so difficult? . . . She closed her eyes again and looked inside until she could see the elephant in the jungle, could hear its thick feet in the long grass, the small snorts it made with its trunk. Noi painted, forgetting about being afraid, keeping the image of the elephant steady within her. (79)

When Kun Ya sees Noi's effort, she responds with delight and tells her that she will be selling the umbrellas soon, and she advises her to "paint whenever you can, while you can" (79). Noi's umbrellas are a hit. Both Kun Ya and Noi are satisfied that Noi's talents as an artist will continue to blossom as she continues to focus on her work.

In Cath Crowley's *Graffiti Moon*, Lucy is fortunate that her parents—who are depicted as kooky but loving toward each other and Lucy—are both artists of sorts. Her father is a magician, and her mother is a writer. They have given Lucy a somewhat unconventional upbringing, often taking her on drives to watch the sky fill with stars. As the novel begins, her father has moved to the gardening shed in the backyard. Lucy is convinced that her parents are heading for divorce. They keep insisting that her father is just working on a new magic act and needs space while her mother is working on a new project and needs quiet, which is the truth. Lucy's parents support her and value art of all kinds. When Lucy becomes bewitched by glassblowing, they truly understand how she has fallen for this unusual art form. To answer her concern about the cost of lessons, they tell her, "Art is more important than money, Lucy,"[13] and they say that somehow they will find a way to give her the support she needs. Lucy's parents provide the gifts of not just glassblowing lessons but, as Noi receives, the attitude that "art is more important than money."

In Summer Light

Lucy and Noi are lucky in that their families appreciate how important their various art forms are to the girls' developing senses of self. But Kate Brewer, from Zibby Oneal's *In Summer Light*, has a different relationship with her artist father. Unlike the parents of Lucy and Noi,

Marcus Brewer is an important and famous painter whose works are in significant art museums in the United States and abroad. Because of his fame, the entire family dynamic has been structured around preserving the time and space that he needs in which to create. As a young child, Kate spent hours in his studio, painting beside him, absorbing his sense of color, composition, and light. But after her first year at boarding school, Kate put away her paints and turned her attention to literature and writing instead. Now, as a senior, she has contracted mononucleosis and has come home for an extended spring and summer of rest, instead of working on the mainland as she had planned. Ian, a graduate student in art history, has also arrived on the island, tasked with cataloguing Brewer's work and helping him prepare for a retrospective.

The story of Kate's relationship with her father plays out in part as she struggles to write a paper on *The Tempest* for her English class. She sees her father as Prospero and thinks that neither is admirable because of the way he manipulates others and is not a good father. As Kate continues to work on the paper, discussing the play with her best friend, Leah, and Ian, she begins to understand what happened to her relationship with her dad. During her first year in high school, at the boarding school, Kate won a prize for her painting. Because she was nervous about her father's reaction, she did not tell her parents about the award before they came to visit. He looked at the painting with an odd expression and remarked only that it was a "nice little picture."[14] Then when she came home for winter break, he told her that she should find somewhere to paint other than his studio because it had gotten too crowded. Kate believes that her father cannot accept the fact that she is so serious about her art. She tells Leah that at first his attitude challenged her to paint more, to learn more, to become so good that he would have to take notice of her, but then she stops painting because she realizes,

> My father has to have the foreground all to himself . . . be the center of attention. It took me longer than it should have to understand that. I thought that the way to please him was to become a better and better painter. After that business at school, I saw that I was wrong. . . . I stopped painting. (68)

Leah and Ian both tell Kate that her reasons for putting down her paints are not good ones. Kate's mother, who had also painted when she was younger, begins to encourage her to try to paint again. When Kate asks her if she minded giving up her paints, her mother says no but notes that she never had Kate's talent. As Kate does begin to work again, her mother provides her with new paints and supportive feedback. As Kate struggles to regain her skill, tackling figures for the first time, she begins once again to study her father's work; she looks closely even at paintings that she does not really like, "because they could teach her something. She studied the way he had applied the paint, what he had done with line" (102–3). She is able to recognize that "from him she had absorbed some idea about how to handle paints, about how to organize a composition and achieve balance" (103).

Even more important, as Kate's mother gives her technical advice, Kate begins to recognize another truth: that most people, with time enough and good instruction, could master the basics of drawing. "It was the other thing that you couldn't learn, that was simply there, like a present. She knew because she recognized this other thing in her father's work . . . whether she liked what he painted or not" (136). Recognizing that she does have her father's gift gives Kate the confidence to begin talking to him again about his work. He has been struggling all summer with a painting, and as Kate watches one afternoon, she blurts out that what he is currently doing looks "desperate" and is "wrong" (141). They end up having a discussion in which her father explains why he has not discarded the painting: "I'm having a war with this painting. It's trying to beat me, and I don't plan to let it" (142). He confesses, in a rare moment of intimacy, that he does not know what he will paint next, which scares him, as he has always had many pictures in his mind. He also confesses that he is scared of the upcoming retrospective because painters are offered such exhibits only when the perception is that they can no longer create.

As a result of her newfound belief in her gift and her reconnection with her father, Kate is not only able to carry on painting but is also able to change her perception of Prospero. She finally finishes the paper by writing that Prospero *is* guilty of ignoring the needs of his people and using others for his own purposes but that, by the end of the play,

> Prospero has become an old man. His magic powers . . . are gone entirely. In the Epilogue he asks us to set him free. I think Shakespeare means for us to forgive him . . . and if we refuse, we will be trapped like Prospero was, on his island. (143)

Kate supports her father when an outspoken young painter suggests that Mr. Brewer may have reached a dead end in his exploration of

abstract expressionism. Kate says that labels and movements have
nothing to do with it: "Painting has to do with knocking yourself out
day after day trying to get what you want down on canvas. Maybe it
works and maybe it doesn't, but every day you try. That's what painting is" (146). Mr. Brewer tells the young artist that his daughter is right.
While Kate and her father may never have a traditional father–daughter
relationship, they have come to admire and respect each other for their
artistic integrity, and it is clear that Kate will continue to forge her own
path as an artist—and with her father's support.

Drawing Lessons

In *Drawing Lessons*, Tracy Mack uses some of her experiences with art
in creating Rory, who, like Kate, has a father who is an artist. When
Rory was five years old, she told her dad, "The pencil tells the paper
what to make." He smiled as he said, "I think you will be a true
artist."[15] For as long as Rory can remember, she has thought in colors:
"blue for a gentle song . . . pink for laughter . . . silver for imagination. . . . I saw pictures in everything" (21–22). Every Sunday in the big
barn studio, she and her father would sit side by side at the drawing
table. Some of her many sketchbooks are filled with the results of these
drawing lessons with her dad. From him, she learned about light and
color, perspective and form. As a birthday surprise for Rory's mother,
they even talked about working together on a mural of a beloved tree
that had to be cut down.

When Rory's sketch of the tree is at the point where she wants to
show it to her father and tell him they can start working on the mural,
everything changes. She hears laughter as she approaches the barn,
looks inside, and sees what appears to be her dad kissing a woman who
is posing for a picture. An uneasy red shakes inside Rory: "a loud color,
jumpy and impatient under her skin" (39). She grabs a match and her
sketchbook and thinks, "*You'll never see my tree!*" (39). Soon the fire
that she sets is "taking the river sketches, the house and barn studies,
taking the tree—[her] best work ever—with it" (40). As Rory kicks dirt
around the fire to keep it from spreading over the grass, her dad approaches and sees what is happening. She takes one last look at the
sketchbook, lying hidden in the heap of dirt, and turns away from the
fire and her father. Soon after, her father leaves and does not even tell
her good-bye.

Rory's art teacher Mr. Miles wants her to submit a piece for an exhibition that will take place after December break. The best works will be entered in a national art contest with those from hundreds of other middle schools. He even lets her know that he is keeping the art room open after school until the contest deadline, and he tells her that the door is always open if she wants to talk. She dreads his prodding her about the contest, but after he stops "bugging" her, the silence of his letting go is even worse. Weeks later he calls to beg her to give him a piece. "It's killing me, Rory, that there isn't one from you. It's just not right. I'm wondering if you might reconsider. I could give you till the end of the week" (127). When Rory says that she will be away, he even offers to give her his address if she wants to mail him something, but she just does not feel that she can do it.

Rory is lost. She has not felt like drawing since her father left, and her mother notes that it has been a long time since Rory has picked up a sketchbook. When Rory finally tells her best friend Nicky that her father has left, Nicky encourages her to try to draw, saying, "You're not you if you don't draw" (114). Rory's mother gives her a brand-new black sketchbook, telling her that she will feel better if she tries to use it. When Rory visits her grandmother in New York, Nana buys her a beautiful watercolor set before Rory can tell her that she is not painting anymore and that she and her Dad painted in acrylics. When Nana is away for the day, Rory does try to paint with the watercolors, stops, and decides to take a taxi and find her father, who is staying with a friend. The brief surprise visit ends with Rory racing to Grand Central Station and returning home. When her worried father finds her, he tells her that he would never forgive himself if anything happened to her. He gives her a package that he was going to send. He had rescued her sketchbook because, as he explains, "it broke my heart to see you try to destroy it, Rory" (155). In the sketchbook, Rory finds the tree with the edges of its page repaired by her father and most of the sketch still intact.

Rory does go back to painting her tree. She has come to understand that "the great thing about painting is you can bring back something you've lost and keep it forever" (166). She decides that maybe her father was not who she thought he was or who she wanted him to be. She will have to let him love her in his own way. She never would have guessed that he would rescue her sketchbook and work to repair it. She loves the words he has written inside:

When you look back over all your old books, this one will always be the most important. It was the first one that was totally your own. You are an artist in your own right now. All you need, you already know. Just remember to watch the light and believe in yourself as much as I believe in you. (167)

Rory has come to understand her father better but also herself, as she explains, having completed the mural on her own:

I looked back at my mural, painted in bold greens and browns and blues and pinks across the barn wall. I saw my tree, standing strong and tall on the riverbank, its sturdy branches reaching for me again like out-stretched arms. I saw this place, our world that was real, that I painted all on my own just for Mom. I saw my painting style, rooted in my father's but branching out in new directions that were entirely my own. I felt him watching from the other side of the river and even though that wasn't where I wanted him to be, at least I knew he was there.

But most of all . . . I saw that I was there, breathing out the colors of my own voice. (167–68)

Rory is another young woman who, like Kate, will continue to develop as an artist. She will use what her father taught her but also find her own way.

Silhouetted by the Blue

The relationship between Serena, who dreams of becoming an actress, and her father, a famous artist, as portrayed by Traci Jones in *Silhouetted by the Blue*, is unique in that her father has become "absent" through his descent into a deep depression after the death of his wife, Serena's mother. The novel opens as Serena, a seventh grader, finds out that she has landed the role of Dorothy in *The Wiz*. She is ecstatic at first, but her euphoria is short-lived as she realizes that she must add memorizing her lines, learning her dances and songs, and attending rehearsals to the long list of chores for which she has taken responsibility since her mother's death, including trying to get her father out of bed at least long enough to go to the bank to get the money that she needs to manage the household. Serena misses her mother desperately and sometimes listens to her mother's voice on her office answering machine. But Serena is a strong young woman who uses her sorrow to inform her acting. When she performs Dorothy's "Home" for the first time at rehearsal, instead of suppressing all the emotions that had been building up since her dad's blue began to reappear, Serena sang it all out—transferring to Dorothy all her worry, all of her anger, and all of her sadness. And as she sang, Serena's frustrations and fears melted away. . . . She felt lighter, as if all her burdens had somehow been lifted. [16]

Serena does not understand why her father, a gifted painter, cannot also use his art to move out of his grief nor why he has lost at least four illustration jobs. She wants to scream and cry when all he can do is crawl back under the covers. But she does not. Instead, she just carries on, trying to maintain her grades, take care of her brother Henry and everything at home, and get the show ready for opening night. Serena is lucky in that she has friends who help her with Henry and a director who senses that something is truly wrong at Serena's home, so he allows Henry to help paint sets after school.

Finally, as Serena's big night approaches and there is no food in the house and Henry begins getting in trouble at school, Serena knows that she needs help. She tries to reach out to her father's brother—an international businessman. When her father begins giving away his art and transfers his art supplies to Henry's room, Serena realizes that he is heading into a suicidal state. That her father, who has had such a deep sense of identity as an artist, is giving up that piece of himself alarms Serena in a way that none of his other actions have done. Fortunately, Uncle Pete shows up just in time to get Serena's dad to the emergency room after he attempts to overdose. From the epilogue, it is clear that *The Wiz* is a hit and that Serena truly carries the show; that her dad is getting better, as he is in the audience with video camera in hand; and that Serena can be a young adult again because Uncle Pete is going to stay with the family until her father is stabilized.

Latent Powers of Dylan Fontaine

In April Lurie's *The Latent Powers of Dylan Fontaine*, Dylan, who is a talented artist and classical guitar player, is somewhat like Serena in that he is dealing with an absent parent who is an artist. In Dylan's case, the novel opens just after his mother has left the family in search of her artistic community and in quest of a space in which she can feel more herself as an artist. Even though she has a studio in their home, she has felt neither understood nor appreciated by Dylan's father. She has long encouraged both her sons to explore the world through art. Dylan says, "As soon as Randy and I were old enough to hold a stick of charcoal, my mother had us drawing, and just like with our musical abilities, Randy's artistic talents have always surpassed mine."[17] In looking at a series of sketches that his mom has taped to her studio wall, Dylan compares a still life that he did to some of Randy's efforts, as well as to his mother's. He says of himself that "the shadows are good and technically it's sound, but next to Randy's portraits and gesture studies, it lacks something—life, emotion, originality, all of the above" (38). By the end of the novel, Dylan has come to accept that his mother is not moving back into their home, in part because of the conversations that the two of them are able to have about art and its importance to his mother. But he understands how deeply his mother loves him by looking at paintings that she has done of her sons, and that realization helps him move toward acceptance—of her, of their relationship, and of his own talents.

TEACHERS, MENTORS, AND CRITICS

As noted in several novels, teachers are often more important than parents in the lives of young adults who are working to understand themselves as artists. This situation is especially true if the parent or family of the young artist is not supportive and if the teacher, a crucial touchstone, recognizes talent and provides opportunities in which the young artist can flourish, as Ms. Taylor does for Frances in *Bitter Melon*. While some of the teachers presented in books with young adult artists as central characters are not such great role models because they squash the budding artist, such as the orchestra teacher in *Stringz*, others work to recognize talent about which the young person is unaware. Some teachers push these young artists by giving them applications for contests and special schools or by offering them private lessons and space in which to practice. Some provide useful models of how to respond to young artists' initial efforts in ways that encourage them to grow and stretch, often doing so by talking about established artists and their visions, struggles, and triumphs. Some not only give the young artist a chance to shine but offer other tangible support. An example might be the director of *The Wiz*, in which Serena of *Silhouetted by the Blue* has the lead, who bends the rules to allow her younger brother to attend rehearsals.

The support and understanding that a significant teacher offers students is often what leads young artists to find a way to use the arts to make sense of their worlds and learn more about themselves. In *Speak* it is Mr. Freeman, Melinda's art teacher, who encourages her to complete her painting of a tree. With her work of art, Melinda finds a way to express herself, with her art and with her voice, and begin to heal. Mr. Steenwilly, the band teacher in *You Don't Know Me*, helps John discover the healing power of music. John does not think that anyone, not even himself, knows who he is, but Mr. Steenwilly certainly knows John well enough to encourage him to learn a tuba solo. In *Dave at Night*, it is the art teacher who comes to the Hebrew Home for Boys and encourages Dave to express his feelings and moods through drawing. When the teacher sees what Dave has drawn and tells him that he has a gift, Dave is delighted: "Gift! I didn't just like to draw, I didn't just have the beginnings of an eye, I had a gift!"[18]

These teachers not only notice the struggling, lost, or lonely artists in their classrooms but find a way to reach out to them, as Mr. Gomez does for Mary in *Irises*. In words similar to those that mean so much to Dave, Mr. Gomez tells Mary she has a gift, "a way of seeing and feeling" that he had not encountered in a young artist before.[19] Mr. Gomez also encourages Marcos to learn more about art and find a way to break away from his gang involvement. Cora in *A Map of the Known World* is glad that Ms. Calico, as a new art teacher, will not label Cora simply as the girl whose brother died. Ms. Calico notices her talent and tells Cora that her "work in this class is quite impressive."[20] She tells Cora about a special program in London that has a cartography class and gives her the application form. For Liz in *Exposed*, it is Mrs. Pratt, the photography teacher, who helps her see which pictures are the best ones to use in the portfolio that she is preparing for her art school application.

In the novel *Zero*, it is interesting to contrast the two teachers in Zero's life. When she works on a piece (that eventually sells), Zero wonders if Mr. Hilmer, her junior high art teacher, would approve. She often thinks about him and what he taught her. She likes to wear a belt on which she painted Salvador Dalí trademark replicas, a work that Mr. Hilmer called one of her best expressions. Zero feels like he was her last good art teacher. She hopes to learn more from Dr. Deborah Salinger in a junior college art class and is eventually encouraged when Dr. Salinger refers to her work as art. Zero begins to think that maybe she will be able to improve her portfolio when Dr. Salinger offers to help her, but she is devastated when Dr. Salinger suddenly moves out of

state. Zero's struggles and feelings of abandonment show how important the fully supportive teacher is to a young artist.

Ms. Dennis of *The Eyes of Van Gogh* stands out among all the
teachers that Jude has experienced in her very transitory life because
Ms. Dennis is a rare teacher, someone who understands young artists in
ways that other adults do not, who can motivate them to see the world
in new ways. Ms. Dennis's remarks make her students think and want
to do more; she does not belittle them nor expect them to work in any
specific way. As an artist, Jude feels truly "seen" by this teacher, and
she finds that a rare and wonderful experience.

Ms. Dennis allows students to interpret assignments in their own
ways. At one point, she asks students to paint the same object from
three different angles, to work on their ability to portray depth. But
Jude picks up on the word *perspective* in the instructions, and she
paints a relatively realistic chair that looks a bit like one that Van Gogh
painted. Her second painting represents shifting reality—the chair in a
corner of the art room with everything bowing toward it. And her third
is just shades of yellow, ultimate reality, just molecules and their energy. This final reality is something that Jude is searching for, "a timeless
reality full of something cosmic. Lots of light and energy. God, it
sounds impossible, but sometimes when I paint, I think I catch a
glimpse of it."[21]

Ms. Dennis eventually is the one who realizes that Jude is searching
for meaning in her life, is in a great deal of pain, and may be considering suicide. After Jude's accident, Ms. Dennis arranges for Jude to stay
with Jazz and her family, and she asks Jude's forgiveness for not realizing sooner exactly how much pain Jude was in, but she promises to
have her paintbrushes waiting when she returns to school. Having this
caring teacher in her life who provides a safe space in which she can
paint is one of the reasons why Jude chooses to live. The reader feels
Jude will be okay.

Like Ms. Dennis, Georgia's art teacher Miss Benedetto, in *Pieces of
Georgia*, recognizes both Georgia's talent and her need for support.
Georgia's father refuses to talk about his daughter's artwork. He does
not try to stop her, but her artistic interests remind him of Georgia's
mother and make him sad. So Georgia needs Miss B in her life. When
Georgia feels weird for noticing things like the irony of a billboard in
an Amish farmer's field advertising Six Flags Theme Park, Miss B
says, "Artists notice things that other people don't. / They're very

observant."[22] When Georgia is not confident that she should even apply for the special art program, Miss B tells her,

> I've seen some pretty incredible sketches / On the covers of your math book, not to mention / The stuff you've done in class. / Of course, I'm not one of the judges / So there's no guarantee. . . . / But how will you know what you can do / Unless you try? (102)

Miss B helps Georgia decide what medium to use for her portfolio work; she helps her plan out a calendar of what to do and when; and she gives her "colored pencils and sketch pads, two boxes of charcoal / and a can of fixative to spray on the best ones / so they don't smudge" (75). She even presents Georgia with a rabbit's foot for good luck. Miss Benedetto's actions are examples of ways that teachers can support gifted young artists, actors, musicians, and dancers.

Sometimes it is the teacher's response to the whole student that is more important than just his or her encouragement of the student's artistic endeavors. Mr. Campbell, Jessa's drama teacher from *Instructions for a Broken Heart*, exemplifies the role of life mentor. During their spring break trip to Italy, Jessa is reading *Portrait of the Artist as a Young Adult* and trying to figure out how to keep from being overwhelmed by the intensity of her emotional response to every aspect of her life. When the group is visiting the Forum,

> Jessa couldn't believe the crazy, open beauty of the Forum, its deteriorating sprawl—the columns shooting up from green ground, the crumbled stone, the way the remaining skeleton of the place stood out against the cloudy sky. . . . Jessa felt herself descending into history.[23]

When Mr. Campbell sees Jessa running her hands along the coolness of the marble, he asks her what she thinks. Jessa says that it makes her feel small. He responds by quoting *Macbeth*: "Life . . . is a tale told by an idiot, full of sound and fury, signifying nothing" (46). Later, when she is concerned that she will constantly feel despair instead of leading a normal, happy life, Mr. Campbell tells her,

> Having an artistic sense about you can make things difficult sometimes, feelings can be more extreme, like all of our nerves are always open to the elements. But that's the secret. . . . We get to *feel* those things. Some people—they get comfort and ease, maybe. We get complexity and really messy feelings that make people uncomfortable. It's a trade-off.

There are people who don't get to look at this sea and wonder what
you're wondering. (262)

He reminds her that "practicality can be its own prison" (263). Having
Mr. Campbell understand how she is feeling—indeed, how she feels
each moment of each day so intensely—is crucial for Jessa as she
makes sense of her broken heart and, at least, begins to sense what
future she really wants for herself.

Nathan Goldfarb, Andi's music teacher in *Revolution*, not only supports her artistic talent but understands her as a person. He knows that
she is a gifted musician who loves music, who loves playing classical
and contemporary music on her guitar, and who wants to continue
learning about musicians and their compositions. But Nathan also
knows that she is grieving the death of her brother, and he knows how
to encourage her to focus on her music, as he had done to survive the
horrors of Auschwitz. Nathan is different from Andi's other teachers,
who tell her that she is a genius and can do anything. Andi notes that
Nathan "is the only one who calls me dummkopf and tells me to practice the Sarabande in Bach's Lute Suite in E Minor five hundred times
a night if that's what it takes to get it through my thick skull. And it's
such a relief I could cry."[24] When Andi practices her Bach so much that
her hand becomes injured and bloodied, her headmistress says that
Andi has even found a way to use her beautiful music to inflict pain.
But Andi knows what Nathan would say about her hand:

> He'd say that bleeding for Bach was no big deal. He'd say that people
> like Beethoven and Billie Holiday and Syd Barrett gave everything they
> had to their music, so what was a fingernail? He wouldn't make a
> tragedy of it. He knew better. He knew tragedy. He knew loss. And he
> knew there was no such thing as forgiveness. (14–15)

Andi's father, aware of how much the music lessons with Nathan mean
to her, threatens that if she does not follow through with his demand
that she talk about her grief with a psychiatrist, he will stop the lessons.
Andi's feelings about Nathan, how he understands her, and the crucial
importance of him in her life, like that of Mr. Campbell for Jessa in
Instruction for a Broken Heart, mean more than anything else to Andi
as she tries to deal with her grief and her inability to forgive herself for
her role in her little brother's death.

In a different setting and situation, Father Antonio Vivaldi in *Hidden Voices* is another example of a teacher who knows the musical

talents and personalities of the girls who are chosen to be in the orchestra at the orphanage. Much of what he does for and with them literally determines their future—whether they will be chosen by suitors because of how they play an instrument or sing or whether they will have the opportunity to perform in places beyond the orphanage. For their rehearsals, he composes a new concerto for them to learn almost every week. He supports each young musician in ways appropriate to her personality and dreams, and as a result of his tutelage, each has a different future than what would be possible without him.

Young adults as developing artists come to expect certain responses from a teacher about a work of art, a theatrical performance, or a piece of music. This predictability—how they will be greeted, what will occur in rehearsal or a weekly lesson (or even class), and how a teacher might react to what the developing artists have done—is important for their sense of stability. For example, when the four young musicians in *Second Fiddle* go to their regular lesson with Herr Müller, they worry when he motions them to sit, pours them all cups of tea, and tells them that they are technically fine players, that he is proud of their progress. Jody notes, "He ended every single piece we had ever played with a list of things in need of 'development.'"[25] Herr Müller's unexpected change in response makes sense only when they learn that he is not well and will not go with them to the competition in Paris. But because they trust him and his judgment of their abilities, they are willing to continue with their plans even without his presence.

Other Mentors

Ed of *Graffiti Moon* works at a paint shop owned by Bert, the only person who, Ed says, "believed I was more than some loser painting on the side of his shop. When I made a mistake, he pointed it out and that was it" (168). Bert never makes a big deal out of Ed's mistakes. When Ed trusts Bert with the secret that he has serious reading difficulties, Bert takes him to an exhibit by the artist Rosalie Gasciogne. Ed describes her works as "road signs or drink crates cut up and spliced on wood so words and letters are jumbled and jutting into each other" (168). Bert asks if one of her works, *Metropolis*, looks like what Ed sees when he looks at words, trying to read. Ed says that it does, and he tells Bert how stupid he feels at school or whenever someone is talking about books. Then Ed says that he *can* read Gasciogne's painting, saying it is a message about being shoved into spaces that are too constricting. Bert buys him a book about the artist's work because "when people are talking about books they've read, you can talk about this one" (168). Bert is the epitome of the mentor. He listens to Ed and shows that he truly understands what Ed has to say. He finds ways to build Ed's self-esteem and support him in his dreams. Even though Bert is not an artist himself, he sees Ed's hunger to paint and does what he can to keep Ed painting, by supplying paint, wall space, and works by other artists to feed his artistic development. Bert is a great model for teachers who are not artists because he shows how to support young artists who need someone to appreciate their dreams and struggles.

Providing Feedback

One of the most important tasks of the teacher or mentor is to give adolescent artists useful feedback as they work to revise their art and develop their talents. It can be tricky to be honest but supportive when working with a young person whose ego may be fragile, especially if the family environment in which he or she lives is not a supportive one. Kimberly Marcus offers insight about how to work with a young artist. She would

> encourage teachers and those who serve as role models to always find something positive to say to young artists. Even if a created work is not to a teacher's particular artistic taste, when constructive criticism is coupled with positive words, students will feel inspired rather than discouraged. You may feel a young writer uses too much description, and not enough action, in a piece of writing, but are there some descriptive phrasings that bring a scene to life? If so, point those out. If a sketch is well-detailed but the perspective is off, praise the student for those details that work before suggesting ways to adjust the perspective.[26]

She makes an important point that not all artistic students need to pursue a career in the arts:

> Art as a hobby has merits. Encouragement and guidance from teachers, and significant others invested in artistic expression, helps all students build self-confidence and embrace a willingness to try new things.

Kim Culbertson also has important advice for teachers:

> I think we have to start from a place of nonjudgment. Often, I might not connect to something one of my students connects to and I have to be

very careful not to level a judgment. This concept is very much the foundation of my newsletter, *Point of View*, because I think our specific sensibilities determine what we're driven to create and enjoy. I often talk with my students about never underestimating the power of being interested and driven by something and that this interest doesn't have to be the same as other people's. In fact, our differences make our art more interesting. I want them to keep an eye out for what they connect to because these connections inform our own creations and views.

Sometimes the professional artist is the only person that a young artist will believe. Oxana is an artist and important gallery owner in Brian Farrey's *With or without You*, and she gives Evan, who has spent years mastering the techniques of many famous artists, important information about his work that his friends and teachers have tried unsuccessfully to make him hear. Oxana begins with praise, telling him that he is very good, with astonishing attention to detail and impeccable technique, and that he is dangerous in that he could become a master forger. But then she says, "If people believe Cezanne did this, where does that put you? You become a nonentity. It's not your work. Where are you, Mr. Weiss? Where are *you*?"[27] She advises, "Inform your pieces with your life, your thoughts, your perceptions. . . . Let your colors be *your* emotions and combine them with *your* technique to give us *your* message" (171). This advice is hard for Evan to hear, but Oxana presses him to keep working, telling him that she can help him get into art school and that she expects great things from him—provided that he stop delivering "someone else's message" (174). Evan, the narrator, notes that he has heard similar comments from his art teacher and from his boyfriend, Erik, who is also an artist, but Oxana's prestige in the art world means that Evan *has* to attend to what she has to say.

Jenny is the artist in the athletic family of Team Fitz, in of *The Other Half of Me.* For her, having input from the professional artists who work in the studio/gallery space that Jenny cleans in exchange for some time to paint there is crucial to her development and confidence. Sid Sleethy, the gallery director, makes comments that keep Jenny trying new strategies. When Jenny begins experimenting with the use of wax to slow her painting's drying time, his cryptic words give her confidence to continue: "If you don't overdo it, you just might have something there" (173). Two other artists also tell her that her experiments with space, "leaving the edges unfinished, like a thought" (174), are working really well, and they help her understand why she stopped before the edges. This new insight pushes her to keep on experimenting. Having one of her pieces selected for the gallery show and another selected by Sid for sale in a new gallery further cements Jenny's commitment to her art and gives her the courage to insist that her parents accept her passion.

Given the abusive nature of the family dynamics in *North of Beautiful*, the artists with whom Terra interacts are also crucial to her ability to even name what she does as *art*. Lydia, one of the artists who runs the gallery where Terra works, introduces Terra to Magnus, a professional artist who works in collage. When Terra meets him, she is terrified; he is a gruff, antisocial individual with a scary honesty. Lydia conveys the news to Terra that not only has Magnus purchased one of Terra's works, which Lydia put into the gallery show without Terra's knowledge, but he also wants to ask Terra to work with him as an apprentice—and Lydia adds that Magnus never mentors anyone. Terra responds by breaking down,

> It takes a lot to make me cry. Years of living with Dad had something to do with that; he inured me of tears. I rested my head on the steering wheel and wept. After working alone in my studio, wondering whether I was wasting my time, wondering whether anyone would respond to my work, this hard won affirmation undid me.[28]

From Magnus, Lydia, and the other artists with whom she interacts, Terra finally understands that "artists do not cower. They live to make statements" (360). So she is able to not only put her complex collages, which are in some ways like topographical maps, out into the world but also put herself out into the world—with the port wine stain that covers one side of her face—without cowering.

GOOD CONCLUDING ADVICE

All adults who work with young artists need to do whatever they can to help the artists face their futures without cowering. Putting students in touch with professionals who can give them the feedback they need to move forward, giving them opportunities to shine, helping them develop the reflective skills they need to become their own best critics, supporting their applications to special programs, and cheering for them when they present their work are all important actions that can nurture their growth as artists.

Rosanne Parry, author of *Second Fiddle*, learned from professionals about mentoring young people in the arts:

> One of the things both arts teachers stressed was how easily strong performers are overwhelmed by requests for performances. Talented musicians and dancers get asked to perform constantly, and often children and teens do not get pay or adequate preparation time for their performances. Most young artists are already busy with academics and multiple music or dance groups.[29]

Parry says that art teachers have taught her to strongly encourage parents and mentors "to defend a young artist's empty hours, in order to preserve their health and strength and joy in creating art." She also notes,

> Becoming an artist is the work of a lifetime. I think it helps to seek fellow artists as friends and mentors. I think it helps to have parts of your life that are not wrapped up in your art. . . . But more than anything, remember that art takes time. The final products you see on the screen or over the radio or in an art museum are the products of years of practice and many failed attempts. Art isn't efficient and the most useful measure of success is your own satisfaction in the creative process. Joy matters.

"Joy matters." Caring adults need to help young artists preserve that sense of joy. If not, they will withdraw from their art, as happened for Eva of *Jersey Tomatoes Are the Best* and Hannah in *Bunheads*. For Patti from *Good Enough*, preserving joy in her playing was the reason why she ultimately decided not to pursue music professionally.

Sometimes it is enough to just pass along a book that will show young artists that their struggles are understood, as Kim Culbertson described one of her college professors doing when he gave her *Portrait of the Artist as a Young Man*, an incident discussed in the preface. She notes that, as a teacher herself, she loves "that a book can be sort of 'passed down' in this way. . . . It's a wonderful thing."

Culbertson and other authors who write about developing artists say that it is important to help them explore their own voices without the need to cut other voices down. She continues:

> I think we can help artists develop without being hard on them. I differ from some of my colleagues around this issue. I think the role of critique plays an essential part in the growth of an artist, but there is a huge

difference between critique and criticism. We live in a world of twenty-four-hours-a-day exposure to feedback. Anyone can log in and spew hateful or hurtful things online about someone's art. It's old fashioned of me, but I tell my students that we do not criticize each other's work in my room. . . . I'll quote a wonderful author, Sands Hall, who always says, "Let's start with the assumption that the writer did everything on that page on purpose . . . and go from there." Thus, we can ask questions, make suggestions, and give our honest ideas about how we interfaced with the work, but it should only be to support that writer's intention for the work. . . . I think critique should be about suggestion, about evolving an artist's lens, and not about the agenda of the person giving the critique.

I don't think a person grows when they are feeling attacked—they go all fetal and put up walls—and I don't think that's the good position to be in for growth.

Lisa Ann Sandell knows the important role that a significant adult can play in a young person's life:

If a young adult has an interest in or passion or talent for anything constructive—art, writing, music, sports—I urge the adults in that young person's life to try to support that individual by asking questions . . . by introducing him or her to further enrichment, such as new artists, other styles, museums or book lists or albums, show how the artist the student likes were influenced by earlier artists; and most importantly, offer constant encouragement . . . [and] let them know that we see value in their thoughts and in their work. [30]

Ms. Calico in Lisa Ann Sandell's *The Map of the Known World* is certainly an example of a teacher who sees value in Cora's thoughts and work. Mrs. Pratt in Kimberly Marcus's *Exposed* is another teacher who is the significant adult for "Photogirl" Liz. Mrs. Pratt does not at first tell Liz what photo she thinks will be the best for Liz to include in her portfolio; instead, she asks Liz which ones she thinks are the strongest pieces, and Liz identifies her portraits as her best work. Mrs. Pratt then surprises Liz by pulling out one that she finds interesting but that Liz had included just to meet the required minimum number of shots. It is Liz's self-portrait. Again, it is this teacher's encouragement, support, and understanding of the young artist that make a significant impact on how the young adult views herself, her art, and her possible future.

But one question that teachers and parents often have is how best to work with a young person who has enough talent to play the lead in the high school musical but not enough talent to make it on Broadway. As a teacher as well as a writer, Kim Culbertson feels that it is incumbent on teachers to introduce kids to the industry behind the art or sport, to help give them terms and titles that they can latch onto, such as "assistant film editor."

For those young people who do have the potential to make it as a professional artist, Stasia Kehoe states, writing about the world of professional ballet,

> I think that parents can do their best to get their young dancer the most professional, highest quality training they can find, but there is a point at which risks must be taken for art—just as risks are taken by kids focused on sports or even on activities such as student government. . . . This might seem cliché but I think the best thing a parent can do to support their young dancer is to try to be very open to conversations— even ones in which there is uncertainty expressed as to whether to continue dancing—and to try to balance teaching responsibility and commitment with the realization that dance is a very tough, competitive artistic endeavor and doubt is natural, even healthy.[31]

AJ's father in Joan Bauer's *Thwonk* is, in the end, a wonderful role model for anyone parenting or mentoring a young adult in his or her artistic endeavors. He has the kinds of conversations with AJ that Culbertson and Kehoe advocate. AJ's dad had tried to be an independent filmmaker and photographer, but he ultimately could not live with the erratic income stream—he also realized that he did not have the push to bring his projects to completion. So he has put aside his art and has been making a living in advertising. AJ has inherited her father's passion for photography, and she craves his approval for her dream of becoming a professional. Toward the end of the novel, her dad sees AJ's newest work and tells her that it is really good. She pushes him to tell her whether she is good enough to make it with her art, whether she is talented enough. But her dad is a realist, saying, "I'm not disputing that you have real talent, AJ, but talent and making it in the art world do not go hand in hand. Do you know how many photographers there are in this world with real talent who can't even scratch out a living?" AJ wonders, "What if I'm good enough *and I don't even try?*"[32]

AJ just continues to work and show her prints to her father. After a disastrous evening on the personal front when she dumps her date at the Valentine's Dance, AJ uses her raw emotions to take some incredible shots that she knows represent her best efforts. Her father watches her

develop these prints and is so in awe of what she accomplishes that he
finally pushes beyond his fears about the uncertainty inherent in a
career in the arts and writes AJ a letter that can serve as a template for
any parent or mentor wanting to encourage the young adult artist:

> I hope, AJ, that as you mature as a photographer, you will always
> appreciate the constantly changing gift of light. I hope that you will
> know a community of artists that can sustain you, that your desire for
> your art will grow stronger, that criticism will make you stretch and go
> beyond yourself, and that you won't ever be afraid to put your butt on
> the line. I wish for you a sensitive soul that cries when things hurt and
> an eye that sees beneath the surface to the humor hiding in difficult
> moments. I hope that you take risks and never care about using too
> much film. . . . And I hope that your work will always speak to someone
> about who you are—if you can accomplish that, it will last long after
> both of us are gone. (202–3)

AJ's dad is willing to bet on her and her future, and he gives her the
hug of all-out acceptance that every young artist needs. Those of us
who care about young adults struggling with their identities as artists
can follow the lead of AJ's dad when we talk with students, in terms of
the language of support that he uses. Providing them access to the kinds
of books listed in the annotated bibliography (see appendix A) is another concrete way of providing support, giving them a wide variety of
worlds of words in which they can find themselves, gather courage
from their fictional peers, and, in the process, imagine futures for themselves in which their sense of self as artist is a valued way of being in
the real world.

NOTES

1. Sherman Alexie, *The Absolutely True Diary of a Part-Time Indian* (New York:
Little, Brown, 2007), 37.

2. Maria Padian, *Jersey Tomatoes Are the Best* (New York: Knopf, 2011), 207.

3. Steve Kluger, *My Most Excellent Year: A Novel of Love, Mary Poppins, and
Fenway Park* (New York: Dial, 2008), 315.

4. Jon Skovon, *Struts and Frets* (New York: Amulet Books, 2009), 186.

5. Cara Chow, *Bitter Melon* (New York: Egmont, 2011), 1.

6. Jordan Sonneblick, *Curveball: The Year I Lost My Grip* (New York: Scholastic,
2012), 2.

7. Kim Culbertson, interview via telephone and e-mail with Lois Stover, April 14,
2012, and June 13, 2012.

8. Laura Goode, *Sister Mischief* (Somerville, MA: Candlewick Press, 2011), 75.

9. Paula Yoo, *Good Enough* (New York: HarperTeen, 2008), 111.

10. Jill Alexander, *Paradise* (New York: Feiwel and Friends, 2011), 140.

11. Emily Franklin, *The Other Half of Me* (New York: Delacorte, 2007), 238.

12. Carolyn Marsden, *Silk Umbrellas* (Cambridge, MA: Candlewick Press, 2004), 2.

13. Cath Crowley, *Graffiti Moon* (New York: Horizon, 2012), 128.

14. Zibby Oneal, *In Summer Light* (New York: Viking, 1985), 167.

15. Tracy Mack, *Drawing Lessons* (New York: Scholastic, 2002), 19.

16. Traci Jones, *Silhouetted by the Blue* (New York: Farrar, Straus and Giroux, 2011), 68–69.

17. April Lurie, *The Latent Powers of Dylan Fontaine* (New York: Delacorte, 2008), 38.

18. Gail Carson Levine, *Dave at Night* (New York: HarperTrophy, 2001), 225.

19. Francisco Stork, *Irises* (New York: Scholastic, 2012), 80.

20. Lisa Ann Sandell, *Map of the Known World* (New York: Scholastic, 2009), 57.

21. Cathryn Clinton. *The Eyes of Van Gogh* (Cambridge, MA: Candlewick, 2007), 88.

22. Jennifer Bryant, *Pieces of Georgia* (New York: Yearling, 2007), 120.

23. Kim Culbertson, *Instructions for a Broken Heart* (Naperville, IL: Sourcebooks Fire, 2011), 45.

24. Jennifer Donnelly, *Revolution* (New York: Ember, 2011), 26.

25. Rosanne Parry, *Second Fiddle* (New York: Random House, 2011), 6–7.

26. Kimberly Marcus, interview via e-mail with Connie Zitlow, June 28, 2012.

27. Brian Farrey, *With or without You* (New York: Simon Pulse, 2011), 170.

28. Justina Chen Headley, *North of Beautiful* (Boston: Little, Brown, 2010), 336.

29. Rosanne Parry, interview via e-mail with Connie Zitlow, April 22, 2012.

30. Lisa Ann Sandell, interview via e-mail with Connie Zitlow, July 6, 2012.

31. Stasia Ward Kehoe, interview via telephone and e-mail with Lois Stover, March 29, 2012.

32. Joan Bauer, *Thwonk* (New York: Delacorte, 1995), 166.

Chapter Seven

Art and Young Adult Literature: Art in Literature, Literature about Art, Literature as Art

The focus on this chapter is the art—words, pictures, and music—in young adult literature. In some works, the main character's art is included and is integral to the story, often showing the young person's development as an artist and understanding about self. In other works, the art supplements the story line or is the basis for what occurs. Some stories reflect how young adults learn from the techniques of established artists. There are works where the language is so powerful that it evokes vivid sounds and pictures in readers' minds. Also there are fine examples of literature for young adults that tell about art and artists.

ART AND WORDS TELL THE STORY

The Absolutely True Diary of a Part-Time Indian

Sherman Alexie's novel, with art by Ellen Forney, is one of the many fine examples of young adult literature where visual art is included in the book. Junior's story in *The Absolutely True Diary of a Part-Time Indian* is one in which the main character's art is integral to the text— where the pictures and words together tell the story. Junior uses his art to help him understand the confusing and conflicting aspects of his life.

Junior draws "all the time"[1] to help him understand what it is he wants to say. He is a fourteen-year-old "budding cartoonist who draws in an effort to negotiate his confusing world and figure out who he is."[2] When he was six months old, he survived surgery to remove the excess fluid in his skull, but he was left with a variety of health problems. He had too many teeth as well as "lopsided eyes," which required his wearing glasses. He was skinny but had huge hands and feet and an enormous skull. He describes his head as being "so big that little Indian skulls orbited around it. Some of the kids called me Orbit. And other kids just called me Globe. . . . So obviously, I looked goofy on the outside, but it was the *inside* stuff that was the worst" (3). Junior had seizures, spoke with a stutter and a lisp, and was called a retard. Because he would get beat up at least once a month, he chose to stay at home, read books, and draw cartoons. Growing up, he felt like a zero on the "rez." He thought that only his tough friend Rowdy and his parents, sister, and grandmother would miss him if he were to leave the reservation.

Although Junior is determined to break away from the life that he seems destined to live, he wonders if he is a traitor when he leaves to attend Reardan High School, twenty-two miles from the reservation in the neighboring farm town, where the only other Indian is the school mascot. His parents do not oppose the idea, but his father tells him that it will be hard to get him there. His mother reminds him that he will be the first one to leave the reservation in this way, and the Indians around there will be angry with him. He feels like a misfit at both the reservation and the all-white high school, but he excels as a member of the basketball team and continues to draw.

Junior's story would not be complete without his drawings. When Junior's friend Rowdy is beaten by his drunken father and Junior wants to make him laugh, he draws cartoons to make Rowdy happy and "give him other worlds to live inside" (23). Junior draws pictures of his sister Mary, who ran away, as well as pictures of his grandmother, his parents, and even the rez teacher Mr. P, who encourages him to leave. Junior's struggles getting to the high school and his experiences there are portrayed in his words and drawings: when the car breaks down or there is no gas money, when he has no lunch money and pretends not to be poor, what he looks like wearing his dad's old polyester suit to the winter formal, and even what his freshman-year report card is. His most powerful drawing is a full-page picture that shows what he sees as the contrast between "White," where there is a bright future, positive role models, and hope on one side, and "Indian," with a vanishing past, a family history of diabetes and cancer, and bone-crushing reality on the other (57). Junior's words make it clear why he must draw, but his cartoon-type pictures show—more than what his first-person narrative can convey—his conflicting emotions and how he envisions what is around him.

The Autobiography of My Dead Brother and *Monster*

Like Junior, Jesse in Walter Dean Myers's *The Autobiography of My Dead Brother* likes to draw. Not only does his art tell us about his dead blood brother, Rise, but it is Jesse's story as well. Jesse in *The Autobiography* and Jamal in *Scorpion* (also by Walter Dean Myers) "use drawing to try to make sense of their life in Harlem, the challenges of their friendships, and the territorial conflicts of gangs wherein guns and drugs are a constant threat."[3] Jesse is disturbed by the territorial conflicts that he sees occurring between Rise and the Diablos gang and the changes in Rise's behavior. In his sketchbook and comic strips, Jesse tells about his friend. Their conversation is conveyed in authentic street dialogue. The illustrations are powerful black-and-white sketches drawn by Christopher Myers. At the beginning and ending of the story, readers feel as if they can hear "Precious Lord, Take My Hand" as it is sung at yet another funeral for a teen whose life ends in violence.

In *Monster*, another powerful story written by Walter Dean Myers, Steve Harmon is in prison. He tells his story with handwritten journal entries and a neatly typed screenplay that he calls "A Steve Harmon Film."[4] The surface effects, such as drawings, photographs, mug shots, and video stills, convey what is happening and how Steve feels about the courtroom proceedings. The size of the print for the word "Monster!" and other words in the title page of "The Story of My Miserable Life" (8–9), in which "he has transcribed the images and conversations as he remembers them" (275), add an impact that is integral to the story line. Five months after the trial, Steve continues his screenplay because he wants to find the "one true image" of who he is and how others see him: "I want to know who I am" (281).

The Berlin Boxing Club

As is true for Junior, Jesse, and Steve, Karl, at age fourteen, draws for a variety of reasons that help keep him stable in a world gone mad, in

The Berlin Boxing Club, by Robert Sharenow. While he has never identified himself as Jewish, Karl finds himself the victim of bullying and violence, as the Nazi violence against Jews escalates in 1939 Berlin. Karl draws cartoons to get distance from the bullies; he draws cartoons to make his younger sister Hildy laugh and, later, to comfort her when their family's situation becomes increasingly bleak. He draws to capture his understanding of the adults in his world, and he draws to envision a new future for himself.

Karl's cartoons are scattered through the book, and they enhance the reader's understanding of the complexities of the plot. Words and pictures combine to show not only Karl's development as a boxer under the tutelage of Max Schmeling—a real-life German/Jewish boxer and national hero—but also his insights and feelings, especially as expressed through his drawings, when he has to assume the role of protector to his family. When things are dire, Karl finds inspiration in the figure of Superman—whom he perceives to be:

> Like me, Superman was an alien, an outsider from another planet that had been completely destroyed. His physiology was different from that of normal humans, just like what the Nazis said about the Jews. Only instead of being corrupted, Superman's blood gave him superior strength and intelligence.[5]

Karl is inspired by this "Champion of the Oppressed" to create Mongrel, his own character, who is a champion of justice and to those in greatest need. Karl draws for hours on end and thinks, "When I finally put my pen down, I felt physically drained but satisfied in a way I never had been in my cartooning before" (315), and the several pages of Mongrel's story that follow in the text show the birth of Mongrel and his—as well as Karl's—determination to be a hero to his people. This picture is the last set of illustrations in the book save one: the rest of the story tells about Karl's efforts to save his family, and the novel, based on much historical research and fact, ends as Karl and his sister escape to the United States. The book concludes with one last image from Karl's notebook: an eagle carrying a small mouse (Karl) across the ocean to freedom in America. It is the interplay of text and illustration that makes *The Berlin Boxing Club* and the character of Karl and his quest to "become [his] own man" (398) so powerful.

Guitar Notes

It is not until Tripp and Lyla find each other and use their art together—
in this case, music—that they find out who they really are, in *Guitar
Notes*, by Mary Amato. Tripp plays the guitar; Lyla is a talented cellist.
They become songwriters, and their words and music in the "Thrum
Society Songbook" are added to the book and can be heard at http://
thrumsociety.com.[6] Tripp is a loner who can barely hang "on to consciousness" (27) in class. Yet, Lyla is perfect at everything, in her
grades and cello playing; she even has a perfect friend who is a violinist. Tripp and Lyla's story begins on the first day of school. Tripp is
upset when he realizes that his mother has confiscated his guitar because he did not do his summer reading or math packet. To get it back,
Tripp must work to do better in school. But playing his guitar is a
matter of survival for him, particularly when he thinks about his dad,
who died of a stroke. Fortunately, at school he sees that he can sign up
for a music practice room and use a school instrument. The first day
that the room is his, he repairs the old guitar's strings, takes out his
pick, and "something inside him comes alive" (22).

On alternate days, Lyla plans to use the room to practice her cello.
Lyla thinks about her mother, a celebrated cellist who died in a plane
crash when Lyla was six years old, and she feels overwhelmed by
pressure from her dad to succeed and fulfill her responsibilities: learning a new piece, doing school work, completing her application to the
Coles Conservatory of Music, preparing for an audition at the Lincoln
Center, plus pressure from her friend Annie to join a club. Instead of
playing her instrument, Lyla "calls up her MP3 files of cello music on
the computer" (26). She becomes disgusted when she sees what she
thinks is trash on the music stand, and she leaves a note about it to
"Odd Day Musician," whose return note, to "Ms. Even Day," explains
that it was not trash but a chord progression that he had written on his
napkin (28). She writes a note back. When she returns to the room, she
is disappointed that there is nothing in response on the music stand. But
upon opening the guitar case, she finds a note suggesting that, instead
of wasting negative energy on being mad, she write a song called "The
Even Day Vibes" (38). She actually tries out the guitar, thinking that
she will soon pick up her cello, but the guitar continues to attract her.

One day Tripp stands near the room, and, in addition to the recorded
cello music, he hears Lyla playing scales on the guitar. In a note, he
writes, "Scales are boring. If you're going to play, *play*" (60). After he

hears the cello solo that she plays perfectly in front of the whole school, he writes how impressed he is with her playing, but he asks her if playing the cello makes her happy. For him, playing the guitar is "thrumming. When the vibrations of the music make your soul vibrate, you feel the thrum. It's like you're perfectly in tune with the song. . . . A serious musician is somebody who really thrums" (73). Their exchange of handwritten notes leads to text messages, followed by longer notes slipped into their lockers, then phone conversations. Because Tripp is uncomfortable with in-person stuff, he agrees to record a song for Lyla on the MP3 player. At her request, he writes out instructions, which he includes in his note "To the One Who Spies on Unsuspecting Aardvarks," so that she can learn a basic chord progression (133). They share secrets and interests that open up a new world for both of them, and these interchanges blossom into an unlikely friendship.

One day at Lyla's suggestion, they break a rule, and Tripp joins her in the practice room. They begin working on songs together, soon meet outside of school, and become "The Thrum Society" (200). They even sneak away from town to play their "Pomegranate Waltz" for a wedding, a wonderful experience until Lyla's angry father finds them and rushes to drive her to the Coles audition. When a deer jumps in the car's path, Lyla is seriously injured. It is only when Tripp sneaks into the hospital room and plays her the song they had begun together that she begins to regain consciousness and recover.

In the course of Tripp and Lyla's story, readers see the sketches of their ideas as they work on the lyrics of their songs. The words in the final versions of their seven songs—complete with diagrams of the chord progressions, beginning with "A Little Room to Play" and ending with "Lucky Me" (227–95)—are integral to their story.

Carmen and *The Fortune of Carmen Navarro*

The songs that young Carmen sings are integral parts of Walter Dean Myers's and Jen Bryant's modern retellings of Georges Bizet's classic story of passionate, doomed love. Myers first heard the opera *Carmen* in a music appreciation class when he was ten years old, and some of the music reminded him of what he heard in his neighborhood. His *Carmen: An Urban Adaptation of the Opera*, written in script form, takes place in Spanish Harlem. He includes arrangements of Georges Bizet's music, which can be heard in the electronic version of the story, along with explanations about what is happening in the story as the music occurs. Carmen is a tough, beautiful Dominican woman, a "chica,"[7] who works in a wig factory and woos the police officer José. Carmen sees him as her way out of "el barrio," but he has a quick temper and likes to get his way. José knows that his passionate love for Carmen is threatened when Escamillo, described as a singer/rapper/producer/businessman, comes to town and has eyes only for Carmen. José is jealous, tries to possess Carmen, and is determined not to let anyone else have her. He says, "Look, I've brought you something. A ring. It's the symbol of my love for you. I give it to you, and my heart goes with it, as your heart came to me with the flower you gave me that sweet day" (109). But Carmen is afraid of him and tells him to take the ring back. José pulls a gun from under his coat, declaring his love for Carmen, who sings the "Destiny Theme":

> Life laughs at me now . . . / Dreams crumble and fall . . .

The tragic story ends as Carmen clutches her side and falls as the melancholy sound of the ominous theme is heard (112–13).

Bryant's *The Fortune of Carmen Navarro* is told by four teens: Carmen, a half-gypsy and high school dropout; her friend Maggie; Ryan, a serious cadet at the Valley Forge Military Academy; and his friend Will. Carmen, along with Maggie, works at the Quikmart, but her first love is music. Ryan is expected to have a promising military future, but when he sees Carmen with her shining black hair and snake tattoo, he becomes obsessed. Their passionate romance begins when she slips a note into his lunch,

> *To a shy soldier:*
>   *If you like good music, you should come to Gallagher's tonight at nine o'clock. I will look for you there.*[8]

Soon Ryan wants to possess her, but she is too busy for him. "This is *my* time and *my* life and I need to be free" (149). She no longer wants to feel like "a hawk tied to a perch. Like a hobbled horse" (151). He is willing to give her time for her music, as long as she says they are together: "Only us. Her and me. Ryan and Carmen. Together" (166). But she will not be owned by anyone.

One night, Ryan waits until Maggie's band has finished performing. He pulls the security guard's gun, demanding that Maggie go with him, until the drummer knocks the gun from Ryan's hand and their fists fly.

When he is in prison, Ryan can still hear Maggie's voice inside his head:

> *Take my hand—come with me, / I can take you where you've never been before— / You are my darling red-faced boy.* (223)

But Maggie is traveling with the band, and Ryan's military career is over.

ART AS THE BASIS FOR THE STORY LINE

In several recent titles, a number of authors have experimented with interesting ways to create story lines based on art. In some cases, the art is of the "found" variety: the author uses the art as the inspiration for the plot, which then unfolds as the author finds a way to include another piece of art in the developing story.

Miss Peregrine's Home for Peculiar Children

Ransom Riggs, author of *Miss Peregrine's Home for Peculiar Children*, writes in his afterword that all of the bizarre and somewhat disturbing photographs reprinted in the novel are

> authentic, vintage, found photographs, and with the exception of a few that have undergone minimal post processing, they are unaltered. They were lent from the personal archives of ten collectors, people who have spent years and countless hours hunting through giant bins of unsorted snapshots at flea markets and antique malls and yard sales to find a transcendent few, rescuing images of historical significance and arresting beauty from obscurity—and most likely, the dump. [9]

This fantasy novel begins as Jacob, the narrator, describes the conversations that he has been having with his grandfather, who tells him tales of his childhood spent at a children's home in Wales, where he was shipped, he says, "because the monsters were after him" (9). As Jacob gets older, he has trouble believing in these monsters, until his grandfather begins to show him photographs from an old cigar box of a suit of clothes with no head, a girl levitating, a scrawny boy hefting a huge boulder above his head, and the back of a head with a face painted on it. When horror strikes Jacob's family, Jacob convinces his father to take him on a quest to Wales, hoping that understanding the past will clarify the stories that his grandfather has told him and will help him determine his own path into the future.

The photos are reprinted in sepia tones and augment the aura of mystery that Ransom's text evokes as Jacob begins to realize that his grandfather's tales have been true; that he and the other children with whom he grew up are special individuals who in some ways live outside of time; and that Jacob can help save the others from the monster that killed his grandfather, if he is willing to give up the life in time that he has known to that point. Ransom constructed his plotline around the photos, developing characters and the setting from what he presents in the pictures; thus, the photos play an essential role in the author's creative process and the reader's appreciation for the novel as it unfolds.

Every You, Every Me

Author David Levithan has a history of successful collaborations with fellow writer Rachel Cohn; together they wrote *Nick and Norah's Infinite Playlist, Naomi and Ely's No Kiss List*, and *Dash and Lily's Book of Dares*. In *Every You, Every Me*, Levithan collaborates with photographer Jonathan Farmer to create a troubling story of love and loss made all the more haunting by the inclusion of black-and-white as well as color photos that push the story forward and create the mystery that Evan must solve to deal with the guilt that he feels in the wake of his best friend Ariel's disappearance. As Evan becomes increasingly aware that he may not have known his friend at all, the photos that he finds—which are clearly meant to taunt him—make him paranoid. This feeling fuels his desire to learn what happened that led to the disappearance of his friend, which in turn leads him out of his isolation and into a collaboration that saves him from despair. But he tells the reader in the end, "I still have the photos, though. Even though they are as unreliable as memories. Even though I will only know my story behind them, not yours. At least, not until you tell me yourself."[10]

The novel was conceived when Levithan saw on Farmer's refrigerator the photo that became the cover picture for the novel: "[I] immediately knew I would draw Jonathan in on an idea I'd had: to do a photographic novel" (247). The way that the novel evolved is that Farmer would give Levithan a photo, and Levithan would write, drawing inspiration from the photo in hand. Then he would ask for another photo, and Farmer would provide him with one. Levithan would write some more and then ask for yet another picture. Farmer had no idea what Levithan was writing, and Levithan had no knowledge of the photos that Farmer would provide for him until he requested a new one. The result is a stunning exploration of how difficult it is to find one truth about any event and how each individual's reality is colored by the context of that person's way of being in the world.

Wonderstruck

In Brian Selznick's *Wonderstruck*, the interplay of text and illustration is taken to a new level. There are two story lines. One unfolds through text, but the other unfolds solely through amazingly detailed line drawings. The reader follows Ben on the quest for the father that he has never known, a quest that he initiates after the death of his mother and the discovery of a book titled *Wonderstruck*, which has a bookmark lettered with a phone number and address in New York City for a bookstore where, Ben thinks, his father may be found.

Meanwhile, the reader follows the story of Rose, set fifty years before that of Ben, who is in search of her mother, as she reads a headline in a newspaper announcing that actress Lillian Mayhew is opening a play on a New York stage the next day. Their stories intersect in a tale that deals with love, friendship, belonging, museums, and the act of "curating"—organizing and commenting on—one's life. The young girl, Rose, is an adult who, fifty years later, helps Ben to a successful conclusion of his own quest, and as the novel's text portion ends, the two of them are leaning on each other, looking up at the stars. The reader turns the page to find this scene illustrated in the present, then the next double spreads show just the night sky against the horizon, followed by one of just the stars in the sky, with the final one being of one star, shining brightly. The drawings take readers out of the specific stories of Ben and Rose to a place of wonder more broadly defined and so provide the perfect ending to the novel.

ART SUPPLEMENTS THE STORY LINE

There are many fine works of young adult literature where art supplements the story line, adding depth to the story. The following selected books represent a range of styles, genres, tone, and art that reflect the subject of the story: humorous fiction narrated by a reluctant reader, powerful historical fiction, and inspiring biographies of artists.

My Life as a Book and *My Life as a Stuntboy*

Janet Tashjian's books *My Life as a Book* and *My Life as a Stuntboy* include cartoons by Jake Tashjian. Derek's humorous narration of both stories is enhanced by his sketchbook drawings. In the first story, the only type of reading that Derek likes is comics such as *Calvin and Hobbs*. Instead of writing the vocabulary words that he does not know, he draws them. He thinks that if his life were a book, he would have his "own cool adventures instead of reading about someone else's."[11] But when his parents send him to learning camp for the summer, he has some surprising adventures. He even admits that he has learned a few things: "We all mess up sometimes and struggle with things that are difficult. . . . Even if reading is hard, everyone needs stories (209). He is proud of his animated report of the one book he read over the summer.

Derek begins his second story by declaring that the first day of school is the worst day of the year. It is "like some crazy surgeon throws you on an operating table and removes a major organ from your chest called summer."[12] His stick figure of a surgeon accompanies his words. After Tony, a film stunt coordinator, sees Derek do a "parkour" with his skateboard (24), he offers Derek the opportunity to get paid to do stunts. Derek says that if his parents give him permission, he will promise to "grow up and become a librarian," which he shows with a drawing he titles "commitment" (39). His words and stick figures show his amazing stunts, his devotion to his dog, and his antics with Frank, a capuchin monkey. Despite Derek's success on the movie set and progress in school, he still worries that he will be a "bad reader" his entire life, which he reflects with his drawing of person in a cubicle (252). But Derek has read a whole book and can tell stories with his sketchbook, which is full of the stick figures that show his actions and emotions as he becomes more confident about who he is and what he is capable of doing.

Breaking Stalin's Nose

Author Eugene Velchin's vivid black-and-white illustrations in *Breaking Stalin's Nose* add power to Sasha Zaichik's story and show his initial naiveté. Sasha is devoted to Comrade Stalin and thinks that he wants to become a young pioneer. He lives in a communal apartment with "forty-eight hardworking, Soviet citizens"[13] who share the kitchen and a single small toilet. Numerous large pictures on facing pages show

how Sasha comes to understand what is really happening under communist rule, from the happy faces in the kitchen to the fear that comrades are spying on one another to the vicious snowball fight when Sasha is called a traitor because he does not want to "shoot the enemy" by throwing an icy snowball at the Jewish boy called "Four-Eyes" (49–51).

One day Sasha marches down the school hallway carrying a heavy banner, imagining that he is in a May Day parade until the banner shoots out of his hands "and its pointy metal tip knocks Stalin's plaster nose clean off his face" (73). Sasha wonders who will expose him. He worries about what will happen because he refuses to renounce his imprisoned father and does not accept the offer to become a secret agent. He wonders what really happened to his mother. His loneliness is reflected in the stark pictures that continue for several pages showing him standing in a very long line and enduring the icy cold as he joins others who, like him, wait to see prisoners (144–51).

Author Eugene Velchin was born and educated in Russia. Before he left the former Soviet Union, he was offered the opportunity to "become a snitch" (152). He realized that many people in the 1960s were not aware of what happened under the ruthless dictatorship of Joseph Stalin. Velchin's illustrations add tremendous power to this story, which transcends time and place, as it exposes the persistent fear when "innocent people face persecution and death for making a choice about what they believe to be right" (154).

Why We Broke Up

Why We Broke Up, a collaboration between author Daniel Handler and artist Maira Kalman, begins with the opening lines of a letter that Min Green has written to Ed, explaining why she is breaking up with him: "In a sec you'll hear a thunk. At your front door, the one nobody uses."[14] Page 2 introduces the reader to the glossy color illustrations that introduce the book's chapters; it shows a simple picture of a blue box set against a black backdrop. Then it shows these words on page 3: "The thunk is the box, Ed." Min goes on to tell him that it contains "every last souvenir of the love we had, the prizes and the debris of this relationship, like the glitter in the gutter when the parade has past, all the everything and whatnot kicked to the curb" (3).

As Min's letter unfolds, each of the items that capture the arc of that relationship is presented to the reader as Ed sees it: a movie poster, an empty box of matches from a restaurant, a Hellman High School Beavers banner, a protractor, rose petals, and many more. The use of the illustrations to introduce each new segment of Min's letter piques readers' curiosity to keep reading to find out just how the next unexpected item fits into the story of the breakup between the artistically inclined Min and the athlete Ed. The illustrations act for the reader in the same way that the objects in the box do for Ed. They scaffold the story line and provide a tangible handhold for Min to use in describing how the relationship first grew, deepened, and then soured in the face of Ed's betrayal. The final illustration provides that same tangible handhold for Min to use in facing the truth about what she has always thought of as just "friendship" with Al, the young man who provided Min with a sounding board as she wrote her cathartic letter to Ed.

A Monster Calls

In *A Monster Calls*, a powerful story of life and death and redemption by Patrick Ness, Conor, age thirteen, wakes up one night to find a monster at his bedroom window. Conor already knows a monster, who has had a starring and recurring role in the nightmares that he has been having ever since his mother became ill with cancer. This new monster, though, is not a creature of the world of sleep. When it first appears, the powerful charcoal illustrations that begin on the left-hand page of the book sweep the reader to the right-hand page, where the wildness of the dark and windy night form a black backdrop to the text that turns white. The reader sees what Conor sees, thus believing in the reality of this monster, who will haunt Conor throughout the rest of the book. It is an ancient and wild creature who continually pushes Conor to face the very difficult truths about his mother and the events that have led to her current stay in the hospital. This monster speaks in parables, illustrated by highly textured drawings that capture the thorniness of these truths.

In the end, Conor comes to realize that he did actually let his mother go, causing her to fall and hurt herself badly, because, as the monster tells him, "You were merely wishing for the end of pain . . . your own pain. An end to how it isolated you. It is the most human wish of all. . . . You wanted her to go at the same time you were desperate for me to save her."[15] But Conor also comes to understand the power of confronting those complex truths and is able to tell his mother all of them before she leaves this world, knowing that "he was going to get through it. It would be terrible. It would be beyond terrible. But he would survive" (104). As the novel ends, Conor is about to hold tightly to his mother, "and by doing so, he could finally let her go." The pages at this point are pure white, with black lettering—and the final page of the book is a soft, wispy drawing in gray of a tree standing dark against a lightening sky, surrounded by white space, illustrating Conor's state of mind in ways that mere words cannot.

Safekeeping

Karen Hesse's *Safekeeping* tells the story of Radley, the much-loved daughter of two Vermont parents who have supported her in her decision to go to Haiti for part of her senior year to volunteer in an orphanage. They actually feel that she is safer in Haiti than she would be at home because of the impending political and social upheaval that they anticipate will occur if the American People's Party gains power. When Radley hears that the president has been assassinated and that vigilante groups are prowling the streets in the United States, all that she can think about is getting home and making sure that her parents are safe. She boards a plane and lands, only to find that her credit cards are frozen, she left her cell phone charger in Haiti and her phone is dead, and she will need travel authorization papers just to cross state lines. Her parents are not waiting for her at the airport, so she begins walking.

Arriving at her home, she finds no sign of her father and mother, and when the police begin showing up at the door, she believes that they have taken her parents. Her mother is a famous photographer, and both her parents have been outspoken opponents of the now prevailing political party. So she takes off on foot, determined to reach Canada, where things are stable and where she hopes that she can track down her family. En route, she meets another young woman, Celia, and they come to trust each other and create a "home" of sorts in an abandoned cabin in the Canadian woods. Radley's adventures along the road are illustrated by fifty black-and-white photographs, sometimes providing haunting images of the places she explores, the loneliness of the road, and the fragile sense of family that Radley and Celia begin to create. While the photographs do not always connect to the story line, their inclusion provides another way in which an author seeks to expand the impact of a novel through the use of art.

The Poet Slave of Cuba

In addition to fictional works in which art is included, there are books about people's lives that are enhanced by the addition of art. Margarita Engle's beautiful story *The Poet Slave of Cuba*, about Juan Francisco Manzano, is told in haunting verse, and Juan's life of slavery and eventual freedom are reflected in Sean Qualls's stunning illustrations. Because he lived from 1797 to 1853 and was a Cuban slave, Juan was denied an education. But he spent his early childhood by the side of his wealthy owner La Marquesa, who considered him the son of her old age. Juan entertained her guests, reciting the lyrics "of verses, plays, sermons and sonnets."[16] The illustrations of his servant mother (11) and rebellious slave father show their sadness that their son is treated like a pet poodle and a parrot (24–25). Juan is called "the Golden Beak" (29). Only the wings of a bird are pictured on the page when his father asks God, "Where is the rest of the bird?" Juan sees the beauty and cruelty around him, as reflected in these words:

> My mind is a brush made of feathers / painting pictures of words / I remember all that I see / every syllable / each word a twin of itself / Telling two stories / at the same time / one of sorrow / the other hope . . . / Poetry cools me, syllables calm me / I read the verses of others / the free men / And know / that I'm never alone . . . (3–4)

But when his owner dies, Juan becomes the property of a cruel woman. When she catches him reading, she beats him and locks him in the cellar "with the charcoal to darken his thoughts and his skin" (40–41). Her cruel face is shown with flames above her head. Juan, given a stub of crayon by her son, listens, watches, and even learns how to draw. He hides behind doors with a book in his hand while "out in the night / slaves are dancing and drumming and singing / I smile / then I cry" (146).

The life story of "the poet-boy, poet-man, almost grown and still composing sad verses" (114) is conveyed by numerous narrators, always in verse made powerful by the art: Juan's sad face, an overseer with a whip, Juan's wounded body, the Cuban instruments that he hears, and the documents proving the freedom that he was denied until he escapes, riding away on a horse "hidden by darkness, gloom, and rain" (171). Included at the end of this remarkable work are historical notes about his life and a few examples of his "capacity for hope . . .

with verses [that] show how he was determined to find beauty and goodness in a world filled with hideous cruelty" (180).

Andy Warhol: Prince of Pop

The biographical portrait of *The Poet Slave of Cuba* is an example of literature with stunning illustrations that supplement the story line. The art in another biographical work—*Andy Warhol: Prince of Pop*, by Jan Greenberg and Sandra Jordan—consists of reproductions of Andy Warhol's contemporary art and family photographs. In each case, what is conveyed by the words is made more meaningful because art is included.

When she was young, Jan Greenberg made lists of words to describe the artworks she saw when visiting museums with her mother. Because art and writing were important to her, especially during times of family illnesses, she was concerned that in the early 1990s there were no books for young readers about contemporary art. Since then, she and Sandra Jordan have authored many acclaimed books about a variety of artists: portrait painter Chuck Close, architect Frank O. Gehry, artist Vincent van Gogh, and the woman sculptor Louise Bourgeois. In *Andy Warhol: Prince of Pop*, Greenberg and Jordan tell about the man who produced iconic art, made controversial films, and launched the magazine *Interview*. The third son of Eastern European immigrants, Andy grew up in Pittsburgh. When his mother gave her sons paper and crayons to calm their rambunctious play, Andy always won the art contests. Instead of staying in his position when he was in the baseball outfield, Andy would be in front of the house painting flowers.

The story of Andy Warhol's rise from poverty to become a pop icon can be an inspiration for young artists. For many years, his New York studio "The Factory" was "*the* place to be,"[17] and his blending of high art and popular culture attests to his understanding of the late twentieth century. Included in the book are thirty-two full-page pictures of him and several of his famous artworks, some important dates in his life, titles of films and books, and a glossary of artists and art forms. Words in the postscript summarize why he is remembered: "Andy Warhol belonged to a long tradition of artists and writers whose charge it was to gain a new perspective on things by standing back and bearing witness" (136). "The sky boy who once dreamed of being a serious artist had become a legend in his own time—far surpassing the fifteen minutes of fame he had predicted for everyone else" (138).

LANGUAGE AS ART: WORDS THAT EVOKE
SOUNDS AND PICTURES

Sometimes the art in a book is not a visual representation on the page but an image in the reader's mind. A close look at words that paint pictures, imitate sounds, and evoke feelings in the mind of the reader leads to an understanding about how the art of fine literature creates an impact. The vivid imagery that touches the senses shows how amazing language can be as it adds depth to a story.

Make Lemonade

The words in Virginia Euwer Wolff's *Make Lemonade* evoke vivid pictures and sounds in readers' minds, and contrasting images reveal much about the poverty in the story. When the babysitter La Vaughn first meets little Jeremy and Jilly, they are "leaking liquids every-where."[18] One day when she takes little Jeremy on the bus to buy shoes, he puts her purse on his head and declares that he is "King of the Bus / King of the Shoe Bus." The other passengers are his "surround-ers, his servants." When it is time to get off the bus, Jeremy gives La Vaughn "back his crown" (78), and she says that they are soon "back down on earth / to buy shoes / we can't afford" (78). One day, in a scene like a picture book, a brief light shines around Jeremy's face as he tells her that his lemon seeds will grow. "Then everything goes back to the way it was, you can smell Jilly's throwup, / there is sticky stuff on the floor, the dishes are dirty because they ran out of soap, / flies buzzing around Jilly's cup" (96). Readers can picture Jilly's headless doll "without clothes on, its arm all twisted in a direction no person could ever reach and beside her leg is her head / with happy plastic eyes staring dead at the ceiling" (133).

In many passages, particularly when read out loud, the words are "like notes in music with tempo, sounds, rhythm, and texture."[19]

> She caves in and boohoos hard, / an avalanche of her voice / coming down her legs into my ears, / and now I don't know what to do. / I was gonna leave, go study my math, study my English / not to end up like Jolly, and here I am on the floor / holding her legs in my arms / and she sounds like a choir crying. (134)

The sounds evoked by the words tell so much about the story: the spoon clicking in an empty jar against voices in the background; Jilly crying as Jolly says that she cannot do it alone; and the powerful climatic scene when Jilly is choking and Jolly says in a voice that La Vaughn

> never heard in her or anybody else, / A voice like an animal somewhere out in the dark / all reaching all alone, / She makes such a sound, so clear I never heard a word so clear in my life, / Or so soft, / "Breathe, Jilly." (188)

The same words can evoke different pictures and sounds in various readers' minds, but the author's craft in creating language as art is clearly apparent to everyone.

Midnight Hour Encores

Passages in Bruce Brooks's *Midnight Hour Encores* have sounds that fit the story about Sibilance, the sixteen-year-old world-class cellist. When she wants to see horses, her father takes her to the coast. There, awakened at dawn, she describes the scene in multisensory language drawing on her musical background:

> The pounding of the surf is getting louder from a specific direction, the way a secondary theme sneaks into melody from the violas in an orchestra. And when I look in that direction, off to my left, instead of surf I see a sudden wild spray of beautiful monsters from Mars swirl out from behind a dune, gracefully rolling toward me, not snorting or shivering but just *running,* running on the flat beach beneath me, splashing in the edges of the tide and emptying those little pools with a single stroke of a hoof.[20]

Brooks's use of the repeated "s" sound and clauses that build on each other mimics the musician's use of sound and repetition, creating a sense of billowing energy and forming an example of how an author's stylistic choices can underscore and expand on the theme of the text more generally. This vivid imagery of sights and sounds shows how the art of literature has style, form, and content that are integral to the work as a whole.

Shabanu: Daughter of the Wind

The figurative language in Suzanne Fisher Staples's *Shabanu: Daughter of the Wind* evokes the sound of Dadi chanting softly in his wood-smoke voice, pictures of Shabanu's dancing camel, her heart crumbling inside her like a burning piece of paper, even the feeling of a sand-storm. Against the cultural expectations of her nomadic people in Pakistan, Shabanu tries to figure out who she is. She tries to escape an arranged marriage, but her Dadi cannot allow it. When she attempts to run away, he finds her and beats her. Then, curiously, she hears sobbing, "as if from a great distance." "My knees crumple. Dadi catches me in his arms and buries his face against my bloody tunic. He holds me against him, and through a haze of pain, I realize it is Dadi sobbing, not me."[21] Such powerful images add depth to the conflicts and events in the plot of the story.

YOUNG ADULTS LEARNING FROM ESTABLISHED ARTISTS

Many stories portray how young adults learn more about their art and craft by studying the works of established artists. In *Sister Mischief*, by Laura Goode, the narrator, Esme, describes the kind of hip-hop/rap music that her all-female group creates, as well as the influence of others:

> We—Marcy, Tess, Rowie, and me—are seriously the four fiercest, bad-dest rhyming lionesses these few miles west of the Mississippi. . . . We write sex-positive reflections on our location in the present; we are a sisterhood of lyrical explosion, and we first throw down mad props to the following: all hail the most righteous Queen Latifah, all hail our fierce sister from the East M.I.A., all hail the powerful partnerships of Salt-n-Pepa. (17)

In that last sentence, Esme makes the connection between contemporary young artists and those masters of a genre known to the world more generally.

In Brian Farrey's book *With or without You*, main character Evan, a self-taught painter, selects a new artist every few months to study and imitate, thus mastering the techniques of artists as varied as Rembrandt, Seurat, and the contemporary Keith Haring. His boyfriend Erik, a sculptor, encourages him to push himself to go beyond mimicry, to learn how these artists share their unique visions of the world through their paintings. The novel describes Evan's journey to find a way to allow his voice to speak while applying the lessons from these masters through his careful and reverent immersion in their worlds. Evan uses the works of these masters in the way that Zero/Amanda is influenced by Salvador Dalí's art in *Zero* and Andi in *Revolution* learns from studying and playing the music of J. S. Bach.

Georgia, in *Pieces of Georgia*, spends hours at the Brandywine River Museum examining the technique, passion, and point of view of three generations of the Wyeth family. When tackling new projects, she tries to use the strategies that she has learned from her investigation of painters N. C., Andrew, and Jamie. The light, line, and emotion in Andrew Wyeth's pictures of the model Helga teach her the value of looking closely and seeing in novel ways. The book is filled with quotes from the Wyeths, such as Jamie Wyeth's words: "[The idea] that I am recording something nobody's looked at before, a unique view, that's why I paint."[22] Thus, when Georgia decides to draw her beloved dog Blake, she does so from the perspective of the gopher that he tries to chase down a hole, taking her cue from Wyeth's desire to paint from a unique point of view. Confronted with the task of creating a portrait of her father, she draws on what she has learned from observing a portrait of Wyeth's wife in which no actual person is present; the portrait of the subject has to be inferred from the objects in the painting and the way they are related. So Georgia reflects on her father by drawing a portrait focused on his tool belt and other objects of importance to him and in the process comes to some important realizations about the way that he has coped with his grief after the death of Georgia's mother.

Like Georgia, Doug, in *OK for Now*, takes inspiration from an established and famous artist. The Sweitecks have just moved to a new town, and Doug is bored, hot, and eager to escape from the abusive atmosphere in his home. He stumbles into the public library, where he sees the works of illustrator James Audubon and meets the energetic and outspoken Lil, who befriends him. For years, Doug has taken solace by drawing air pictures when life gets rough. When he sees the huge color plates of one of Audubon's works on display, without thinking he begins to trace the image with his finger. An assistant librarian watches him, coaxes him into trying to put pencil to paper, and then gives him tasks related to the problems that the illustrator had to solve to present his birds for the world to see. Each chapter is introduced by a reproduction of one of Audubon's colored images.

Doug begins to develop a sense of a possible self that he has not been able to envision before, as he works on his drawing, comes to know Lil, and takes on some of the difficult customers to whom he delivers groceries on Saturdays for Lil's father. His art and his relationships with Lil, his librarian instructor, and Audubon's works keep him focused in the wake of accusations, abuse, and the arrival home of his adored older brother, who has been damaged almost beyond repair in the Vietnam War.

As Doug works to reconstruct the Audubon book—the pages of which have been sold to support the library and town budgets—he learns a great deal about the townspeople, his family, and most important, himself, primarily through making connections between the dynamics of the birds in Audubon's work and his own interactions and experiences. Doug has an exciting adventure on the Broadway stage, copes with the serious illness of Lil, solves a mystery involving his brother and father, and finds a way to give his older brother a sense of purpose in life. The reader is left knowing that Doug is in fact "OK for now" because of his evolving identity as an artist and the way that he describes the picture of the Arctic tern on which he has been working. The drawing will replace the one plate in the Audubon book that cannot be found. Doug says,

> That Saturday afternoon, I finished my Arctic tern. He was beautiful. He was diving into the water because there was so much for him to find. The waves rolled all around him and were already starting to break, but he was going to be fine. He had so much to do. He had so much to see. He was going to go wherever he wanted to go. And he wasn't alone, you know. If you could see the picture like I saw it, there was a whole flock of Arctic terns all around him, all flying above the waves. . . . And after I finished, Mr. Powell opened *Birds of America* again. He laid my painting in at the place where Audubon's tern was missing. "Nothing is ever perfect" he said. "But this comes pretty close."[23]

Doug's experience shows what a young adult artist can accomplish as he learns about art from an established artist and continues to develop as an artist himself.

The telling of stories and art cannot be separated, whether it is the art in the literature, such as the visual descriptions that help tell the story, or the powerful words in literature that evoke images in readers' minds. Certainly, young adults who identify themselves as artists, as well as those who do not, will appreciate art and narrative more as they read these books. They have the opportunity to respond with a deeper understanding of the story and learn about literature, art, and artists because of the role that art plays in the creation of the book.

CONCLUSION

As teachers, using the arts in our classrooms is one way to increase our own joy and that of our students—doing so is a way to honor the multiple kinds of talents students bring to the table, to help readers make the abstract more concrete and knowable, and to differentiate our instruction in ways that help all our students meet curricular outcomes. As Cornett summarizes, the arts are basic vehicles of communication. They engage emotion and motivation. Their use encourages aesthetic understanding and attention to detail; their use promotes higher order thinking, promotes respect for diversity, helps develop concentration, and can foster the confidence to be unique. [24]

Space constraints for this volume mean a lack of opportunity to review the considerable literature available that documents the value of integrated arts pedagogical approaches. Claudia Cornett's *Creating Meaning through Literature and the Arts* is a wonderful source for strategies for using the arts as a way to bridge the gap between the reader's world of experience and the world of the text, and then as a way to help students process what they are reading as they move through a text, as well as how to synthesize and make sense of the whole experience of the text once they have completed the entire piece. Reader's theater is one such strategy, but drawing, music, dance, and creative movement activities can all be used to both draw young adult artists into the book and to appeal to students with diverse learning styles, helping all readers better understand, from the inside out, what it feels like to take the artist's perspective. Such activities stretch all our students to think creatively and explore alternative strategies for self-expression and, in the process, perhaps provide them a route to self-understanding and healing.

For more information about using an integrated arts approach in the English language arts classroom, see appendix B, which provides a wealth of ideas tied to specific young adult novels and other texts often used by teachers; additionally, appendix A includes an extensive anno-tated bibliography, organized by arts categories, of young adult novels, including all the titles mentioned in this text, in which a young person identifies as an artist or uses the arts to help move toward a stronger sense of self and place in the world.

In her speech at the November 23, 2002, ALAN breakfast, Virginia Euwer Wolff spoke eloquently about the need for art of all kinds. She quoted the powerful words written by Katherine Paterson: "Art takes the pain and chaos of our broken world and transforms it into something that brings forth life."[25] The arts bind us together—the literary arts as well as the sister arts of painting, sculpture, music, dance, and theater—and in this increasingly fractured world we hope that as teachers we can harness the power of the arts to do our little part to create community, increase tolerance, and build empathy and understanding for the self and the other.

NOTES

1. Sherman Alexie, *The Absolutely True Diary of a Part-Time Indian* (New York: Little, Brown, 2007), 5.

2. Connie Zitlow and Lois Stover, "Portrait of the Artist as a Young Adult: Who Is the Real Me?" *ALAN Review* 38, no. 2 (2011): 32.

3. Connie Zitlow, "Sounds and Pictures in Words: Images in Literature for Young Adults," *ALAN Review* 27, no. 2 (2000): 7.

4. Walter Dean Myers, *Monster* (New York: Amistad, 2002), 277.

5. Robert Sharenow, *The Berlin Boxing Club* (New York: HarperTeen, 2011), 313.

6. Mary Amato, *Guitar Notes* (New York: Egmont, 2012), 275–96.

7. Walter Dean Myers and Georges Bizet, *Carmen: An Urban Adaptation of an Opera* (New York: Egmont, 2011), 123–52.

8. Jennifer Bryant, *The Fortune of Carmen Navarro* (New York: Ember, 2010), 54.

9. Ransom Riggs, *Miss Peregrine's Home for Peculiar Children* (Philadelphia: Quirk Books, 2011), 350.

10. David Levithan and Jonathan Farmer, *Every You, Every Me* (New York: Ember, 2011), 239.

11. Janet Tashjian, with cartoons by Jake Tashjian, *My Life as a Book* (New York: Holt, 2010), 5.

12. Janet Tashjian, with cartoons by Jake Tashjian, *My Life as a Stuntboy* (New York: Holt, 2012), 1.

13. Eugene Velchin, *Breaking Stalin's Nose* (New York: Holt, 2013), 5.

14. Daniel Handler, *Why We Broke Up*, art by Maira Kalman (New York: Little, Brown, 2011) 1.

15. Patrick Ness, *A Monster Calls*, based on an idea by Siohban Dowd (Somerville, MA: Candlewick, 2011), 191.

16. Margarita Engle, *The Poet Slave of Cuba*, with illustrations by Sean Qualls (New York: Holt, 2006), 24.

17. Jan Greenberg and Sandra Jordan, *Andy Warhol: Prince of Pop* (New York: Laurel Leaf, 2007), book jacket.

18. Virginia Euwer Wolff, *Make Lemonade* (New York: Scholastic, 1993), 7.

19. Zitlow, "Sounds and Pictures in Words," 22.

20. Bruce Brooks, *Midnight Hour Encores* (New York: HarperCollins, 1998), 5–6.

21. Suzanne Fisher Staples, *Shabanu: Daughter of the Wind* (New York: Random House, 1989), 240.

22. Jennifer Bryant, *Pieces of Georgia* (New York: Yearling, 2007), 141.

23. Gary D. Schmidt, *OK for Now* (New York: Clarion Books, 2011), 355.

24. Claudia Cornett, *Creating Meaning through Literature and the Arts: Arts Integration for Classroom Teachers, 4th Edition* (Boston, MA: Allyn and Bacon/Pearson, 2010), 144–48.

25. Katherine Paterson, "Repairing Spirits in Disarray." In Michael Cart (Ed.) *911: The Book of Help: Authors Respond to the Tragedy* (Chicago, IL: Cricket Books), 12.

Appendix A: Annotated Bibliography

Young Adult Books about the Arts

Note: Titles followed by *(MC)* include multicultural perspectives.

VISUAL ART

Alexie, Sherman. *The Absolutely True Diary of a Part-time Indian*. New York: Little, Brown, 2007. Junior—a budding cartoonist who chooses to attend an all-white school instead of the one on his Spokane reservation—draws pictures of his life and the people in it. (MC)

Anderson, Laurie Halse. *Speak*. New York: Puffin, 2006. With the support of her art teacher and her completion of his art assignment, Melinda gradually confronts the emotional trauma of rape and regains her voice.

Bingham, Kelly. *Formerly Shark Girl.* Somerville, MA: Candlewick Press, 2013. This novel, told in verse, continues the story begun in *Shark Girl* when Jane lost her arm to a shark attack. It is more than a year since the attack, and Max seems to be interested in her again, but maybe he just feels sorry for her. Should she have to give up her dream of becoming an artist and instead pursue nursing?

Blumenthal, Deborah. *Lifeguard.* Chicago: Whitman, 2012. Sirena spends the summer at her aunt's beach house, using her art and her friendship with an artist she meets there to sort through her parents' divorce, mysterious happenings at her aunt's house, and her fascination with a gorgeous lifeguard.

Brown, Jennifer. *Hate List.* New York: Little, Brown, 2009. After her boyfriend goes on a school shooting spree, killing a number of their classmates and seriously wounding her, Valerie struggles to make sense of her memories and feelings, especially about their "hate list," which sparked Nick's actions. Her art and some unlikely friendships help her move toward healing.

Bryant, Jennifer. *Pieces of Georgia*. New York: Yearling, 2007. In this novel in poems, Georgia, like her deceased mother, is an aspiring artist, but her grieving father will not look at her sketchbooks. Georgia's life begins to change with the mysterious gift of a museum membership.

Clinton, Cathryn. *The Eyes of Van Gogh.* Cambridge, MA: Candlewick Press, 2007. Jude has long coped with the pain and loneliness of her peripatetic life through her art. When her mother moves the two of them to another new town, to live with her grandmother, Jude hopes that things will be different. She makes friends and finds an art teacher who encourages her, but the despair just keeps pulling down—the way that she can see Van Gogh drowning in despair when she looks at his eyes in his self-portraits.

Cole, Brock. *Celine*. New York: Farrar, Straus & Giroux, 1989. Celine's artistic talent helps her deal with her parents' neglect while gaining confidence about who she is and what she is capable of doing. She is expected to show a little maturity, and she explores her identity as she paints a self-portrait that she calls "Celine-Beast."

Crowley, Suzanne C. *The Very Ordered Existence of Merilee Marvelous*. New York: Greenwillow, 2007. Merilee, a thirteen-year-old with Asperger's who fills her journal with drawings of dragons, finds that her very ordered existence is threatened after meeting Bismark, an emotionally damaged eight-year-old who follows her everywhere.

Engle, Margarita. *The Poet Slave of Cuba.* With illustrations by Sean Qualls. New York: Holt, 2006. The story of Juan Francisco Manzano's life is told in powerful verse and stunning illustrations. He was born in Cuba in 1797 and denied an education, yet he had an exceptional talent for poetry. (MC)

Farrey, Brian. *With or without You*. New York: Simon Pulse, 2011. For nine years, Evan and Davis, now eighteen, have faced the world together as gay loners and best friends. But Evan, a painter, meets Erik, a sculptor, and they develop a relationship—just as Davis gets pulled into a fringe group, the Chasers, whose leader promises Davis not only revenge against those who have bullied him but also acceptance. With whom does Evan's future lie?

Franco, Betsy. *Metamorphosis: Junior Year*. Illustrated by Tom Franco. Somerville, MA: Candlewick Press, 2009. Junior Ovid is an artist; in his journal, which he illustrates, he uses classical mythology as a way to describe his fellow students and to try to make sense of the disappearance of his sister, who is addicted to meth.

Franklin, Emily. *The Other Half of Me*. New York: Delacorte, 2007. Jenny, who loves to paint, is an artist with nonartistic athletic half siblings who, unlike her, were not fathered by Donor 142. She learns more about herself and her family when a she finds a new half sister.

Gallagher, Liz. *My Not-So-Still Life* New York: Wendy Lamb Books, 2011. Vanessa, an artist, eager to get out of high school and start living, gets her dream job at an art store where she meets new people who push her to take risks—not just as a painter but in life.

———. *The Opposite of Invisible*. New York: Wendy Lamb Books, 2008. The friendship between Alice and Jewel (Julian), who create and appreciate art, is threatened when Alice is noticed by a handsome, popular athlete. She wonders where she fits in. (Art: also photography and glass blowing)

Giff, Patricia. *Pictures of Hollis Woods*. New York: Yearling, 2004. Gifted as an artist, Hollis is a ward of the state who finally feels needed with she meets Josie, an aging artist whose memory is slipping.

Grab, Daphne. *Alive and Well in Prague,* New York: HarperTeen, 2008. After her father is diagnosed with Parkinson's disease, Matisse and her parents, a painter and a sculptor, move from New York City to Prague, New York.

Greenberg, Jan, and Sandra Jordan. *Andy Warhol: Prince of Pop.* New York: Laurel-Leaf, 2007. This accessible biography about Warhol explores his life, the context in which he works, the issues that his work raises, and the reasons for his popularity.

Gulledge, Laura Lee. *Page by Paige.* New York: Amulet Books, 2011. This graphic novel tells the story of Paige, whose family has just moved to New York City. Paige struggles to make friends and find herself in this new world by using her sketchbook to explore what she is experiencing, how she is feeling, and who she is becoming.

Handler, Daniel. *Why We Broke Up.* Art by Maira Kalman. New York: Little, Brown, 2011. In trying to explain to Ed why they are breaking up, Min writes a long letter punctuated with illustrations of all the objects that she has collected over the course of their relationship, the significance of which she explores to move the narrative forward.

Headley, Justina Chen. *North of Beautiful.* New York: Little, Brown, 2010. Terra is beautiful, smart, and talented, except her face is marred by a port wine stain that she keeps covered with her long blond hair. She expresses her sense of being an outsider in exquisite collages. Headley layers the themes and plotlines of Terra's journey to self-acceptance in the same way that Terra's artistry allows her to explore layers of meaning and relationships.

Hubbard, Kirsten. *Wanderlove.* New York: Delacorte, 2012. When Toby and Bria break up, she leaves him and her art behind to explore the world. She meets Rowan in Central America, and the two take off on a journey of discovery of both self and the world, illustrated by Bria's own drawings. (MC)

Johnson, J. J. *The Theory of Everything.* Atlanta, GA: Peachtree, 2012. Everyone thinks that Sarah should be "over it," the freak accidental death of her best friend. But Sarah is not and thinks that she may never be, but she finds hope through new friendships. The first-person narrative is illustrated with Sarah's drawings from her journal.

Johnson, Maureen. *The Last Little Blue Envelope.* New York: HarperTeen, 2011. Ginny has been sent on a series of adventures by her Aunt Peg, an artist who died and left Ginny a series of envelopes with instructions that she needs to follow to gain her inheritance. The last envelope is stolen with Ginny's backpack. Oliver, who purchased the stolen backpack, tracks Ginny down and entices her into one final adventure to find Peg's final works.

Jones, Traci. *Silhouetted by the Blue.* New York: Farrar, Straus & Giroux, 2011. Seventh-grader Serena is trying to keep up with the demands of the lead role in the school play, her studies, and the care of her younger brother, while trying to deal with the deep depression into which her artist father has sunk since the death of her mom. (MC)

Koja, Kathe. *The Blue Mirror.* New York: Frances Foster Books, 2004. Sixteen-year-old Maggy escapes from her alcoholic mother by losing herself in her sketchbook and sitting at a downtown café where she meets charismatic Cole, a runaway who introduces her to his homeless friends.

Leveen, Tom. *Zero.* New York: Random House, 2012. Seventeen-year-old Amanda ("Zero"), whose hero is Salvador Dali, is lost after her application to the Chicago Art Institute is rejected, until she meets Mike, a talented drummer, at a punk concert. As their romance increases, she begins to gain confidence in herself and her art. (Art: also music)

Levine, Gail Carson. *Dave at Night.* New York: HarperTrophy, 2001. Only after he experiences the world of musicians, painters, and writers of the Harlem Renaissance can Dave tolerate his life in the Hebrew Home for Boys. Set in 1926 in New York City's Lower East Side. (Art: also music)

Lockpez, Inverna, and Dean Haspiel. 2011. *Cuba: My Revolution.* Vertigo Press, 2011. Based on her experiences, this graphic novel tells the story of Sonja, who gives up her dream of becoming an artist to join Castro's revolution and become a surgeon, but after five years of difficult lessons, including imprisonment, Sonja is forced to flee her beloved homeland. Note: There are graphic illustrations of violence and some nudity. (MC)

Lord, Cynthia. *Rules.* New York: Scholastic, 2008. Catherine, at age twelve, has conflicting feelings about her younger brother David, who has autism. Through her art, she processes her thoughts and feelings about him, as well as her new friend Jason.

Mack, Tracy. *Drawing Lessons.* New York: Scholastic, 2002. When her artist father leaves the family, twelve-year-old Rory must find a way to regain her ability to draw, paint, and otherwise express herself.

Marsden, Carolyn. *Silk Umbrellas.* Cambridge, MA: Candlewick Press, 2004. Eleven-year-old Noi discovers that she has her grandmother's gift for painting scenes from the jungles of northern Thailand onto delicate silk umbrellas, a gift that will bring income to her family and save her from a soulless job in the local radio factory. (MC)

Mori, Kyoko. *Shizuko's Daughter.* New York: Holt, 1993. When Shizuko turns her memories into art, she is finally able to come to terms with her mother's death and her cold, distant father and stepmother. (MC)

Myers, Walter Dean. *Autobiography of My Dead Brother.* Art by Christopher Myers. New York: Amistad, 2006. Like Jamal in Myers's *Scorpion,* Jesse uses drawing to try to make sense of his life in Harlem. Jesse's black-and-white sketches tell the story of his blood brother's deterioration into a life of crime. (MC)

———. *Monster.* New York: HarperCollins, 1999. In this highly acclaimed and multi-layered book, sixteen-year-old Steve Harmon is in prison and facing trial for murder. The story takes place in contemporary Harlem and is told in Steve's handwritten journal entries and his typed screenplay of the courtroom proceedings. Is he guilty or innocent? Who is the real Steve Harmon?

Ness, Patrick. *A Monster Calls.* Based on an idea by Siohban Dowd. Somerville, MA: Candlewick Press, 2011. After his mother dies, Conor is visited by a monster who helps him begin to heal, in this richly illustrated tale of loss, guilt, and love.

Oneal, Zibby. *In Summer Light.* New York: Viking, 1985. This story of reconciliation, with help from *The Tempest,* depicts the emotional struggle between Kate and her father, two artists who are much alike. It takes time before they recognize this fact and come to understand each other and their relationship.

Parra, Kelly. *Graffiti Girl.* New York: MTV Books, 2007. Angel Rodriguez has long channeled her hopes for the future into her art, but when she is passed over for an award to do a community mural, she succumbs to the powerful charms of Miguel, who introduces her to the gritty world of graffiti wars; she learns a lot about art and develops her skills, but what kind of life does she really want for herself?

Pixley, Marcella. *Without Tess.* New York: Farrar, Straus & Giroux, 2011. Tess's descent into childhood psychosis is documented by the drawings and poems in her journal; five years after her death, her younger sister Lizzie, now fifteen, uses the journal to make sense of their childhood relationship and reach catharsis after the loss of her beloved sister.

Rodowsky, Colby. *Julie's Daughter.* New York: Farrar, Straus & Giroux, 1986. After seventeen-year-old Slug goes to live with her mother, who had abandoned her as a baby, Slug helps her care for an elderly, terminally ill artist.

Sáenz, Benjamin Alire. *Aristotle and Dante Discover the Secrets of the Universe.* New York: Simon & Schuster, 2012. Set in El Paso in 1987, this is a story of two teenage boys who are bored and lonely until they find each other. They talk about their Mexican heritage and skin color and share questions about life, nature, poetry, and art as they discover their love for each other. Their fathers are an interesting contrast: Ari's, a Vietnam veteran, is quite and distant; Dante's, an English professor, is openly affectionate. (MC)

Sandell, Lisa Ann. *The Map of the Known World*. New York: Scholastic, 2009. After her reckless older brother dies in a car crash, Cora finds solace in art. After meeting another artist, Damian, who was in the same car crash, she begins to put together the fragments of her live.

Say, Allen. *Drawing from Memory*. New York: Scholastic, 2011. When Say's father shunned Say because of his commitment to his art, Noro Shinpei, Japan's leading cartoonist, became his mentor. In this illustrated mix of narrative, memoir, and history, Say describes his development as an artist and his relationship with his teacher. (MC)

Selznick, Brian. *Wonderstruck*. New York: Scholastic, 2011. In interwoven stories—one told in charcoal illustrations, one told in text—the lives of a young boy and an older woman come together in unexpected ways that enrich them both.

Sepetys, Ruta. *Between Shades of Gray*. New York: Philomel Books, 2011. Set against the backdrop of a little-known aspect of World War II history—the invasion of Lithuania by Russia—this harrowing story of Lina and her family portrays their struggle to survive in the work camp to which they are exiled. Lina finds solace in documenting events and recording her feelings in her artwork and using her art as a way to maintain her sanity and her dignity.

Sharenow, Robert. *The Berlin Boxing Club*. New York: HarperTeen, 2011. At fourteen, Karl has never identified himself as a Jew but has always identified himself as an artist, a cartoonist. But it is the eve of World War II, and it has become dangerous to be Jewish, so when a friend of Karl's father, boxing champion Max Schmeling, offers to give him boxing lessons, Karl jumps at the chance to reinvent himself. In the end, both his boxing and his art help him protect himself and his sister and forge a new life outside the reach of the Nazi regime.

Stork, Francisco X. *Irises*. New York: Scholastic, 2012. Mary wants only to stay home and paint, but none of her art seems to work since an accident that left her mother in a vegetative state. Her older sister Kate wants to go away and study to become a doctor. When their loving but repressive minister father dies, the girls wonder what they will do.

Tashjian, Janet. *My Life as a Book*. Cartoons by Jake Tashjian. New York: Holt, 2010.

———. *My Life as a Cartoonist*. Cartoons by Jake Tashjian. New York: Holt, 2013.

———. *My Life as a Stuntboy*. Cartoons by Jake Tashjian. New York: Holt, 2011. Derek Fallon adds his clever, sticklike sketches to his narration in these stories that reveal his frustrations with school and difficulties reading. In the first story, he finds adventure at a summer learning camp. In *Stuntboy*, he gets the opportunity to be a stunt boy in the movies, meets a famous actress, and almost loses Frank, the monkey that he and his family are fostering. In *Cartoonist*, Derek's drawings become a comic strip, with his capuchin monkey Frank and beloved dog Bodi as favorite subjects. But Derek's life becomes complicated when Umberto, a new kid in class who uses a wheelchair, is not interested in Derek's idea that Frank might be trained to assist him and he steals Derek's cartoon ideas.

Vega, Denise. *Fact of Life #31*. New York: Knopf Books for Young Readers, 2008. Until things in her life change, Kat is a content to be the freaky yoga girl and talented artist with a mother who is a midwife.

Velchin, Eugene. *Breaking Stalin's Nose*. New York: Holt, 2013. Ten-year-old Sasha thinks that he wants to become a Young Pioneer and be like Comrade Stalin until life becomes increasingly difficult for his family and those in their crowded communal apartment. Velchin's powerful illustrations show Sasha's growing doubt and fear.

Woodson, Jacqueline. *I Hadn't Meant to Tell You This*. New York: Bantam Doubleday Dell, 1994.

———. *Lena*. New York: Delacorte, 1999. In these novels of interracial friendship, one of the significant subplots follows Lena as she copes with sexual abuse and holds on to hope and her sense of self by drawing on any piece of scrap paper or brown paper bag that she can find. (MC)

DANCE

Blundell, Judy. *Strings Attached*. New York: Scholastic, 2011. Kit leaves high school and Rhode Island to live in New York, but she can get only a bit part as a chorus girl until she meets Billy, whose father is a lawyer for the mob. What price will she have to pay to accept his help?

Draper, Sharon. *Panic*. New York: Atheneum Books for Young Readers, 2013. Diamond, who is rehearsing for the ballet of Peter Pan, makes one bad decision that threatens not only her own future but that of her family and friends. (MC)

Flack, Sophie. *Bunheads*. New York: Little, Brown, 2011. Nineteen-year-old Hannah, a prestigious ballerina with the Manhattan Ballet, has always followed the unofficial mantra "Don't think, just dance." Then she meets cute musician Jacob, and her universe begins to change. The elite world of professional ballet is portrayed in this debut novel by a former dancer.

Howrey, Meg. *The Cranes Dance*. New York: Vintage Books, 2012. Kate Crane and her sister Gwen are talented dancers in a demanding New York City ballet company until Gwen suffers a mental breakdown. As Kate's anxiety about her sister increases, she begins to doubt her own sanity.

Hurwin, Davida Wills. *A Time for Dancing*. New York: Puffin, 1997. In alternating chapters, friends Sam and Jules, two gifted dancers, reveal their inner thoughts after Jules is diagnosed with cancer.

Kehoe, Stasia Ward. *Audition*. New York: Viking, 2011. In this novel in verse, readers journey with Sara throughout the year that she spends with the prestigious Jersey Ballet, a year of "auditions" of many different kinds.

Kephart, Beth. *House of Dance*. New York: HarperTeen, 2008. Rosie, emotionally distant from her mother, finds a way to awaken her dying grandfather's fond memories of watching his wife dance, reconciling the family in the process.

Lundgren, Jodi. *Leap*. Toronto, ON: Second Story Press, 2011. Natalie, fifteen, who has identified herself as a dancer for most of her life, is challenged to rethink who she is and what she wants from life when she is introduced to modern dance and falls in love with the genre.

Matthews, Andrew. *A Winter Night's Dream*. New York: Delacorte Books for Young Readers, 2004. Based loosely on *A Midsummer Night's Dream*, this tale of young lover's confusion is narrated by Casey and Stewart, the latter of whom does the lighting for a dance concert. Lucy, one of the teens, is a dancer extraordinaire. (Art: also theater)

Nolan, Han. *Dancing on the Edge*. New York: Harcourt Brace, 1997. Raised by her grandmother amid mystical rules and beliefs, Miracle's desperate dancing is part of her search for an identity.

Padian, Maria. *Jersey Tomatoes Are the Best*. New York: Knopf, 2011. Jersey girls and best friends Henry and Eva are both talented athletes: Henry cannot be beaten on the tennis court, and Eva wins a spot in a prestigious and highly competitive New York School of Dance. But when Eva's search for physical perfection leads her into anorexia, their friendship is tested. Eva has to find a way to be true to her artistic self without destroying her body.

Shabas, Martha. *Various Positions*. New York: Farrar, Straus & Giroux, 2011. Set against a backdrop of the Toronto ballet dance world is fourteen-year-old Georgia and her struggle to understand her developing sexuality and find people that she can trust and a place where she feels safe to be herself.

Southgate, Martha. *Another Way to Dance.* New York: Laurel-Leaf, 1998. While fourteen-year-old Vicki spends the summer at the School of American Ballet in New York City, she tries to come to terms with her parents' divorce and consider her future as an African American dancer. (MC)

Wunder, Wendy. *The Probability of Miracles.* New York: Razorbill, 2011. Cam Cooper is dying of cancer, but when her mom takes her to live in Promise, Maine, for the summer, she gets the chance to experience many emotions and what might be called miracles that she did not think she would have. Cam and her mother are both hula dancers and often dance to tell stories or respond to those of others.

MUSIC

Alexander, Jill S. *Paradise.* New York: Feiwel and Friends, 2011. Paisley has long dreamed of escaping her small Texas town, and when the band in which she is the drummer starts to make a name for itself, she is well on her way, until Paradise shows up and life gets more complicated.

Amato, Mary. *Guitar Notes.* New York: Egmont, 2012. On alternate days, Tripp, a loner who uses a borrowed guitar, and Lyla, a gifted student and talented cellist, use the same school practice room. Their unlikely friendship begins when they exchange snippy notes to each other. Before they even meet in person, they challenge each other to write songs. They become songwriters whose words and music in "Thrum Society Songbook" are added to the book itself and can be heard at http://www.thrumsociety.com.

Bass, Karen. *Drummer Girl.* Regina, SK: Coteau Books, 2011. Sid, whose favorite class is shop, is easily the best drummer in school, but the all-guys group Fourth Down will only take her on if she agrees to dress like a girl. Doing so makes her fair game for sexual harassment, so she has to fight for her right to be both a girl and a drummer on her own terms.

Brezenoff, Steve. *Brooklyn Burning.* New York: Carolrhoda Books, 2011. Over the course of two Brooklyn summers filled with fires, music, anger, and loss, Kid and Scout ultimately connect in ways that honor the importance of creating their own family and making their own punk rock music.

Brooks, Bruce. *Midnight Hour Encores.* New York: HarperCollins, 1998. When Sibilance, a world-class cellist, travels across America with her father, she learns about the music and life of the 1960s. In searching for her mother, she also finds out more about herself.

Bryant, Jen. *The Fortune of Carmen Navarro.* New York: Ember, 2010. Four teens tell the story of half-gypsy high school dropout Carmen, who invites Ryan, a serious cadet at the Valley Forge Military Academy, to hear her band. He falls passionately in love with Carmen, who will not be owned by anyone. In this contemporary tale of tragic, obsessive love, Ryan's actions end his once-promising military future. (MC)

Calame, Don. *Beat the Band.* Sommerville, MA: Candlewick Press, 2010. After learning that he has been paired with "Hotdog" Helen for a semester-long high school health project, Cooper Redmond determines that the only way to escape the taunting of his classmates is to gain back a "cool" rating by winning the upcoming Battle of the Bands, but it turns out that he wins self-knowledge and Helen's heart instead.

Cannon, A. E. *Loser's Guide to Life and Love.* New York: HarperTeen, 2008. Ed, bored with his work at Reel Life Movies, pretends to be "Sergio" and is caught in a love triangle with friends Quark and Scout in this contemporary twist on Shakespeare's *Midsummer Night's Dream.*

Chari, Sheela. *Vanished.* New York: Hyperion, 2011. Neela, eleven years old, is an Indian American who dreams of playing her veena, a traditional Indian instrument, for audiences around the world, but when the instrument is missing, Neela has to solve the mystery of its disappearance, a journey that takes her to see her grandmother in India. (MC)

Collins, Pat Lowery. *Hidden Voices.* Somerville, MA: Candlewick Press, 2009. Set in early-eighteenth-century Venice, three girls who live in an orphanage study music with "Father Vivaldi": Luisa is a voice student; Anetta has the ear and touch for playing the voila d'amore; and Rosalba is an especially talented cellist whose romantic notions lead to unexpected consequences.

Conner, Leslie. *Waiting for Normal.* New York: Katherine Tegen Books, 2008. Sixth-grader Addie, living in a less-than-"normal" world, tries to work on her flute music for the orchestra performance.

Cooner, Donna. *Skinny.* New York: Point, 2012. Skinny is the voice living inside fifteen-year-old Ever Davies, who weighs over three hundred pounds, but Ever has another voice, a beautiful singing one. She makes the risky decision to have gastric-bypass surgery, includes charts of her progress, and hopes to find the courage to audition for the school musical.

Cooney, Caroline. *The Lost Songs.* New York: Delacorte Books for Young Readers, 2011. The stories of Doria, an organist, and Lutie, a singer, intertwine with the story of the "Laundry List," a set of songs that Lutie's ancestors used to express their daily sorrows and joys in this story of community, friendship, faith, and the healing power of music. (MC)

Cronn-Mills, Kirstin. *Beautiful Music for Ugly Children.* Woodbury, MN: Flux, 2012. Elizabeth, a music geek, is transitioning, becoming Gabe, the person that he has always meant to be. This process is facilitated by Gabe's friendship with mentor John, who gets him a gig as a radio DJ, defends him in the face of bullying, and supports his full transition.

Crowley, Cath. *A Little Wanting Song.* New York: Knopf, 2010. Charlie, sad and lonely, voices her feelings in the songs of longing that she writes. Through her music, she breaks down barriers so that friendship with Rosie, tough and science loving, blossoms, allowing each young woman to gain insight into herself, boys, and the future. (MC) (Australian)

Curtis, Christopher Paul. *Bud, Not Buddy.* New York: Laurel-Leaf, 2004. After his mother dies, Bud searches for his father and wonders if he could be the famous jazz musician. When Bud finds the band, he wonders if he will become a member. (MC)

Donnelly, Jennifer. *Revolution.* New York: Ember, 2010. Andi is a gifted musician and senior at a prestigious private school, but after her little brother is killed, her life is filled with rage and grief. Her father forces her to go with him to Paris, where, after discovering a diary in an old guitar case, she relives the French Revolution

Dowell, Frances O'Roark. *Ten Miles Past Normal.* New York: Atheneum, 2011. Janie Gorman enters ninth grade just wanting to have a normal high school experience, which is hard when her mom blogs about their life on their farmette and Janie often inadvertently tracks smelly goat poop on her shoes. But when she joins the jam band, playing bass, she begins to make friends and discover that life is actually better ten miles past normal.

Forman, Gayle. *Where She Went.* New York: Dutton, 2012. Picking up at the end of *If I Stay,* this time Foreman explores the possibility of a new kind of relationship between classical cellist, Mia, and now rock-star Adam, from Adam's point of view.

Goode, Laura. *Sister Mischief.* Cambridge, MA: Candlewick Press, 2011. Esme, a Jewish lesbian living in a conservatively white religious Minnesota suburb, narrates this story of first love, love of hip-hop and rap, love of making music, and a love of challenging those in power who would stand in the way of any of those other loves, as she gives us the story of "Sister Mischief," an all-girl hip-hop crew, coming of age together and independently. (MC)

Hesse, Karen. *Out of the Dust*. New York: Scholastic, 1997. Billie Jo's love of playing the piano is a thread that runs through this poetic and beautifully told story of harsh reality, tragedy, and reconciliation set in Oklahoma during the Dust Bowl.

Kelly, Tara. *Amplified.* New York: Holt, 2011. Although she has been accepted to Stanford, Jasmine cannot stomach the thought of four more years of academic push, so she takes off on her own to see if she can make it as a guitarist and performer.

———. *Harmonic Feedback*. New York: Holt, 2010. Drea, who has Asperger's and attention-deficit/hyperactivity disorder, and her mom land at her grandmother's home after her mom loses her job. Drea gets a chance to start over, making friends, even a boyfriend, and bonding over their shared passion for music.

Klass, David. *You Don't Know Me*. New York: HarperTeen, 2001. John's clever, amusing thoughts about life, school, and his participation in the school band, playing his tuba—which he calls a bullfrog—help him hide the reality of life with his abusive stepfather. The support of his band teacher is significant as he finds a way forward with his life.

Leveen, Tom. *Zero*. New York: Random House, 2012. Seventeen-year-old Amanda ("Zero"), whose hero is Salvador Dali, is lost after her application to the Chicago Art Institute was rejected, until she meets Mike, a talented drummer, at a punk concert. As their romance increases, she begins to gain confidence in herself and her art. (Art: also visual)

Levine, Gail Carson. 2001. *Dave at Night*. New York: HarperTrophy, 2001. Only after he experiences the world of musicians, painters, and writers of the Harlem Renaissance can Dave tolerate his life in the Hebrew Home for Boys. Set in 1926 in New York City's Lower East Side. (Art: also visual)

Maia, Love. *DJ Rising*. New York: Little, Brown, 2012. For Marley, music is like oxygen. When he is at his DJ job, he can escape his heroin-addicted mother, busing tables, and the pressures of school. But after his career suddenly skyrockets, tragedy strikes, and he is afraid that his world will come crashing back down. (MC)

Martinez, Jessica. *Virtuosity.* New York: Simon Pulse, 2011. Carmen has soloed with major symphonies all over the world and has been preparing for the prestigious Guarneri Competition for years. She does what her mother tells her to do, including taking antianxiety drugs to prevent stage fright. The only person who might keep her from winning is Jeremy King, the famous British violinist. Can she trust him when he seems to be falling in love with her?

Murray, Victoria Christopher. *Destiny's Divas*. New York: Touchstone Books, 2012. The three young women who compose the Christian singing sensation "Destiny's Divas" are known for their incredible music and their testimonies, but it turns out that their offstage lives are not exactly as they present them for their audiences. In a story of murder—which touches on faith, justice, compassion, female circumcision, and the goodness of God—music is the touchstone that these individuals need to keep them grounded. (MC)

Myers, Walter Dean, and George Bizet. *Carmen: An Urban Adaptation of the Opera.* New York: Egmont, 2011. Carmen, a beautiful "chica" who works at a wig factory, falls in love with Jose, the policeman who is different from the gansta types she knows. But when she meets the singer/rapper/producer/businessman Escamillo, she gives up on the jealous Jose, who is not going to get her out of "el barrio." The electronic version of this modern retelling of the enduring, tragedy love story includes music. (MC)

Parry, Rosanne. *Second Fiddle*. New York: Random House, 2011. Soon after the Berlin Wall comes down, three musician friends—Giselle, Vivian, and Jody—prepare to go to Paris for a classical music contest. It will be the last time that they play together before two of their army fathers go back to the states. After the girls witness a terrible crime and think that they must save a Soviet soldier's life, their trip to Paris becomes urgent.

Sawyers, June, ed. *The Best in Rock Fiction*. Hal Leonard, 2004. This short story collection features works by many of today's top writers whom the editor identifies as having a "rock and roll sensibility." New short stories and excerpts from novels such as Alexie's *Reservation Blues* are included.

Skovon, Jon. *Struts and Frets*. New York: Amulet Books, 2009. Sammy is trying to make his band ready for the Battle of the Bands, cope with his grandfather's descent into dementia, figure out what it means to be a real musician, as well as how to move into a different kind of relationship with his longtime best friend, Jen, who is an artist.

Sonnenblick, Jordan. *Drums, Girls, and Dangerous Pie.* New York: Scholastic Press, 2004. Thirteen-year-old Steven plays the drums in an all-star jazz band, but his world is turned upside down when his little brother becomes ill with leukemia. Steven tries to juggle homework, girls, worrying about his brother and parents, and still finding time to practice with his drumsticks and practice pad.

Tashjian, Janet. *For What It's Worth*. New York: Holt, 2012. This one is set in 1971, during the Vietnam War, when Quinn, a fourteen-year-old who loves rock and roll, makes the case that listening to music is a critical step in growing up. He makes lists of favorite songs, writes a journal piece about famous musicians, has a girlfriend, and even gets messages from Jim Morrison, Janis Joplin, and Jimi Hendrix on his Ouija board. But what will he do about the draft dodger who needs his help?

Taylor, Greg. *The Girl Who Became a Beatle.* New York: Feiwel and Friends, 2011. After her high school band breaks up, Regina wishes to become as famous as the Beatles—and her wish comes true. For one crazy weekend, Regina lives the life of pop music fame but then has to decide whether she needs to heed that old warning of "be careful what you wish for."

Vega, Denise. *Rock On: A Story of Guitars, Gigs, Girls, and a Brother*. New York: Little, Brown, 2012. In a story of brothers, bands, and friends, Ori want to be out of his older brother's shadow, but he wonders if his TBTBNL (The Band to Be Named Later) will ever get a real name.

Wealer, Sara Bennett. *Rival.* New York: HarperCollins, 2011. Brook is Queen B, a popular alto in her high school honors choir. She prefers the choir people, but her cruel, powerful friend Chloe does not want Brook to be friends with Kathryn, a gifted beautiful soprano. Former best friends Brook and Kathryn both feel great pressure to succeed in the prestigious Blackmore vocal competition.

Wenberg, Michael. *Stringz*. Lodi, NJ: Westside Books, 2010. Jace Adams and his mom frequently move to new locations. So when he enters a new high school three weeks into the school year, he thinks that he has a game plan for survival—namely, to stay unobtrusive. But after he rescues a valuable violin and its owner from destruction, he finds that he is making friends, and they recognize his gift on the cello. With their help, he begins to find a place of his own, and his musical talents blossom. (MC)

Wesselhoeft, Conrad. *Adios, Nirvana.* Boston: Houghton Mifflin, 2010. Since his twin brother died in a skateboard accident, Jonathan has been struggling to keep himself from jumping off a bridge. His "thicks"—a dying World War II veteran, a girl with cancer, a guitar teacher, and his principal—challenge him to use his talents to get back his grip on reality.

Wolff, Virginia Euwer. *Mozart Season*. New York: Holt, 1993. Allegra is ready for a relaxing summer after her demanding softball season, but her violin instructor tells her that she has qualified for a young musicians competition, where she will perform Mozart's Fourth Violin Concerto.

Wright, Bil. *When the Black Girl Sings.* New York: Simon Pulse, 2009. Lahni, fourteen years old, is the only black student at her elite private school, so she is taunted there, and things are falling apart at home as her white adoptive parents are splitting up. When her mom takes her to a multiracial church and she joins the gospel choir, Lahni finally feels a sense of belonging and gains enough confidence to enter a vocal competition.

Yoo, Paula. *Good Enough.* New York: HarperTeen, 2008. Patti, whose Korean American parents expect the best from her, loves her violin and rock concerts, and her very ordered existence becomes more complex when she meets the Cute Trumpet Guy. (MC)

Music Websites

The following sites provide information about a plethora of titles just on music alone:

http://www.goodreads.com/list/show/2142.YA_Music_Books#7818683—110 books!
http://www.goodreads.com/list/show/4232.Fiction_Involving_Music#7818683—255 books!

OTHER ARTS

Andrews, Jesse. *Me, Earl, and the Dying Girl.* New York: Amulet Books, 2012. When Greg's mom insists that he befriend Rachel, just diagnosed with cancer, his life changes. When she decides to stop treatment, Greg and Earl—a longtime film-making duo—decide to make a movie in her honor, and their decisions require them all to become visible within the high school community in ways that they previously avoided with a passion. (Art: film) (MC)

Austen, Catherine. *All Good Children.* Victoria, BC: 2012. In this dystopian novel set in the near future, Max, a graffiti artist, becomes concerned as he watches what the "treatment" does to the young people forced to receive it. He, his family, and fellow artist Dallas decide to resist by moving beyond the town's walls, where his creativity becomes crucial to their survival. (Art: graffiti art).

Calame, Don. *Call the Shots.* Somerville, MA: Candlewick Press, 2012. In this sequel to *Beat the Band*, the boys' plan—to make a low-budget horror film that will win them lots of money and the girls—starts to spin out of control. Sean has to step in to "call the shots." (Art: film)

Crane, E. M. *Skin Deep.* New York: Delacorte, 2008. Andrea feels like a Nothing until, when caring for a sick neighbor's dog and garden, she learns about pottery, about life, and about herself. (Art: pottery)

Crowley, Cath. *Graffiti Moon.* New York: Horizon, 2012. Crowley tells the story, in alternating voices, of an all-night adventure after Lucy's high school graduation, during which she shares her love of glass blowing with Ed, who turns out to be the graffiti artist nicknamed Shadow, with whose work she has fallen in love. (Art: graffiti art, glassblowing). (MC) (Australian)

Darrow, Sharon. *Trash.* Cambridge, MA: Candlewick Press, 2006. Boy and Sissy have been shunted from foster home to foster home. When they experience abuse, they set out to find their older sister in St. Louis, where they feel at home for the first time in years. But they are fascinated by the whole concept of tagging, and their hobby leads to tragedy for Boy, leaving Sissy to deal with her loss through graffiti art and, ultimately, sculpture. (Art: graffiti art, sculpture). (MC)

Doctorow, Cory. *Pirate Cinema*. New York: Tor Teen Books, 2012. Trent is a brilliant maker of pirate cinema, gathering materials from movies that he illegally downloads from the Internet and then remixing them to create new art. When he is caught and his entire family is cut off from the internet for a year, Trent runs away to London and joins with others who fight the government and its constricting regulations with their movies.

Hemphill, Stephanie. *Sisters of Glass*. New York: Borzoi Books, 2012. This novel in verse is based on story of the real-life Maria Barovier, daughter of a master glass-blower, who gains permission to build a small furnace for firing enamel on the Venice island Murano. It is a tale of a young woman's love of her art and love of the glassmaker who helps pull her family out of difficult financial times. (Art: glassblow-ing).

Hirahara, Naomi. *1001 Cranes*. New York: Delacorte Books for Young Readers, 2008. Angela, a twelve-year-old Japanese American, spends her summer in a small town outside Los Angeles working in her grandmother's flower shop and creating 1,001 paper crane displays for newlyweds. (Art: origami) (MC)

Johnson, Alaya Dawn. *The Summer Prince*. New York: Levine Books, 2013. In a futuristic Brazil, June and Enki stage explosive, provocative exhibitions and risk everything for love and art. (Art: technological/installation) (MC)

Krossing, Karen. *The Yo-Yo Prophet*. Victoria, BC: Orca, 2012. Calvin feels in control only when performing on the streets with his yo-yo, but when he is dubbed the "Yo-Yo Prophet," he has to really think about what kind of future he truly wants for himself. (Art: street performance)

Lurie, April. *The Latent Powers of Dylan Fontaine*. New York: Delacorte, 2008. When Dylan's best friend Angie takes a summer course on filmmaking and casts Dylan as the lead and subject of her project, Dylan begins to take more risks with his art and music, as well as in basketball and with Angie herself. (Art and music—Dylan's mother is an artist, and he and his brother both draw and are both musicians, with Dylan classically oriented and his brother, rock.)

Selzer, Adam. *How to Get Suspended and Influence People*. New York: Delacorte, 2006. When the gifted eighth-grade class is assigned the project of developing infor-mational videos for the sixth and seventh graders, Leon picks sex education as his topic. He decides to craft a video in the style of avant-garde director Fellini, and he learns a lot about creating meaning and effect through the art of movie making. (Art: film)

Stanton, Ted. *Jump Cut*. Victoria, BC: Orca, 2012. Spencer finds movies a lot more interesting than real life, but in this funny novel filled with film allusions, Spencer takes off on a wild adventure as dictated by his grandfather's will, which challenges that perspective.

Woodson, Jacqueline. *Show Way*. New York: Putnam Juvenile, 2005. In this autobio-graphical tale written in part to tell her infant daughter about the strong women from whom she descends, Woodson uses the image of the "show way" quilt as a metaphor for the importance of the art of "showing the way" to each succeeding generation. (Art: quilting) (MC)

Wright, Bil. *Putting Makeup on the Fat Boy*. New York: Simon & Schuster, 2011. Carlos Duarte enters the competitive world of makeup artists, landing his dream job but then having to confront a lot of different truths about himself, his relationships, and his talent in the process. (Art: makeup) (MC)

PHOTOGRAPHY

Bauer, Joan. *Thwonk*. New York: Speak, 2005. When a cupid allows Allison (AJ) one wish, she must decide between her passions: her photography and getting into art school or handsome Peter.

Beam, Chris. *I Am J.* Boston: Little, Brown Books for Young Readers, 2011. J—half Jewish and half Puerto Rican—has always felt that he was a boy born into a girl's body. After he has a falling-out with his best friend, he decides to commit himself to becoming the man that he knows he is, enrolling in a high school for transgendered teens while applying for photography programs in college. (MC)

Gallagher, Liz. *The Opposite of Invisible*. New York: Wendy Lamb Books, 2008. The friendship between Alice and Jewel (Julian), who create and appreciate art, is threatened when Alice is noticed by a handsome, popular athlete. She wonders where she fits in. (Art: also visual and glass blowing)

Krisher, Trudy. *Spite Fences*. New York: Laurel-Leaf, 1996. Until Maggie Pugh can face the racial violence that she witnessed in her small Georgia town during the summer of 1960, she looks at life through the lens of her camera, a gift from her black friend. With her photography, she gains independence from her abusive mother. (MC)

Levithan, David, and Jonathan Farmer. *Every You, Every Me*. New York: Ember, 2011. After his friend Ariel disappears, Evan—the boy who loved her but had settled for just being her friend—sets out on a quest to learn what really happened after he begins to find photographs that taunt him and make him question his previous reality.

Marcus, Kimberly. *Exposed*. New York: Random House, 2011. The story of sixteen-year-old Liz, "Photogirl," is told in raw free verse. Her friendship with talented dancer Kate is destroyed after Kate accuses Liz's brother of rape. Liz wonders if her brother is guilty and if she will ever be able to get a perfect photo shot again.

Myers, Walter Dean. *One More River to Cross: An African American Photograph Album*. New York: Harcourt Brace, 1995. Myers's poetic narrative accompanies black-and-white pictures in this beautiful portrait of people of African descent in the United States. (MC)

Riggs, Ransom. *Miss Peregrine's Home for Peculiar Children*. Philadelphia: Quirk Books, 2011. Jacob travels to an island off the coast of Wales in search of the story behind the photographs that his grandfather, who has recently been killed, has left him in this intriguing story that mixes narrative and pictures of some very peculiar children.

Rylant, Cynthia, and Walker Evans. *Something Permanent*. New York: HarperCollins Children's Books, 1994. With Rylant's poetry to accompany Evans's photos taken during the 1930s, this book tells about ordinary moments in the lives of people living in America during the Great Depression.

Sonneblick, Jordan. *Curveball: The Year I Lost My Grip*. New York: Scholastic, 2012. Pete loves baseball until an arm injury destroys his chance of playing in high school with his best friend, Adam. After Pete's favorite person, his grandfather, gives him all his camera equipment, Pete enrolls in a photography class and meets the super-hot star of the girl's dance team who is also a photographer.

Uhlig, Richard Allen. *Last Dance at the Frosty Queen*. New York: Laurel-Leaf, 2008. In this sometimes steamy novel, Arty Flood, a design assistant, wants to escape his middle-of-nowhere Kansas town as soon as he graduates. Then strange, disturbed Vanessa swims into his life using her photography to help her regain emotional equilibrium. (Art: also visual and design).

THEATER

Boyd, Maria. *Will.* New York: Knopf, 2006. After his dad dies, Will begins to act out at his Australian boys'school and retreat inside himself. Finally faced with either expulsion or using his musical talents to support the high school musical, Will is forced to face reality, acknowledge his gifts, and better appreciate the world of the theater. (Art: also music) (MC) (Australian)

Chow, Cara. *Bitter Melon.* New York: Egmont, 2011. High school senior Fei Ting (Frances) has lived all of her life in service to her mother's needs and dreams, but with the help of a supportive forensics teacher, she begins to find her voice and assert herself against her immigrant mother's demands and expectations. (MC)

Cooner, Donna. *Skinny.* New York: Point, 2012. At fifteen years old, Ever, over three hundred pounds, decides that it is time to try weight-loss surgery if she is ever going to achieve her dream of starring in her high school musical, but to do so, she has got to vanquish the voice of "Skinny," who tells her that she will never be more than an ungainly elephant.

Culbertson, Kim. *Instructions for a Broken Heart.* Naperville, IL: Sourcebooks Fire, 2011. Jessa finds herself on a spring break trip with her drama club, having to watch her former boyfriend constantly kissing his new girlfriend. Through theater, music, and art and the instructions of her best friends, Jessa comes to terms with the situation and finds a new understanding of herself.

———. *Songs for a Teenage Nomad.* Naperville, IL: Sourcebooks Fire, 2010. Calle and her mother have lived in more towns than the number of years that Calle has been in school, but during her freshman year, Calle settles into being part of the drama stage crew and confronts her mother about her absent father, and life becomes more certain—all of which Calle chronicles in her "song journal." (Art: also music)

De Baun, Hillary Hall. *Starring Arabelle.* Grand Rapids, MI: Eerdmans Books for Young Readers, 2012. Arabelle's first year of high school is filled with adventure, when she moves from being the prompter for the school play to taking on a lead role and when she uses her theatrical talents at a nursing home to coax the residents out of their loneliness.

Joseph, Danielle. *Shrinking Violet.* New York: MTV Books, 2009. Tere is a painfully shy high school senior who finds her voice only when she is behind a microphone as a radio DJ. But then the radio station decides to offer a date with "Sweet T" as a reward for a song-writing contest, and Tere begins to panic. (Book behind Disney Channel's original movie *Radio Rebel*)

Kluger, Steve. *My Most Excellent Year: A Novel of Love, Mary Poppins, and Fenway Park.* New York: Dial, 2008. Three ninth graders gain clarity about aspects of their identity through their involvement in musical theater, as one begins to recognize that he is gay and one realizes that she has theatrical talents that she needs to use in spite of her parents' disapproval. Political activism, baseball, and romance are also key elements in this happy novel.

Lecesne, James. *Absolute Brightness.* New York: HarperTeen, 2008. Strange Leonard, who moves in with Phoebe and her mother, wants to change everyone, but he disappears after being cast in *The Tempest* at drama camp.

Leveen, Tom. *Manicpixiedreamgirl.* New York: Random House, 2013. Tyler writes short stories and a screenplay and joins the high school drama club operating the lights so that he can be near the talented actress Rebecca Webb. He has been obsessed with "Becky" since his freshman year. Yet, what will his girlfriend Sydney think when she reads his published short story in which he idolizes Becky, named after a character in *A Midsummer Night's Dream*? Why do some people call her "Becca," saying that she is not who Tyler thinks she is?

Matthews, Andrew. *The Flip Side*. New York: Laurel-Leaf, 2005.While studying Shakespeare and playing the part of Rosalind, Robert, a British fifteen-year-old, becomes confused about who he really is. (MC) (Australian)

———. *A Winter Night's Dream*. New York: Delacore Books for Young Readers, 2004. Based loosely on *A Midsummer Night's Dream*, this tale of young lovers' confusion is narrated by Casey and Stewart, the latter of whom does the lighting for a dance concert. Lucy, one of the teens, is a dancer extraordinaire. (Art: also dance) (MC) (Australian)

Mitchard, Jacquelyn. *Now You See Her*. New York: HarperTempest, 2007. Hope is a talented actress who, as a ninth grader, wins the role of Juliet in the prestigious Starwood Academy's production of *Romeo and Juliet*. When she begins to realize that her life is less than perfect, she cries out in a destructive way, just wanting to be heard, and eventually is diagnosed with borderline personality disorder.

Nadin, Joanna. *Wonderland*. Cambridge, MA: Candlewick Press, 2009. The only bright spot in Jude's life is drama; she excels on stage, and she has been invited to audition for a prestigious drama school in London. But to face the future, Jude has got to face Stella and figure out where the boundaries between them lie.

Shanahan, Lisa. *The Sweet, Terrible, Glorious Year I Truly Completely Lost It*. New York: Delacorte, 2008. Gemma Stone, usually a calm person, is cast as Miranda in the school's production of *The Tempest* in this Australian author's first book for teens. (MC)

Spiegler, Louse. *The Jewel and the Key*. Boston: Clarion, 2011. Seventeen-year-old Addie is able to move between the present and 1917 after an earthquake rocks Seattle. Her time in the past, as an assistant to the director of the Jewel Theater, gives her insights that she needs when the present-day Jewel is about to be razed. Working in antiwar movements in both periods, as well as in the theater, Addie comes to know more about love, loyalty, and the nature of her true theatrical talents.

Telgemeier, Raina. *Drama*. New York: Scholastic, 2012. This humorous graphic novel traces the efforts of middle school student Callie as she tries to create a set for the school production of *Moon over Mississippi* that is worthy of Broadway, even though she actually knows little about construction. There is as much drama backstage as onstage.

Voorhees, Coert. *Lucky Fools*. New York: Hyperion, 2012. David Ellison is a talented actor at Oak Fields Prep School, where a mysterious prankster attacks high achievers. David's life becomes complicated when he is torn between his girlfriend Ellen and Vanessa, his new costar in *The Great Gatsy*. David's classmates hope to be the one student accepted to attend nearby Stanford University. But against his father's advice, David dreams of acting at Juilliard. Yet he must decide who he really is when he freezes during his initial Julliard audition and a Stanford recruiter watches his performance as Nick.

Wilkinson, Lili. *Pink*. New York: HarperCollins, 2009. At sixteen years old, Australian Ava wants to try being somebody other than the edgy, liberal, black-wearing girl that she has been. She wants to try dating a guy rather than staying with her sleek, radical girlfriend. She transfers to a new high school where it is cool to be smart; she begins to wear pink; and she explores heterosexual relationships. It is her involvement in the theater tech crew that helps her figure out who she really wants to be and the importance of being honest with your friends and yourself.

Zadoff, Allen. *My Life, the Theater, and Other Tragedies*. New York: Egmont, 2011. Sixteen-year-old Adam is a techie to the core, a lighting guy who struggles to overcome the fear of the dark that he has been experiencing since the death of his father. He works to overcome the unwritten code saying that techies and actors do not mix, when he begins to fall for the lead in *A Midsummer Night's Dream*.

Appendix B: Using the Arts Pedagogically

Moving Students into and out of Texts through Arts-Based Strategies

This appendix moves into the realm of pedagogy, discussing specific strategies for using the arts in the classroom and the multiple ways that teachers can help students learn about the role of art in their lives. Claudia Cornett (2010, 1), in *Creating Meaning through Literature and the Arts*, writes eloquently about the importance of the arts:

> Visual art gives new perspectives while satisfying our need for beauty. Drama welcomes us to suspend disbelief, to pretend and consider "what if." Dance extends communication of thoughts and feelings through the use of the body. Music "soothes the soul" while giving insights into ideas and emotions beyond words. The arts engender concentrated work punctuated with play. Curiosity is aroused and interest is piqued as we consider the possibilities arts materials, tools, techniques, and products present to express thoughts and feelings.

She goes on to note that, in general, we use the arts to "make sense of the otherwise incomprehensible" aspects of life (10). Think of Picasso's *Guernica*, which can provoke a viewer to tears in looking at the artist wrestling with the horrors of war; think of da Vinci's *Mona Lisa* and all the questions that viewers want to ask and all they want to know when looking at her. Art can be used to jar audiences out of complacency and foster both intellectual and emotional engagement with the world and with others involved in the aesthetic experience.

So, consider how students introduced to the concept of imagery might react differently to each of the following teachers' approaches. Ms. Martin starts class by asking, "Who can recall the five senses?" Students call out the senses—seeing, hearing, touching, tasting, and smelling. She then directs them to work with a partner and read a passage from the novel that they are reading as a class, William Golding's *Lord of the Flies*, and to fill out a chart in which they list words or details from the passage that relate to each of the different senses. She then discusses with them why Golding would have chosen the words that he used and what the effect is on the reader of those choices, including how these words relate to the tone and mood of the passage. She tells them that they have been working with the concept of imagery, and she gives them a formal definition. Finally, she assigns the students the task of writing a descriptive paragraph using sensory imagery to create a mood of their choosing.

Ms. Wells, however, has music playing as the students enter the room. For their warm-up activity, they listen to the dissonance of "Rite of Spring," by Igor Stravinsky, and then to the melodic strains of a mazurka by Frédéric Chopin , jotting down descriptive words and phrases that reflect what they hear and how they feel and respond as listeners as they do so. She then has them view *Lavender Mist*, by Jackson Pollock, and *Four Darks in Red*, by Mark Rothko, again asking them to try to capture what they see and how they react to the paintings. She ends this part of the lesson by having them get out of their seats to perform some specific movements. This time, they write descriptions of what they are actually doing, as well as how their bodies felt while involved in the activities, as they first stretch and yawn and then do five jumping jacks. At this point, Ms. Wells asks for volunteers to read one of their responses to either Pollock or Rothko—asking the other students to try to guess which one is the subject. She does the same for the pairings of musical compositions and for the movement activities, prodding those who are listening to add words that might tap into other senses—what does *Lavender Mist* taste like? Would feeling a cheese grater or an eggplant most capture how the piece by Rothko makes you feel? She tells them that they have been practicing with the concept of "imagery," and she asks them to try to generate a definition of their own. At that point, she turns their attention to *Lord of the Flies*, giving them different passages to tackle in groups, looking for sensory imagery—and asking them to come up with examples of pieces of music, art, food, and objects that could be used to symbolize the effect of the imagery on them as readers. Their homework is to find a passage from the novel that they have already read that has a lot of imagery. She then asks them to write a paragraph about Golding's word choices and use of imagery to create mood and to practice reading it out loud, trying to convey the mood of the piece using their voices. The next class will begin with students volunteering to read their selected passage while the other students, as audience members, listen to determine what mood the speaker is attempting to portray—and how well the speaker managed to do so.

The difference between the lessons by Ms. Martin and Ms. Wells has to do with the use of the arts to provoke engagement and understanding. Ms. Martin's lesson involves a perfectly good sequence of events: the teacher has tapped prior knowledge; she has students work collaboratively in a close reading; and she provides useful practice with the concept of imagery. But the students use only one of their senses and are focused on the words on Golding's pages. Ms. Wells has also helped students better appreciate Golding's craft—but she has introduced them to a number of other works of art, visual and musical; she has had them active and out of their seats; and she has asked them to take a stab at reading orally with expression, trying to convey how the words on Golding's page work to create a sense of mood and place, an important element of the Common Core learning standards. Ms. Wells has put the power of the arts to work in her classroom in ways that show that she understands recent research on using the arts pedagogically as well as on learning styles and multiple intelligences.

Numerous researchers provide support for ways in which engagement in the arts fosters the development of skills and ways of thinking that are necessary for survival in today's increasingly interconnected world. The National Governors Association, in Psilos's report *The Impact of Arts Education on Workforce Preparation* (2002), calls for more arts-based education in the K–12 classroom because current workplace demands include flexibility of thought, interpersonal skills, and problem solving—all of which are, they say, fundamental elements of any artistic endeavor. Psilos documents that working in any art form requires the kind of skill, discipline, perseverance, and sacrifice necessary for success in any realm of endeavor. Soep (2005) articulates how artists involved in self-evaluation have to work at the upper levels of

Bloom's taxonomy as they analyze details, look for patterns, gather evidence, and ultimately make judgments. Students in a New York City "ArtsConnection" program used more self-regulatory behaviors and had a sense of identity that made them more confident and resilient, according to Oreck, Baum, and McCartney (1999) and Deasy and Stevenson (2005) found that significant involvement in the arts by students from low-income families narrowed the achievement gap between them and students from more affluent homes.

Learning styles research focuses on how students vary in the ways that they take in information and make sense of it and then how they synthesize information and use it in problem-solving situations. Researchers such as Evans, Kirby, and Fabrigar (2003) distinguish between students who use what they term "deep" versus "surface" information-processing strategies. Deep processing involves making systematic connections among ideas that cross disciplinary boundaries. For example, in studying the American Revolution, connections would be made between geography and historical events and between the U.S. Revolution and other historical events, such as the French Revolution or the more current revolutions happening as part of the "Arab Spring" (i.e., does the American revolution parallel these other revolutions or not?). Surface processing focuses on memorization of important facts and concepts. Students who engage in deep processing, according to Schunk, Pinntrich, and Meece (2008), tend to be more intrinsically motivated and able to self-regulate, while surface processors are more likely to be motivated by external factors, such as grades or competition. In a report by the Dana Foundation on brain-based research in arts education, Gazzaniga (2008, 47) notes that it is "remarkable and challenging to find that learning in the arts changes the brain." Arts activities are also important for differentiation, especially for students with limited language proficiency, who can perform at higher cognitive levels in the arts long before they have similar capabilities using words and texts (Cunningham and Shagoury 2005). Cornett (2010) provides a thorough summary of the current research on the value of arts integration in the areas of academic achievement, cognitive effects, literacy and math effects, motivational and affective effects, and social effects. The evidence seems overwhelming that teachers need to incorporate the arts in all classrooms as much as possible for the benefit of not just the young adult artists but all students.

Research on the specific topics of learning styles and multiple intelligences also calls for teachers to actively use more arts-based teaching strategies. "Learning styles" is a term around which some controversy exists. Workshops on learning styles often focus on students' preferences in terms of the environment in which they learn best; teachers are then encouraged to adjust the environment in terms of noise level, lighting, temperature, or seating (single desks, groups of desks, quiet corners, etc.). Elements of the learning task can also be juggled; specifically, the amount of structure provided, student choice allowed, and individual versus collaborative or cooperative activity can all be adjusted. Additionally, teachers can vary the way that they provide information to students; some students could read a text, while others might watch a video. Assessment strategies can also be varied based on student preference for strategies that they can use to show their comprehension of the material and concepts involved in the lesson.

While the research on learning styles has produced varied results, with proponents arguing that matching students with instruction based on learning styles increases achievement and attitude toward learning (Lovelace 2005) and with others showing that such matches have little effect (Kratzig and Arbuthnott 2006), the concept of learning styles does have implications for teachers. Brophy (2005) argues that at the very least, it is important to vary instructional strategies because no strategy will be preferred by all students. Teachers also need to help students best understand how they learn and what strategies work best for them. Research on metacognition indicates that learners who are aware of these factors can take more control over their learning and thus increase achievement (Kuhn and Dean 2004; D. Anderson and Nashon 2007). And as teachers think about learning styles, they become more sensitive to the myriad ways in which students differ, making it more likely they will acknowledge students as unique individuals.

Gardner's theory of multiple intelligences (Gardner and Moran 2006) too is important in helping teachers focus on the individual strengths and needs of students in planning for and delivering instruction and designing assessments to determine how well they are learning. Gardner's list of intelligences now includes linguistic, logical–mathematical, musical, spatial, bodily–kinesthetic, interpersonal, intrapersonal, and naturalist. He is also considering the idea of a spiritual intelligence, characterized by individuals attracted to questions such as "Who are we, and where do we come from?" Again, there are critiques of Gardner's theory. Some researchers, such as Chen (2004), argue that Gardner's ideas do not qualify as a "theory"; others argue that abilities in specific domains, such as art or music, do not qualify as "intelligences." Gardner (1995) does caution, "There is no point in assuming that every topic can be effectively approached in [multiple] ways, and it is a waste of effort and time to attempt to do this."

But the implications are clear for the ongoing strands of research in the arena of learning styles and multiple intelligences for teachers. Teachers need to present material to students in as many ways as possible and help students understand, again, their own strengths and weaknesses that meet their multiple needs. Given (2002) described students as having cognitive needs (to know, to self-monitor), emotional needs (to feel pride in one's efforts), social needs (to belong), and physical needs (the need to move) that require teachers to orchestrate experiences that are thought-provoking, aesthetic, concrete, and physically interesting. Arts-based activities do so. In the various fictional worlds explored in the body of this text, teachers are shown to play a pivotal role in helping young people in these ways. It is the English teacher in *Auditions* who gives Sara the knowledge that she has talent as a creative writer; it is art teacher in *Pieces of Georgia* who recognizes the talent in Georgia's doodles and pushes her to apply for a special program for gifted middle school artists; it is a drama teacher in *Instructions for a Broken Heart* who helps Jessa get a handle on her emotional responses to the world; it is the teacher/director of *The Tempest* in *The Sweet, Terrible, Glorious Year I Truly Completely Lost It* who recognizes that Raven needs a space and a venue in which to process his roiling emotions and convinces him to play Caliban. In *Revolution* Andi's music teacher is the only one who really understands the depth her grief and guilt; when everything else in the world that Liz has known is falling apart, it is her photography teacher in *Exposed* who supports her as she chooses the best works for her portfolio; and it is the art teacher of *Speak* who helps Melinda, in a very literal sense, regain her voice.

So, in the real-world classrooms over which teachers have jurisdiction, it just makes sense to use arts-based activities to introduce students to the texts they will be reading and to help them better comprehend and synthesize what they are reading. Doing so will draw students who identify themselves as artists of various sorts into the classroom conversation and will help tap the strengths and interests of all students in the process, perhaps giving them new information about themselves and their learning preferences while stretching them to think more creatively, explore new modes of self-expression, and try new strategies for catharsis and reflection. Teachers need to introduce students to characters who use the arts to make sense of their joys and pains, their confusion, and their insights as they search for a sense of self, which will also give students insights into the artist's way of being in the world. But teachers must also

> make the gift of the journal, the crayons, the part in the play, the space to dance or move creatively available to our students, inviting them to explore and, perhaps, discover an ability or talent previously latent in them that, when tapped, can help them better negotiate the difficult waters of adolescence. (Zitlow and Stover 2011, 32)

It may feel a bit scary to consider weaving arts activities into the classroom, especially for reading language arts teachers who love words but may feel awkward on the stage or in front of an easel or musical instrument. But teachers do not have to be artists of any sort themselves to present arts-based opportunities to young adults or model a delight in the exploration of concepts through the arts. All teachers need, as Cornett (2010) says, is to show that they are enthusiastic, have a desire to learn, believe in the power of the arts, can be flexible in their thinking and open to experiment, and are "optimistic about teaching and reaching all students with the courage to make mistakes in the process of doing so" (31). What follows are descriptions of specific strategies that any teacher can try or offer as options in the process of making his or her classroom a more arts-based environment.

DANCE

Dance is the movement of the universe concentrated in an individual.

If I could tell you what it meant, there would be no point in dancing it.

These lines—both offerings from Isadora Duncan, widely acclaimed as the founder of modern dance—capture the power of dance as a means of expression. Dance is wildly popular outside the school building. Dance schools, dance clubs, dance shows on television—all are thriving. On the nightly news, viewers watch individuals come together in large groups to dance in celebration of happy news—or to dance in mourning behind the body of a beloved public figure. Lois's four-year-old granddaughter Willow just started taking dance lessons, and she says of dancing, "It makes my whole self happy." Connie's granddaughter Eva Grace says that when she is in a recital, dancing makes her feel "elegant" and when she is having a bad day or when something is bothering her, dancing makes her feel "better." Murray (1993, 5) describes dance as a special kind of art form because it is a "primary medium for expression involving the total self (not just a part, like the voice), or totally separated from the physical self (like painting)."

So how can teachers capture the power of creative movement and dance inside the classroom walls? Cornett (2010, 255) writes, "Dance is the art that puts the curriculum in motion. Dance engages cognition within the context of compelling experiences that teach how to move one's body with intention." When individuals are dancing, they go beyond just moving their bodies for the purpose of accomplishing some specific task, such as getting a drink of water when thirsty; they move with intention to create a sense of beauty and emotion in a more abstract and even playful way. Teachers can move students up a ladder of abstraction with dance similar to how they move students toward higher levels of thinking on Bloom's taxonomy. Young children like to pretend to *be* a dog; they will happily sit up, beg, roll over, or chase their tails with abandon, imitating their pet black lab or cocker spaniel. But by middle school, rather than simply miming how Doug Swieteck from *OK for Now* makes his Saturday delivery rounds, students can explore, through dance, how he *feels* about having to slog his way through the snow to the homes of people who are going to turn their backs on him and withhold his tip because of their anger over his brother's alleged criminal behavior. They can go beyond mime to dance out the range of emotions that he feels when his older brother returns to the family with his face badly burned and both legs amputated above the knee after a tour in Vietnam. By high school, students can create dance variations to show how the characters in *Fallen Angels*, by Walter Dean Myers, respond to the intense and difficult situations they face during the Vietnam War.

But just walking into third period one morning and announcing, "Today everyone is going to dance!" is likely to lead to lesson failure. So a useful sequence is to incorporate dance-based activities in smaller chunks and on a regular basis, perhaps starting by just offering options for responses to assignments that include dance possibilities and then gradually pulling all students into the fray. Begin in an easy, comfortable way; start by asking students to note passages in their reading in which the author describes movements—of characters or elements of the setting—in dancelike ways. Teach them the dance vocabulary

"B.E.S.T." outlined by Randy Barron (2010): body parts, energy, space, and time. Pay attention to the more specific elements of rhythm—that is, pulse or beat, speed or tempo, accent or emphasis, duration or length—and then ask students to highlight ways in which good authors capture, in words, how their characters move through space in dancelike ways or how the elements of the setting are far from stationary.

After talking about the language of dance and attending to the "B.E.S.T." elements, begin to offer activity options for students that allow them to use dance. For example, if students are learning more advanced punctuation rules, such as those for a nominative absolute or when to use a colon, come up with motions that students can make for commas, semicolons, quotation marks, and so on. Get them to listen to a passage and make the appropriate motions at the appropriate times—or ask them to work in groups to act out the punctuation for a passage of their choice. To move from simple body motions into something more dancelike during a review session on vocabulary or the elements of a particular novel, ask students to group themselves by activity: for vocabulary, some may choose to write sentences or paragraphs effectively using the words; some may choose to draw or make collages to illustrate the words and their uses; some may choose to write dialogue incorporating the words and perform; and some may choose to dance out the meanings. Adverbs lend themselves particularly well to dance—students can use their bodies, individually or collectively, to move jauntily, surreptitiously, or lugubriously. But verbs, "lumber" versus "saunter," do as well, and more abstract concepts, such as "plot" or "foreshadowing," can become the basis for interesting dance presentations. Character sketches can also be presented in a number of ways—when reading *The Outsiders* by Hinton, one group can verbally describe Ponyboy, and another can create a dialogue between Ponyboy and, say, Maniac McGee. One group can draw or make a collage, while another can create a dance that captures the essence of Ponyboy's character and central tensions.

To stretch all students into using their bodies to solve a problem, collaborating, and presenting an abstraction in the more tangible, physical expression of dance, the teacher can use a standard warm-up used by generations of theater teachers: the machine. In groups, students can be challenged to create a "machine" in which all of the group members have to participate by making a repetitive motion, with each member's motion in some way connected to at least one other motion. The machine overall needs to capture the mood of a particular scene—for example, all groups could be assigned the same scene, and then the machines can be compared and contrasted in their effectiveness; or, groups can pull scenes from a hat, and as each group performs, the rest of the class has to try to guess which scene is being performed. To get a better feel for the machine concept, try viewing the videos at http://www.youtube.com/watch?v=qxZnfh2weO8 or http://www.youtube.com/watch?v=mA9Xy1NxQaA&feature=related.

Once students become more comfortable using their bodies and moving in conjunction with others—dance requires the practice of important skills, such as focusing attention, collaboration, self-control, and improvisation—they can begin offering suggestions for ways to incorporate dance more often. Students might be called on routinely to create comparison/contrast dances of characters or settings, dances that capture mood or tone of a poem or story (how would the mood of "The Yellow Wallpaper" be danced differently than the mood of "The Tell-Tale Heart?"), dances that demonstrate the emotions bubbling beneath the surface actions at key points of a story, dances that illustrate how different lines can be interpreted in different ways by both the producer and the receiver of the line—how many ways can "I love you" be conveyed and with how many interpretations? Or they can create dances that show different organizational strategies for newspaper articles. They might dance out their predictions of what will happen in the next chapter in a novel. They might dance out alternative endings (especially when they are not happy with the way that a book ends, as in *The Chocolate War).* Or they can try to capture in dance the whole spirit of a given period in literary history. How does the Renaissance look and feel versus the medieval period? In a variation of the "machine" concept, each student might pull an index card out of a hat, on which an event from a novel is written. Each student would have to create a movement reflective of that event—and then line up in sequence, creating a plot outline/timeline for the whole of the story. Even if the actual products—that is, the dances themselves—are not Tony Award quality, the kind of thinking required to generate the dance involves all of the Bloom levels, attends to a variety of different learning styles, and taps multiple intelligences.

Of course, students can then write about these performances using the language of dance as well as the language of the content area in the process, thus cementing their understanding of the concepts through another medium. In fact, the processes of composing with words and in dance is somewhat parallel so that students practice composition as choreographers, moving through the stages of brainstorming, selecting and organizing what works and fits best, revising the original dance conception, fine-tuning it for performance, and then actually showing it to an audience, ideally receiving feedback that leads to further revision. As such, they are actually gaining practice with the stages and processes involved in bringing a piece of writing from conception to publication.

Teachers know that students come to class last period of the day either so tired and lethargic that they can barely speak or so full of fidgets and wiggles that it is impossible for them—and for us—to concentrate. Using creative movement and dance activities generates energy and focuses attention. As Robert Sylvester (1998, 33) puts it, "misguided teachers who constantly tell their students to sit down and be quiet imply a preference for working with a grove of trees, not a classroom of students!"

DRAMA

Like dance activities, drama or theater activities usually involve students in movement, in a whole body–whole mind engagement that leads to positive effects on language development, reading comprehension, listening/speaking/writing skills, vocabulary development, skills in taking on the perspectives of others, empathy, social skills, and reflection on moral issues and values (Deasy 2002; Fiske 1999; Kardash and Wright 1987; Podlozny 2000; Cornett 2010). But in spite of the benefits, it can sometimes be hard to coax students into theatrical performances. Again, as with dance, it is helpful to ease young adults, often nervous about their bodies and shy about moving in front of others, into drama activities slowly. There is a hierarchy of activities that start at a very basic level with just a warm-up or getting-to-know-you activity, such as the "Circle Game."

Push the desks out of the way, and stand with the students in a circle or oval—in some round shape that allows every individual to see every other participant. Person 1 is going to call out the name of another person while moving across the circle to take that individual's spot. Upon hearing his or her name, person 2 walks out of his or her starting spot, calling out the name of another individual and moving toward that person's location. The process continues until every individual has been called and has had to switch positions. The fun begins when the group pits itself against the clock to see how many seconds can be shaved off the total time necessary for completing the process. If a teacher knows that someone might be self-conscious about moving or if a student is on crutches or not able to move freely, the teacher can create a team of observers and timers, who not only time the group but offer suggestions for how the group can move more quickly. After several tries—the teacher participates, too, of course—ask the students what they just did that mirrors the requirements of being in a drama activity: they had to move, they had to listen, they had to attend to others' movements, and they had to speak. Thus, they basically had to do everything that an actor does.

After the "Circle Game," try activities that leave out one of those elements. Tableaux or "freeze frames" are another easy first activity. The instructions can be that students are either creating an exhibit for the new Shakespeare Wax Museum or posing for yearbook photos. They might then have to create tableaux of important or turning-point scenes from *Romeo and Juliet* or a scene in which some essential character trait is revealed about a major character from *Macbeth*. Or, they might have to imagine that it is yearbook picture day, and they have to pose in groups as characters from the short stories that they have recently read for their short story unit. The key point is that nobody speaks in both these activities. The students collaborate to come up with a pose, and then they freeze in it. The teacher can then ask one group member to be the docent—who has to explain to the rest of the class, who have arrived at the wax museum for a field trip, what is going on in the exhibit—or the rest of the class can try to guess what part of the story or what character relationships are being portrayed by those who are posing.

Creating a successful pose involves abstracting essential elements from the reading, creatively solving the problem of how to portray those elements using just bodies and any props available in the class-room, collaborating, and attending to one another in the process. This kind of activity makes a great warm-up—an alternative to the dreaded pop quiz can be to ask students to do a tableau from the previous night's reading and to randomly call on members of the group to explain the significance of what is being portrayed. It also makes a great closure activity, a way to summarize the day's discussion of important themes and issues for those few moments just before the bell is going to ring. As an aside, Viola Spolin's classic *Improvisation for the Class-*

room and the more recent *Theater Games for the Classroom: A Teacher's Handbook* include over one hundred games and activities designed to support teachers in their efforts to change the pace and culture of their classrooms and engage students more actively through dramatic activities.

An easy way to move students into the concept of taking a role and becoming more comfortable speaking is for teachers to take on role. By wearing a hat or using some other sort of prop to signify that they are no longer only the teacher—even a name tag will do—they then begin questioning students in search of clarification about a topic. A teacher might be Shakespeare, wanting to know if some aspect of whatever play is being read by the class makes sense or needs revision to be clearer. Or one might be a character wanting help to understand the motives of some other character. Or perhaps be like a confused exchange student wanting more clarity about the difference between tone and mood or between dependent and independent clauses. One teacher might play the role of a different teacher—for instance, one of Doug Swieteck teachers from *OK for Now*, wanting to know why his grades have started to slip. The students can, at first, just be asked to respond as themselves—as readers of the particular text or as native English speakers who have been studying tone and mood. But, gradually, they can be asked to take on roles themselves. If a teacher is Shakespeare, groups of students might have to answer the bard's questions from the perspective of Lady Macbeth, Macbeth himself, Banquo, Duncan, and so forth. For extra credit, students might be able to earn points if they can use vocabulary words that are currently being studied as they respond.

As students become more accustomed to speaking in role, the tasks can become more complex. "Breaking News" involves having a journalist who is asking for opinions and insights from people on the sidewalk or at the airport or coffee shop as important new events unfold or new information becomes known. Other students can be assigned specific roles (perhaps they have to work in groups to help one individual from each group get ready to respond), or they can react off the cuff, depending on the context. The reporter may have just learned that Romeo and Juliet are both lying dead, and he or she wants a response to the tragedy from the friar, the nurse, the prince, Tybalt, or Lady Capulet. Or the reporter may just have learned that historians have uncovered a lot of new information about salt (after students have been reading *Salt: A World History*, by Mark Kurlansky), and he or she is asking scientists, sailors, kings, and other groups of people to describe the value of salt and why it has been so important in different ways throughout history. Depending on the comfort level of the class, students can just stay seated as they give their answers—they do not have to feel any pressure to act or become someone else; they merely have to answer as their assigned characters would do.

To ease students into adding even more movement and acting to their role taking, variations of reader's theater are helpful. Aaron Shepard (2004) defines this strategy by saying,

> Reader's theater is minimal theater in support of literature and reading. There are many styles of reader's theater, but nearly all share these features:
>
> - Narration serves as the framework of dramatic presentation.
> - No full stage sets. If used at all, sets are simple and suggestive.
> - No full costumes. If used at all, costumes are partial and suggestive, or neutral and uniform.
> - No full memorization. Scripts are used openly in performance.

Shepard provides lots of useful information for how to coach students in the process of creating reader's theater scripts. But to get them started, it is easy to use this strategy as a warm-up activity. For instance, working in groups, students might have to select "center of gravity" passages: passages that encapsulate some significant plot event or character revelation or relationship tension, from whatever they had to read for homework or the previous day. One person then reads the passage while another student or two pantomime what is going on in the passage, while a fourth person has to introduce the passage and explain why the group chose it and what its significance is. Similarly, students can be coached in the concept of more formal reader's theater, in which the text is read out loud, as though it were a script, with someone reading as narrator and others taking on the dialogue parts. Specifically, they work together to transform a text into a reader's theater script and then practice reading it out loud—staying seated but reading with emotion. Finally, "performing" for the rest of the class helps students come to understand the text in a deep way and requires them to listen and respond to their peers as they perform in ways consonant with the new Common Core curriculum standards that emphasize cross-disciplinary skill development in speaking and listening.

Moving students away from a script and giving them practice with improvisation can be accomplished by using the television talk show format, which allows for interesting conversations and can truly illustrate how well students understand the complexity of character relationships in a given text. "Oprah" might be interviewing characters from multiple novels or texts centered on similar themes, about their definitions of terms such as "bravery" or "honor," their relationships with their parents and how those relationships shaped them, and their understanding of the importance of family (or education or honesty—whatever is appropriate given the titles being synthesized). For instance, imagine Oprah interviewing the protagonists from *Out of the Dust*, *Maniac McGee*, *The Absolutely True Diary of a Part-Time Indian*, and *Lyddie* about their definitions of family or talking to Marty from *Shiloh*, Ponyboy from *The Outisders*, Lena from *I Hadn't Meant to Tell You This*, and Charlie from *A Little Wanting Song* about courage. After Oprah finishes with the group of young protagonists, she might call up other categories of individuals from the casts of the same books—the parent or teacher of the protagonist, the antagonists, or the friends and siblings. So students are working in groups, each of which is assigned a story or novel, to prepare for roles drawn from the given text. But when they are not onstage being interviewed, they can generate questions for Oprah to ask, or they can evaluate how well the people onstage capture the essence of the characters being portrayed.

Cornett (2010, 240) describes an activity that she calls "The Chair," which is also a very useful review activity. Two chairs are in the front of the room (or perhaps there are three sets of chairs around the room so that more students can be involved at any given time). Person A sits in one chair. Person B takes on a role (assigned by the teacher, pulled out of a hat, or determined by person B or a group of people supporting person B). Person B then approaches the other chair, starting a conversation in the role. Person A must figure out who person B is and then respond accordingly. This strategy works in any content area. Person B might be Hester Prynne, an antibody, the *X* axis, Napoleon, a particular part of speech, Monet, or a minor chord. Audience members can give suggestions to person A and keep track of the probable point at which person A figured out person B's identity. Again, as students become used to this kind of activity, which certainly helps them meet the speaking and listening standards as outlined in the new Common Core learning standards, they can expand on the activity. Person A has been approached by person B as Boo Radley from *To Kill a Mockingbird*;

person A figures out person B's identity and then might choose to respond as Scout would do. The teacher then can tap someone else's shoulder, and, as person C, that individual has to approach the two who are already talking together and who then have to determine who person C is (Atticus, Jem, a teacher from the school, etc.).

At the most complex level of drama as pedagogy, students can be guided to perform actual dramatic texts or their own interpretations/translations of such works. Harold Foster and Megan Nosol (2008), in *America's Unseen Kids: Teaching English Language Arts in Today's Forgotten Classrooms*, provide a host of activities that ultimately lead the urban students with whom Foster works—students who are English-language learners who have not been successful in school and who sometimes live by themselves and work while attempting to graduate—into live performances of Shakespeare that clearly show their understanding of the relationships and underlying themes of the difficult texts. Offering students the option of rewriting a text into dramatic form—including stage directions and notes for the director as to music and lighting—and then moving them into actual production of these scripts is a great way to tap the strengths of kinesthetic and visual learners, who can truly "show" what they have learned about a literary work in ways that they may not be able to do in a more standard essay or multiple-choice testing format. They have to attend to important details in completing such a "translation" that they often miss during a straight read-through of the text, and when they then have to talk about who they would cast for particular roles, they move beyond just the physical resemblance that an actor might have to a character. They consider how particular actors are able to convey certain emotional realities and inner struggles—again, thinking at a much higher level and truly demonstrating understanding and analysis skills.

MUSIC

Take a look at this YouTube video in which Tom McFadden teaches about genetics using the rap "Regulatin' Genes": http://www.youtube.com/watch?v=9k_oKK4Teco. As you watch, keep track of your response. Do you start singing along? Does your foot start to tap? After it is over, think about what you remember. What new terms and concepts are now in your brain because they have been attached to this energizing rap piece. Investigate the raps of Alex Kajitani, California teacher of the year in 2007, at http://www.mathraps.com (Cornett 2010, 309).

Now take a step away from these videos and consider your relationship to music more broadly. Do you sing in the car or shower? Do you listen to music while you commute or jog or make supper? Do you attend concerts of any kind? Do you respond to music emotionally at holidays or sad events, such as funerals, or happy ones, such as weddings? Do you use music as a way to reach out to other people, as a way to connect with your students, or to feel connected to your own cultural heritage? Do you play an instrument or sing in a performance group perhaps? Music is ubiquitous in our lives; it makes us happy, provides solace in times of sadness, and pulls us together in community.

Additionally, there is a growing body of research documenting the positive relationship between engagement with music and academic and personal development. Individuals who study music as instrumentalists or vocalists tend to develop desirable character traits, such as self-discipline, respect, and collaboration, according to Scripp (2003). Research done through the Dana Foundation and published by Gazziniga (2008) shows that regular music instruction and practice increase children's brain plasticity. Deasey (2002) finds that fourth graders with emotional issues improve their writing quality and quantity when they listen to music with headphones rather than writing in silence, while Catterall (2009) studied twenty-five thousand twelfth graders from all over the United States, only 20 percent of whom could do high-level mathematics. But among the students from the lowest socioeconomic backgrounds, those who were involved in instrumental music were much more likely than their peers to perform well in higher-level mathematics exercises. Catterall and Peppler (2008) cite Trusty and Oliva's meta-analysis of fifty-seven studies of engagement in arts experiences; taken together, results show that such engagement increases self-concept, language development, general cognitive development, critical thinking, and social skills. And the College Board reports that the more years that students spend in music education, the higher their SAT scores (Cornett 2010, 312).

Thus, there is a compelling rationale for using music in classrooms, especially as music and art programs are being decimated in the wake of the very difficult economic issues that many school systems are facing. It is not likely that English language arts teachers will have the time and skill necessary to teach students how to read music; it is even more unlikely that they can teach students to *compose* music. But English language arts teachers can certainly tap the skills that their musician students have in using the similarities among the processes of reading music and reading text, as well as composing music and composing texts; both processes involve decoding abstract symbols to make sounds and then putting those sounds into sequences that make sense, flow effectively, and have an effect on the audience. And teachers can certainly bring music into their classrooms as a way to change classroom culture, enliven lessons, pull students who enjoy music into the world of the text, and provide scaffolding for musical students to learn new concepts or remember course content.

At a very basic level, teachers can teach students to truly listen to the music that good authors create with their words. And they can listen to the ways that good authors evoke setting and mood through the use of sound imagery. Listen to this passage from Siobhan Dowd's *Solace of the Road* (2009), in which Holly, who has renamed herself Solace, is waiting for a train to arrive at the station in the deep darkness of the middle of the night. Keep track of the way that Dowd uses sound to capture the isolation that Solace feels, to capture the tension that she is experiencing as she waits to find out if the train will stop—and if she can get aboard and thus escape from the town where a well-meaning but somewhat clueless social worker has placed her in foster care:

> Then a rumble came in the distance. At first I thought it was thunder. Then I thought of the old trains in movies, how steam rises around the wheels. I listened. The noise stopped. . . . Electricity hissed down the rails. . . . A carriage whizzed by. It was first class, with fancy lamps and curtains and a woman reading. It didn't look like stopping. Then the brakes screeched. Another carriage passed, then another. The train slowed and stopped with a jerk and a shiver.
>
> I heard a door slam somewhere up front. . . . I pressed down on a big metal door handle. Inside was dim and damp. Warm air curled round me, pulling me in. I stepped up and closed the door behind me. A second later, the train glided and the station platform fell away. (217–18)

A timeline of sounds conveys the quickness of how the train appears auditorily out of the darkness, thunders into the station, hisses, and screeches to a stop. Next the train shivers into rest; doors clang and slam; then quickly, Solace is pulled into a cabin, and the train just glides effortlessly away.

In *Between Shades of Gray* (Sepetys 2011), Lina, who has been taken to a Soviet work camp from her native Lithuania, has just been tapped by the Soviet jailers to draw maps for them. Sepetys, the author, says that the following scene takes place in "silence," but students can listen for all the ways that the room in which Lina finds herself crackles with sound, creating tension for both Lina and the reader:

> "Davai!" yelled Kretzsky. He slapped me across the face. My cheek stung. My neck twisted from the unexpected blow.
> The two NKDV drew near, watching. Kretzsky called me a fascist pig. They laughed. One of them asked for a match. Kretzsky lit the guard's cigarette. The NKVD brought his face an inch from mine. He muttered something in Russian, then blew a long stream of smoke in my face. I coughed. He took the burning cigarette and pointed the glowing tip at my cheek. . . . My heart hammered. Kretzsky laughed and slapped the guard on the shoulder. The other NKVD raised his eyebrows and made obscene gestures with his fingers before laughing and tromping away with his friend. (338)

Just asking students to read a passage or listen to one read orally and focus on the use of sounds can help them become more aware of the way that the "music" of the everyday world affects our response to it.

Bridging into a unit of study or a particular text by using music to set the scene, capture the tone of the historical period in which the piece is set, and evoke atmosphere is one of the easiest possibilities for using music effectively and efficiently. During a unit on *Romeo and Juliet*, each day as students enter the room, music by a different renaissance composer could be featured—Tallis, Monteverdi, Byrd, Palestrina, or Gabrieli—as students complete a warm-up activity or just settle into their desks. Eventually, after hearing enough examples, students could probably inductively identify common features of the music and then be pushed to discuss how these characteristics reflect the style of Shakespeare's writing. If students seem especially interested, it would be interesting to have them compare these renaissance pieces with music by women of medieval times—an interesting selection of such music is available at http://womenshistory.about.com/od/musicclassical/tp/medieval_music.htm. Music of the jazz age, from Louis Armstrong to Scott Joplin to Billie Holiday, begs to be incorporated when studying the literature of that period; again, asking students to listen to the music and compare it stylistically to Fitzgerald's style is a way to get them into thinking more abstractly and analytically, while a unit centered on

Walter Dean Myers's *Fallen Angels* can be enhanced with music of the Vietnam era.

During the reading of any kind of text, students' interest in music can be used, again, to push them into more abstract thinking by asking questions or assigning tasks such as those that follow, adapted from Cornett (2010, 318); these examples relate to Woodson's *If You Come Softly*:

- "What musical instrument would Miah choose to play? How about Ellie? Why? Once you get to the end of the novel, would you change your mind?"
- "Imagine that you are creating a musical composition based on the book, a composition that will tell the story as the music in 'Peter and the Wolf' does. What musical cues would you choose to indicate the appearance of the major characters: Miah, Ellie, Miah's mom, his dad, Ellie's mother and her sister, the guys on Miah's basketball team?"
- "If you were making a movie of this book, what music would you use in the background for the scene in which Ellie and Miah meet, when they literally run into each other?"
- "What song is Ellie singing in the shower the morning after she's met Miah?"
- "Choose a passage that seems to you to have a lot of sound imagery. Prepare to re-create the mood and effect of these words—such as an eggbeater for a whirring effect."
- "Create a sequence chain of the ten most significant events in the story and then create a musical timeline for the novel."

After finishing any novel or a text of any sort, students can use music-based activities as a way to document their increased insight into the nature of the characters, or they can at least be given options for final projects that allow them to tap into their musical interests or talents. For example, after studying a unit on the development of the novel and reading Defoe's *Robinson Crusoe*, a student might come to class dressed as Robinson Crusoe and perform "The Ballad of Robinson Crusoe," showing a grasp of not only the ballad form but also the key events and themes of the novel. Greg Robison, now an English teacher in Montgomery County, Maryland, created "Lord Byron's Playlist" as a model assessment for a romantic poetry unit that he developed while in his teacher education program. Robison's introductory comments show how the opportunity to think about music that he already knows and loves in a new way engaged him. Samples of his playlist show how well he has come to understand Byron and his work. Greg says,

> I spent way more time on this than I intended to, I wanted to get it just right: a mix of music as eclectic as the man himself that played like a mixtape (for the most part, there are some hiccups) and showed philosophical or aesthetic similarities to Lord Byron and the Romantics. That would be a great name for a band. What follows is a list that explains why the tracks I chose embody something about this poetic movement and this fascinating man.
>
> *Queen: Flash*
>
> Flash Gordon, in many ways, reminds me of a Byronic hero: outcast from Emperor Ming's society, a paragon of masculinity, dashing. . . . Not my favorite song by Queen, but I felt that I should fit a Byronic hero somewhere in here.
>
> *ZZ Top: Sharp Dressed Man*
>
> I think this would be Lord Byron's theme song if he was alive in the 1980s. A song about dressing well, having loads of money, and attracting lots of attention. These all describe Lord Byron; he practically invented being a celebrity.
>
> *The Hives: Won't Be Long*
>
> The lyrics are about disillusionment with cosmopolitan life and a restless feeling to move on. Lord Byron did flee life in England to seek adventure, though there were probably other reasons for hitting the road than just restlessness.
>
> *The-Dream ft. Kanye West: Walkin' on the Moon*
>
> The lyrics detail the imagery of space and the feelings that accompany love. Kanye West's verse also details a glamorized bad-boy lifestyle.
>
> *Daft Punk: Voyager*
>
> A peaceful song that reminds me of driving through the country, probably because of all the times I've listened to it while driving through the country. There's some tension between the melancholy synthesized strings, the bouncy jubilant bass, the repeated guitar note, and the drums that gives me the same feeling of multiplicity from viewing a collection of Lord Byron's poems, which are just as diverse in tone, rhythm, and sentiment. I think the man himself would fall in love with this song. (Greg Robison, class assignment for "Content Investigations" at St. Mary's College of Maryland, used by permission of the student)

For even more ambitious students, an option could be provided to rewrite a story or novel into a musical, operetta, or opera. Or, in a creative writing class, an option could be to translate an opera into a novel, with Jennifer Bryant's *The Fortune of Carmen Navarro* or Walter Dean Myers's *Carmen* as a model. A good resource for introducing students to the world of opera is *Grabbing Operas by their Tales: Liberating the Libretti*, by Charles Lake.

Music can also be used to help students better retain what they are learning. Cornett (2010) suggests creating songs about parts of speech or other grammatical concepts and provides a version of "Yankee Doodle Dandy" that reels out a list of prepositions. Creating "call and response" songs to use in gaining student attention or having students create a "class theme song" to establish community at the beginning of the year can also enliven the classroom. Elementary teacher Linda Cruikshank (2010) notes that it is possible to use the language of music to jazz up directions to students. Rather than asking them to move more quickly during transitions to group work, she tells them to be "allegro." If they were trying to move too fast through an assignment or reading without giving it the required attention, she would remind them to slow down by using "largo." Rather than using more standard English terms to describe a character or event, she would use musical terms such as "adagio" or "legato." Students attended to her because of the novelty of the language, but they also began to vie with one another to find new musical terms that they could contribute to their class's developing vocabulary.

In general, teachers can help students become "multilingual" by helping them compare the language used to analyze literature with the language used to analyze music, in terms of the way that these genres of expression work, as well as in terms of how students, as consumers of such genres, respond. Some useful questions to ask include "What are the musical equivalents of terms such as *theme, character*, and *plot*?" and "What are the literary equivalents of terms such as *volume, speed, stress*, or *pitch*?" Teachers can also help students focus attention on the ways that writers use language, asking them if a given writer is "on pitch" or "off pitch" in terms of how his or her word choices are and are not appropriate given the context and characters being created. When asked about his use of language from this standpoint, Conrad Wesselhoeft, author of *Adios, Nirvana,* said,

> The feedback I've received on the language in "Adios, Nirvana" runs the gamut from "poetic" to "peculiar," from "raw" to "dangerous." Possibly everybody is right. I write what feels and sounds true. After years of doing this, you become surer of what you want to say and what

you want to leave out. Still, I find writing hard work. I rewrite obsessively—in part, because I don't have perfect pitch—and in part because I know that young-adult readers hold writers to a high standard. They can spot a fake a mile away. I like Hemingway because he opened the door for awkward voices, Kerouac because he said "Hurry up!" and Charles Bukowski because he said "Warts and all, warts and all!" (personal correspondence)

If teachers do nothing else in terms of bringing music into the English language arts classroom, they can and should talk about the nature of the voices that good authors create and whether or not they stay on pitch throughout their work. But beyond doing so, using musical experiences to help students connect with a text and then allowing students to respond to texts using music in myriad ways will, as Cornett (2010, 303) writes, "help engage, celebrate, unify, comfort and make ideas memorable."

VISUAL ARTS

Think about the fact that the English part of the curriculum is often referred to as "English language arts." Why? How is it similar to that of the field of visual art? Why is it an "art" at all? Cornett (2010, 175) says that individuals create texts and pictures in similar ways and for similar reasons—to capture thoughts and emotions, to capture the essence of a moment, to express feelings and ideas. Individuals respond to literary and visual texts in similar ways and look to both kinds of texts for stories and ideas that can help them better understand themselves, others, and life itself. Thus, using the visual arts in the English language arts classroom is a natural connection, and it behooves English teachers to help students recognize that the more means that they have at their disposal for communication, the better they can communicate with ourselves and others.

In their 2002 study on mental imagery and reading, Gambrell and Koskinen found that students who were explicitly instructed to make visual images as they read had significantly higher reading comprehension and memory of those texts than did students who did not engage in this kind of active reading (Cornett 2010, 142). This study builds on an earlier one by Sadoski and Quast, from 1990, in which they documented that readers retain the most what they both imagine and feel. Later, in 2004, Sadoski and Paivio showed that an "imaginative response is central to comprehension of literary works and is related to more objective responses such as evaluation of plot importance" (1361). What all of these studies have in common is the exploration of how teaching young readers to make the words on the page come alive through the process of generating pictures from authors' words results in deeper understanding, both cognitive and affective.

Thus, one easy way to incorporate attention to the visual arts, similarly to having students listen for the music of a passage, is to have students close their eyes and really "see" the setting, the characters, and their relationships as painted in words by those authors whose prose is full of vivid imagery. As a next step, the teacher can ask questions that guide students to consider the effect that a writer's use of such imagery has on them as readers, perhaps sharing examples of such an analysis—for example, that by Basia Walker (2011) in her blog "Basia's Bookshelf." She comments on Danielle Joseph's *Pure Red*, pointing out the ways in which Cassie, the main character, makes sense of her world—a world dominated by her famous artist of a father—by using color. Everything in Cassie's world has color associated with it in ways that mean something: the gray of an opposing basketball's T-shirt, the purple that she attaches to her crush Graham, and the red that she associates with her dead mother and the work of her father. Walker says in response, "This isn't a book driven by external conflict or one that has any great drama. It's a quiet book, with the relatively quiet personal issues of one girl in one summer. I loved the way Joseph used colors for emotional imagery, especially as it's used almost defiantly by Cassia at times." Walker's comments give a potential reader a scaffold to use in searching out such color imagery: What does it mean to use color "defiantly"? Who are some visual artists who use color in this way?

But beyond just attending to the visual imagery that authors use to evoke time and place, characters and mood, the teacher can use visual arts activities to help set the stage for reading and to help students better plumb their responses to texts in ways that allow for the fact that a text often affects a reader in a visceral, wordless manner. One easy strategy for incorporating attention to visual art in the classroom—that is, teaching the language of art while also teaching important literary concepts—is to use picture books as a bridge into the world of the text and its mood. Woodson's book *The Other Side*, illustrated by E. B. Lewis, evokes the world of pre–civil rights relationships between blacks and whites, making clear, through the perspective of the child narrator and her friend, that there are definite demarcations between the races. It also makes clear that it is often the case that children have to help lead their parents into new ways of being and understanding. The fence in the book—a concrete reminder of the divide between white and black and the way that the two girls figure out how they can use it as a starting point for their personal connection—is a powerful symbol of the past and the future. Using this lovely story book to open a unit on *To Kill a Mockingbird* can help establish setting and mood and make clear the value of both Harper Lee and Jacqueline Woodson's choice to use a child as narrator. Discussing Lewis's attention to detail—his choices regarding the perspective used in each softly colored page, the way that he uses line to pull the viewer's eyes to his point of focus, the positioning of the main character within a given plate—and then asking students to compare his choices to Lee's use of detail can provide a very useful way into the first chapter of the novel. The teacher can then incorporate into this segue the way that Scout's voice affects our response, as well as the ways in which having Scout as the narrator can give us a limited sense of what is happening.

Comparing and contrasting Lewis's artistic choices and Lee's literary ones and how these choices affect the mood created and determine the author's or illustrator's tone can help make the abstract concepts of tone and mood more concrete. In general, it seems to be hard for less sophisticated readers to distinguish between these terms, *tone* and *mood*. Knowing that mood is the overall effect that a piece has on the reader whereas tone has to do with the author's attitude toward the subject of the piece is an outcome on which students begin working in middle school and often still struggle to meet in high school. Showing Lewis's illustrations as they capture the gentleness of Woodson's story and convey a sense of hope without any sense of irony is one way to lead teenage readers into recognizing that while there are certainly somber moments in Lee's novel, overall there is a gentleness of tone and a sense of optimism with which Lee leaves the reader. Using visuals in general to help explain a concept or introduce a story can provide for higher levels of attention, interest, and motivation. For a nicely done visual approach to teaching the concepts of tone and mood more generically, see http://www.brainpop.com/english/writing/moodand-tone/preview.weml. The Internet has a plethora of such materials available to the teacher who does not self-identify as a creative soul. But the intrepid teacher can also create videos and other materials that help reel students into the net of learning. Eighth-grade teacher Stefanie Wells used the program Animoto when she needed a bridge into Tennyson's

"Charge of the Light Brigade," which, on the surface, may have little appeal to a middle school audience in 2012. Stefanie writes,

> Animoto is an excellent tool that enables the quick and easy creation of videos that incorporate music, images, text, and/or movie clips. I first used this tool in the classroom for a pre-reading activity in a lesson on Tennyson's "The Charge of the Light Brigade." Prior to the lesson, I used Animoto to create what I called a trailer for the poem. In my video, I included images of paintings that depicted the battle in the poem and used dramatic music to set the stage. I also interspersed these images with slides of text that gave basic historical details and asked questions related to the poem's theme. The minute and a half long video I created immediately captured the attention of my eighth grade students; their eyes were riveted to the screen, and at the end of the video, students were eagerly asking for the page number of the poem. Introducing a poem, or any literature, through the use of such a video can greatly influence the attitude with which students approach a text. Used properly, Animoto can be a valuable resource for educators to use to engage students and create the positive, motivated atmosphere that fosters learning. (personal correspondence)

The following link takes the reader to Stefanie's Animoto product: http://animoto.com/play/NB0JRrXXsw3shkqVT7D9fQ.

Beyond simply creating visual arts products for students to view, it is useful and just plain fun to engage them in actually *doing* visual art. In the 2011 *ALAN Review* article "Portrait of the Artist as a Young Adult" (36–37), we describe specific visual arts–based activities as examples for ways to tap the inner artist in all students while giving them some specific insights into the power of color as a bridge into the novel *Skin Deep*, about a dying potter and the young woman whom she befriends and with whom she shares her artist's view of the world. Before class, the teacher has to do some preparation.

First, the teacher needs to create groups of three crayons close in hue (e.g., yellows, greens, purples) from the box of sixty-four crayons. Then, the teacher makes two swatches of color on small pieces of paper from each of the three crayons in the group. One set of swatches gets labeled with the name of the crayon on the back and numbered 1a–1c to correspond with the names of three crayons in the group. The other set of swatches for that group are labeled with just the number and letter (i.e., no name for the color). For example, group 1 (all shades of orange) might include 1a = neon carrot, 1b = mango tango, and 1c = sunset orange. The teacher next puts the crayons themselves and the set of color swatches that include the color names on the back in a baggie, labeling it with the number of the set. The other set of swatches for that group goes into a second baggie, also labeled with the appropriate number.

When class begins, the teacher distributes to groups of three students the baggies with just the swatches of color that do not have the crayon names on them. The students then work in their groups to explore the differences, although the colors may seem too close together to distinguish. Their task is to come up with names for these colors and the reasons for those names; the trick is to be precise enough that someone else can label them in the same way.

Next, the teacher distributes the bags of crayons to the appropriate groups, which is fairly easy to do because he or she will have two different baggies: one labeled 1a–1c and one 2a–2c. The teacher asks the groups to compare the names that they gave the colors to the actual names provided by the crayon company, also asking which names they prefer and why and which are most descriptive. Then the teacher tells the groups, "Collectively, let the colors take you somewhere on the paper; draw something using the colors you have." Finally, the teacher asks the students what colors they might want to add, telling them to see if they can swap their bag of colors for another group's and continue to build their own piece.

This activity serves as an introduction to Crane's *Skin Deep* (2008), in which Angela learns to see color and experience a wonderful diversity of points of view, as she cares first for Zena, the St. Bernard who is owned by Honora, a potter, and then as she cares for Honora herself, who is dying of cancer. Angela is not an artist, but by listening to Honora and her friends and opening her mind and heart to the world as Honora sees and experiences it, Angela grows in wisdom, confidence, and self-understanding. At a memorial service for Honora, Angela reads this poem:

> Live like you are extraordinary.
> Love like you admire someone's most painful burden.
> Breathe like the air is scented with lavender and fire.
> See like the droplets of rain each are exquisite.
> Laugh like the events of existence are to be cherished.
> Give freedom to your instincts, to your spirit, to your longing. (254)

Another approach is to distribute the same bags of crayons to groups of three students, who have to share the colors that they have been given, swapping them, to draw a geometric shape that will capture, in some way, their sense of core identity. Next, ask them to use the colors that they have been given to shade and elaborate on the shape. As a safe option, let them make a shape symbol for a friend or family member, and then ask them to discuss what is hard about this activity and what is useful about it.

At this point, the teacher should show students the cover of *The Other Half of Me* (Franklin 2007), asking them to make a prediction about what the story will be about and then reading a description of the artist's self-portrait. The teacher can then tell students that, by reading the book, they can find out about the main character's longing for certainty about the identity of her father and how, through her art, she explores her own identity. At one point Jenny is standing in front of a piece that she has created, and she tells us,

> I stand in front of it and remember each slash of color, each stroke of purple and orange, the wax I put in to delay the drying time. Tate once commented that my paintings are filled with circles, and I guess he's right. Now I realize the spheres are like family, everything joined together in teams. Maybe the point of art—and of everything—is that you can't predict the outcome, that the crazy upheaval of it all is part of life. (237)

Providing options for visual arts–based responses to texts is another important way to honor the students with visual or spatial intelligence while inviting students to explore their own creativity. Even in college classes for future teachers, a powerful assignment is to have students "create a visual" that somehow captures the essence of a reading and their sense of what is important in it.

Middle school teacher Laura Swann (personal correspondence) uses poster making as a way to motivate her students to read sometimes-dense nonfiction texts and to help them make sense of such readings. To begin the lesson, Laura works through a PowerPoint presentation on different types of text features, such as headings, subtitles, or bolded words, while students follow a note-taking guide. Then she splits students into groups, each of which is given a text that she has retyped so that it is broken into paragraphs but no longer evidences any text features. The group task is to create a new layout for the text using at least five different text features. Groups could choose how they wanted to present the text on the poster: magazine or newspaper style. Students report that this activity helped them not only understand that the pictures typically found in such texts are not present "just for fun" but also appreciate how text features can help them preview a text and scaffold their understanding of its meaning.

One goal of the language arts curriculum has to do with providing students with an array of strategies to use in demonstrating comprehension of a text and interpreting it. Asking students to revisit a text for the purpose of drawing a vivid image that the author has created—one that serves as a center of gravity for the text in that it opens up the reader's understanding of a character, the relationships among characters, or the setting and the author's use of imagery to evoke response—can help them become more sophisticated in their response to the text as they narrow down and visually articulate their understanding of the text. For example, after reading Wolff's *Make Lemonade*, asking students to draw or make collages of the images of poverty that characterize Jolly's apartment helps them really see and appreciate the difficulties that she faces in raising her two children. When they have to make those images of poverty come to life—the dirt and filth, the way the little ones, Jeremy and Jilly, are leaking liquids everywhere, the headless doll with its arm twisted in an inhuman way, and that small lemon seed that finally sprouts—they develop empathy and understanding for Jolly's everyday struggles. Rief's *Vision and Voice: Extending the Literacy Spectrum* (1998) gives the teacher many powerful strategies tested by Rief of ways that she invites her students to participate in a literary work by using visual images and other forms of art, including musical creations to explore and extend their understanding and appreciation of a piece of literature.

Teaching the Selected Works of Katherine Paterson (Stover 2008) provides several easy-to-use arts-based strategies, as well as samples of student work generated in response. For instance, the "Mandala" activity allows students to think symbolically by asking them to complete an abstract design using three colors that, to them, capture the essence of a character. Talking about color imagery and the ways in which different cultures interpret colors differently—for example, red can mean anger, or it might mean royalty—and then asking students to identify colors as metaphors for their personalities and relationships helps them make their abstract understanding of a character more concrete. Here is an A–Z list of possible visual art responses to texts that students might be given:

> Advertisements (for some important item in the text), award certificates (for some major achievement of the characters), Animoto

Board games, book jacket

Cartoons, collages, children's book version of the text

Diorama, diary entries—illustrated

Eulogy with portrait of character

Flash cards, filmstrips, fanzines

Graphic organizer, graphs, graffiti (what graffiti would a character post?), greeting cards

Haiku—illustrated

ID badge, illustrations

Jigsaw puzzle of character or setting or entire text (somehow)

K/W/L charts, Kraft elbow macaroni sculpture, kernel sentences with expansions (i.e., give the students a subject and predicate and then tell them to expand by adding an adverb phrase, an adjective, a subordinate clause—have "sentence races!")

Love letter to a subject, lists, limericks, letters of all sorts—all illustrated in some way

Map, mobiles, movie version poster, metaphors (visual)

Newspaper article with photograph

Overview (visual), objects in the bag (pick fifteen items of significance in the story and tell the story by pulling the objects out of the bag, either randomly or in sequence)

PowerPoint summaries, puppet show, photo essays, propaganda posters, podcasts, pecha kucha

Quest maps (a kind of timeline of the events that the main character experiences in questing toward a personal goal)

Related art—find art mentioned in the text and, after viewing, discuss significance or why the author referenced that particular piece

Sketches, slide-tape scripts, set designs, stained glass window designs

Timeline, TV storyboard

Urgent news bulletin with photo, Frisbee golf with visuals from the text sequenced as targets, underground comix

Venn diagram, vitae, vocabulary stories—illustrated

Watercolor, WebQuest, walking tour scripts

X, Y coordinate plane drawing from text, "Xeroxing" (i.e., imitating the style of another's work)

Yellowbook of information, yearbook, yodel, year-at-a-glance in pictures

Zoological study/handbook, zines, zeugmas—illustrated (see http:// grammar.about.com/od/tz/g/zeugmaterm.htm for definition and examples)

Many books in which the main characters are themselves visual artists who look to specific artists as mentors or books in which well-known art is referenced more generally beg for teachers and students to explore that artwork together. *Pieces of Georgia* is filled with quotes from various members of the Wyeth family of artists and references to their art. Georgia is fascinated by the fact that Jamie Wyeth painted a portrait of his wife, Phyllis, without having her actually appear in the picture; instead, he used specific objects to represent her. He created visual metaphors for her, such as the delicate hat with a highlighted sash hanging over the back of a chair to illustrate her gracefulness. Students can examine Wyeth's portrait and then attempt to do a portrait of their own, either drawing or using a collage technique, to capture the essence of a friend, family member, someone they identified with in the book, or another important person in their lives. Crowley's *Graffiti Moon* is another such novel, which also introduces interesting questions about the nature of art, social justice, and the place of art in society. In what ways is graffiti art? In what ways could it be argued that it is not? The following website includes many useful discussion questions but ends, in section 5, with an outline of visual arts activities that can profitably be used to help students better connect with Lucy and Ed, Poet and Shadow: http://www.panmacmillan.com.au/resources/CC-Graffiti-Moon.pdf.

It is useful for the teacher working with visual art in the classroom to appreciate that there is a developmental sequence to how students respond to artwork that is related to their cognitive and emotional/ social developmental stage. Michael Parsons outlined this sequence in a 1987 book about the development of art appreciation, noting that, at first, young children respond to a work of art as they do to a story—by discussing favorite colors or objects in the piece and connecting those to personal stories. Later, they focus on how realistic a work is. They like realistic subject matter and appreciate the artistic skill involved in creating a realistic representation. As they become more experienced viewers, they realize that, as is true for a good story, a provocative work of art plays on their emotions and they gain appreciation for how artists evoke an emotional response. As they mature cognitively, students can be guided to discuss how art is socially and culturally influenced, how it is important within the context of a specific culture, and how it works to create meaning. Finally, Parsons (1987) discusses the "autonomy" level of artistic appreciation, at which the viewer first recognizes that judgments about art should be made on a mix of personal and social bases and then appreciates how art is a useful tool in thinking about the nature of the human condition and how it can be used to "provoke conversations about life."

But in general, the point about using arts-based strategies for moving into and out of texts is that doing so invites more students into these conversations—allowing musicians, thespians, dancers, and artists to draw on their strengths—and invites all students to develop an increased awareness of the value of the arts in our lives. However, Conrad Wesselhoeft cautions that with these kinds of activities, it is important that teachers balance respect for academic goals with respect for individual students' comfort.

> Not all kids need to have their talents trotted out before an audience. Sometimes the only audience they need is themselves. We pursue art to feed our souls. To force an unwilling kid on stage can distance that kid from the pleasure of his or her gift. So teachers and adults need to be respectful of a child's artistic needs. If a child wants to perform—great. Encourage that. If not, that, too, is okay. Time may change their minds—but don't shove performance at them. Let them move toward it at their own pace. To quote a prodigiously artistic friend: "It's not about perfection; it's about joy." (personal correspondence)

Using the arts in the classroom is one way to increase the teacher's own joy as well as that of the students. Doing so is a way to honor the multiple kinds of talents that students bring to the table, to help readers make the abstract more concrete and knowable, and to differentiate instruction in ways that help all students meet curricular outcomes.

NOVELS CITED

Alexie, Sherman. *The Absolutely True Diary of a Part-Time Indian*. New York: Little, Brown, 2007.

Anderson, Laurie Halse. *Speak*. New York: Puffin, 2006.

Bryant, Jen. *The Fortune of Carmen Navarro*. New York: Ember, 2010.

———. *Pieces of Georgia*. New York: Yearling, 2007.

Cormier, Robert. *The Chocolate War*. New York: Dell, 1995.

Crane, E. M. *Skin Deep*. New York: Delacorte Books for Young Readers, 2008.

Crowley, Cath. *Graffiti Moon*. New York: Horizon, 2012.

———. *A Little Wanting Song*. New York: Knopf, 2010.

Culbertson, Kim. *Instructions for a Broken Heart.* Naperville, IL: Sourcebooks Fire, 2011.
Defoe, Daniel. *Robinson Crusoe.* New York: Simon and Brown, 2012.
Dowd, Siobhan. *Solace of the Road.* Oxford, England: David Fickling Books, 2009.
Franklin, Emily. *The Other Half of Me.* New York: Delacorte, 2007.
Gilman, Charlotte Perkins. "The Yellow Wallpaper." 1892. http://www.library.csi.cuny.edu/dept/history/lavender/wallpaper.html.
Golding, William. *Lord of the Flies.* New York: Capricorn Books, 1959.
Hesse, Karen. *Out of the Dust.* New York: Scholastic, 1997.
Hinton, S. E. *The Outsiders.* 40th anniversary ed. New York: Viking Juvenile, 2007.
Joseph, Danielle. *Pure Red.* New York: Flux, 2011.
Kehoe, Stasia Ward. *Audition.* New York: Viking, 2011.
Kurlansky, Mark. *Salt: A World History.* New York: Penguin, 2003.
Lee, Harper. *To Kill a Mockingbird.* 50th anniversary ed. New York: Harper, 2010.
Myers, Walter Dean, and Georges Bizet. *Carmen: An Urban Adaptation of the Opera.* New York: Egmont, 2011.
———. *Fallen Angels.* Anniversary ed. New York: Scholastic, 2008.
Patterson, Katherine. *Lyddie.* New York: Puffin, 1995.
Poe, Edgar Allan. "The Tell-Tale Heart." 1843. http://etext.lib.virginia.edu/toc/modeng/public/PoeTell.html
Schmidt, Gary. *OK for Now.* New York: Clarion Books, 2011.
Sepetys, Ruta. *Between Shades of Gray.* New York: Speak, 2011.
Shakespeare, William. *MacBeth.* http://shakespeare.mit.edu/macbeth/full.html.
———. *Romeo and Juliet.* http://www.pubwire.com/downloaddocs/pdfiles/shakespr/tragedy/rmeojlet.pdf.
Shanahan, Lisa. *The Sweet, Terrible, Glorious Year I Truly Completely Lost It.* New York: Delacorte, 2008.
Spinelli, Jerry. *Maniac McGee.* New York: Little, Brown Books for Young Readers, 1999.
Wolff, Virgina Euwer. *Make Lemonade.* New York: Faber Children's Books, 2003.
Woodson, Jacqueline. *If You Come Softly.* Reprint ed. New York: Speak, 2009.
———. *I Hadn't Meant to Tell You This.* New York: Bantam Doubleday Dell, 1994.
———. *The Other Side.* Illustrated by E. B. Lewis. New York: Putnam Juvenile, 2001.

REFERENCES CITED

Anderson, David, and Samson Nashon. 2004. "Predators of Knowledge Construction: Interpreting Students' Metacognition in an Amusement Park Physics Program." *Science Education* 91, no. 2 (2004): 298–320.
Barron, Randy. "B.E.S.T." 2010. http://owldancer.net/RandyBarron/Downloads_files/Elements%20of%20Dance_1.pdf
———. "What Is Arts Integration?" http://www.owldancer.net/RandyBarron/Arts_Integration.html.
Bloom, Benjamin S. *The Taxonomy of Educational Objectives.* New York: Longman, 1956.
Brophy, Jere. "Goal Theorists Should Move on from Performance Goals." *Educational Psychologist* 40, no. 3 (2005): 167–76.
Catterall, James. "Conversation and Silence: Transfer of Learning through the Arts." *Journal for Learning through the Arts* 1, no. 1 (2005): 1–12.
———. *Doing Well and Doing Good by Doing Art: A 12-Year Longitudinal Study.* Los Angeles: Igroup Books, 2009.

Catterall, James, and Kylie Peppler. "Learning in the Visual Arts and the Worldviews of Young Children." *Cambridge Journal of Education* 37, no. 4 (2008): 543–60.

Chen, J. Q. "Theory of Multiple Intelligences: Is it a Scientific Theory?" *Teachers College Record* 106, no. 1 (2004): 17–23.

Cornett, Claudia. *Creating Meaning through Literature and the Arts: Arts Integration for Classroom Teachers.* 4th ed. New York: Pearson, 2010.

Cruikshank, Linda. "Creating Classroom Harmony." *The Rising Tide* 4 (2010). http://www.smcm.edu/educationstudies/rising-tide/volume-4.html.

Cunningham, Andie, and Ruth Shagoury. "The Sweet Work of Reading." *Educational Leadership* 63, no. 2 (2005): 53–57.

Deasy, Richard J., and L. Stevenson. *Third Space: When Learning Matters.* Washington, DC: Arts Education Partnership, 2005. http://mediation.centrepompidou.fr/PDF/symposium/session2/RichardDeasy.pdf.

Dowd, Siobhan. *Solace of the Road.* New York: David Fickling Books, 2009.

Duncan, Isadora. "Isadora Duncan Quotes." http://womenshistory.about.com/od/quotes/a/isadora_duncan.htm.

Evans, C. J., J. R. Kirby, and L. R. Fabringar. "Approaches to Learning, Need for Cognition, and Strategic Flexibility among University Students." *British Journal of Educational Psychology* 73, no. 4 (2003): 507–28.

Fiske, Edward. *Champions of Change: The Impact of the Arts on Learning.* Washington, DC: President's Committee on the Arts and Learning, 1999. (ERIC Document Reproduction Service No. 435581)

Foster, Harold, and Megan Nosol. *America's Unseen Kids: Teaching English Language Arts in Today's Forgotten Classrooms.* Portsmouth, NH: Heinemann, 2008.

Gambrell, L. B., and P. S. Koskinen. "Imagery: A Strategy for Enhancing Comprehension." In *Comprehension Instruction: Research-Based Best Practice*, edited by C. C. Block and M. Pressley, 305–18. New York: Guilford, 2002.

Gardner, Howard. "Reflections on Multiple Intelligences: Myths and Messages." *Phi Delta Kappan* 77, no. 3 (1995): 200–203, 206–208.

Gardner, Howard, and Seana Moran. "The Science of Multiple Intelligences Theory: A Response to Lynn Waterhouse." *Educational Psychologist* 41, no. 4 (2006): 227–32.

Gazziniga, Michael. *Learning, Arts and the Brain: A Dana Consortium Report.* New York: Dana Foundation, 2008. http://www.dana.org/uploadedFiles/News_and_Publications/Special_Publications/Learning,%20Arts%20and%20the%20Brain_ArtsAndCognition_Compl.pdf.

Given, Barbara K. *Teaching to the Brain's Natural Learning Systems.* Alexandria, VA: Association for Supervision and Curriculum Development, 2002.

Hanna, Judith L. "A Non-verbal Language for Imagining and Learning: Dance Education in K–12." *Educational Researcher* 37, no. 8 (2008): 491–506.

Kardash, Carol and Lin Wright. "Does Creative Drama Benefit Elementary School Students: A Meta-analysis." *Youth Theater Journal* 1, no. 3 (1987): 11–18.

Kratzig, Gregory, and Katherine Arbuthnott. "Perceptual Learning Style and Learning Proficiency: A Test of the Hypothesis." *Journal of Educational Psychology* 98, no. 1 (2006): 238–46.

Kuhn, Deanna, and David Dean. "Metacognition: A Bridge between Cognitive Psychology and Educational Practice." *Theory into Practice* 43, no. 4 (2004): 268–73.

Lake, Charles. *Grabbing Operas by Their Tales: Liberating the Libretti.* Toronto, ON: Sound and Vision, 2004.

Lovelace, M. K. "Meta-analysis of Experimental Research Based on the Dunn and Dunn Model." *Journal of Educational Research* 98, no. 3 (2005): 176–83.

McFadden, Tom. "Regulatin' Genes." 2009. http://www.youtube.com/watch?v=9k_oKK4Teco.

Murray, R. "A Statement of Belief." In *Children's Dance*, edited by G. Fleming, 5–7. Washington, DC: American Alliance for Health, Physical Education, Recreation and Dance, 1973.

Oreck, Barry, Susan Baum, and Helen McCartney. "Artistic Talent Dvelopment and Urban Youth: The Promise and the Challenge." In *Champions of Change: The Impact of the Arts on Learning*, edited by Edward Fiske. Washington, DC: President's Committee on Arts and the Humanities, 1999. (ERIC Document Reproduction Service No. 435581)

Parsons, Michael. 1987. *How We Understand Art*. New York: Cambridge University Press.

Podlozny, Ann. "Strengthening Verbal Skills through the Use of Classroom Drama: A Clear Link." *Journal of Aesthetic Education* 34, nos. 3–4 (2000): 239–75.

Psilos, Phil. *The Impact of Arts Education on Workforce Preparation: Impact Brief.* Washington, DC: National Governors Association Center for Best Practices, 2002. http://www.eric.ed.gov/PDFS/ED465119.pdf. (ERIC Document Reproduction Service No. 465119)

Rief, Linda. *Vision and Voice: Extending the Literacy Spectrum.* Portsmouth, NH: Heinemann, 1998.

Sadoski, M., and A. Paivio. "A Dual Coding Theoretical Model of Reading." In *Theoretical Models and Processes of Reading*, edited by R. B. Ruddell and N. J. Unrau, 5th ed., 1329–62. Newark, DE: International Reading Association, 2004.

Sadoski, Mark, and Zeba Quast. "Reader Response and Long-Term Recall for Journalistic Text: The Roles of Imagery, Affect and Importance." *Reading Research Quarterly* 25, no. 4 (1990): 256–72.

Schunk, Dale, Judith Meece, and Paul Pinntrich. *Motivation in Education: Theory, Research, and Applications.* 3rd ed. New York: Pearson, 2008.

Scripp, Larry. "Critical Links, Next Steps: An Evolving Conception of Music and Learning in Public School Education." *Journal of Learning through Music* (Summer 2003): 119–40. http://www.music-in-education.org/articles/2-AF.pdf.

Sepetys, Ruta. *Between Shades of Gray.* New York: Philomel, 2011.

Shepard, Aaron. "What Is Reader's Theater (and How Do You Spell It)?" 2004. http://www.aaronshep.com/rt/books/ReadersOS.html.

Soep, Elisabeth. "Critique: Where Arts Meet Assessment." *Phi Delta Kappan* 87, no. 1 (2005): 38–63.

Spolin, Viola. *Improvisation for the Theater.* Evanston, IL: Northwestern University Press, 1963.

———. *Theater Games for the Classroom: A Teacher's Handbook.* Evanston, IL; Northwestern University Press, 1986.

Stover, Lois. *Teaching the Selected Works of Katherine Paterson.* Portsmouth, NH: Heinemann, 2008.

Sylvester, Robert. "Art for the Brain's Sake." *Educational Leadership* 56, no. 3 (1998): 31–35.

Walker, Basia. "Asia's Bookshelf: *Pure Red*." December 2, 2011. http://www.basiasbookshelf.com/pure-red/.

Zitlow, Connie, and Lois Stover. "Portrait of the Artist as a Young Adult: Who Is the Real Me?" *ALAN Review* 38, no. 2 (2011): 32–42.

Young Adult Books Cited

Alexander, Jill. *Paradise*. New York: Feiwel and Friends, 2011.

Alexie, Sherman. *The Absolutely True Diary of a Part-Time Indian*. New York: Little, Brown, 2007.

Amato, Mary. *Guitar Notes*. New York: Egmont, 2012.

Anderson, Laurie Halse. *Speak*. New York: Puffin, 2006.

Bauer, Joan. *Thwonk*. New York: Speak, 2005.

Boyd, Maria. *Will*. New York: Knopf, 2006.

Brooks, Bruce. *Midnight Hour Encores*. New York: HarperCollins, 1998.

Brown, Jennifer. *Hate List*. New York: Little, Brown, 2010.

Bryant, Jen. *The Fortune of Carmen Navarro*. New York: Ember, 2010.

———. *Pieces of Georgia*. New York: Yearling, 2007.

Calame, Don. *Beat the Band*. Somerville, MA: Candlewick, 2010.

Chow, Cara. *Bitter Melon*. New York: Egmont, 2011.

Clinton, Cathryn. *The Eyes of Van Gogh*. Cambridge, MA: Candlewick, 2007.

Collins, Pat Lowery. *Hidden Voices: The Orphan Musicians of Venice*. Cambridge, MA: Candlewick, 2009.

Cooney, Caroline. *The Lost Songs*. New York: Delacorte Books for Young Readers, 2011.

Crowley, Cath. *Graffiti Moon*. New York: Horizon, 2012.

———. *A Little Wanting Song*. New York: Knopf, 2010.

Culbertson, Kim. *Instructions for a Broken Heart*. Naperville, IL: Sourcebooks Fire, 2011.

———. *Songs for a Teenage Nomad*. Naperville, IL: Sourcebooks Fire, 2010.

Darrow, Sharon. *Trash*. Cambridge, MA: Candlewick, 2006.

Donnelly, Jennifer. *Revolution*. New York: Ember, 2011.

Engle, Margarita. *The Poet Slave of Cuba*. With illustrations by Sean Qualls. New York: Holt, 2006.

Erskine, Kathryn. *Mockingbird*. Reprint ed. New York: Puffin, 2011.

Eulberg, Elizabeth. *Take a Bow*. New York: Point, 2012.

Farrey, Brian. *With or without You*. New York: Simon Pulse, 2011.

Flack, Sophie. *Bunheads*. New York: Little, Brown, 2011.

Franklin, Emily. *The Other Half of Me*. New York: Delacorte, 2007.

Gallagher, Liz. *My Not-So-Still Life*. New York: Ember, 2012.

———. *The Opposite of Invisible*. New York: Wendy Lamb Books, 2008.

Goode, Laura. *Sister Mischief*. Somerville, MA: Candlewick Press, 2011.

Greenberg, Jan, and Sandra Jordan. *Andy Warhol: Prince of Pop*. New York: Laurel Leaf, 2007.

Handler, Daniel. *Why We Broke Up*. Art by Maira Kalman. New York: Little, Brown, 2011.

Headley, Justina Chen. *North of Beautiful*. Boston: Little, Brown, 2010.

Hemphill, Stephanie. *Sisters of Glass*. New York: Borzoi Books, 2012.

Hesse, Karen. *Out of the Dust*. New York: Scholastic, 1997.

———. *Safekeeping*. New York: Feiwel & Friends, 2012.

Howrey, Meg. *The Cranes Dance*. New York: Vintage Books, 2012.

Hurwin, Davida Willis. *A Time for Dancing*. New York: Puffin, 1997.

Jones, Traci. *Silhouetted by the Blue*. New York: Farrar, Straus and Giroux, 2011.

Joyce, James. *Portrait of the Artist as a Young Man*. Viking critical ed. New York: Viking Press, 1968.

Kehoe, Stasia Ward. *Audition*. New York: Viking, 2011.

Kelly, Tara. *Amplified*. New York: Holt, 2011.

———. *Harmonic Feedback*. New York: Holt, 2010.

Kephart, Beth. *House of Dance*. New York: HarperTeen, 2008.

Klass, David. *You Don't Know Me*. New York: HarperTeen, 2001.

Kluger, Steve. *My Most Excellent Year: A Novel of Love, Mary Poppins, and Fenway Park*. New York: Speak, 2009.

Krisher, Trudi. *Spite Fences*. New York: Laurel Leaf, 1996.

Leveen, Tom. *Zero*. New York: Random House, 2012.

Levine, Gail Carson. *Dave at Night*. New York: HarperTrophy, 2001.

Levithan, David, and Jonathan Farmer. *Every You, Every Me*. New York: Ember, 2011.

Lockhart, E. *Dramarama*. New York: Hyperion, 2007.

Lundgren, Jodi. *Leap*. Toronto, ON: Second Story Press, 2011.

Lurie, April. *The Latent Powers of Dylan Fontaine*. New York: Delacorte, 2008.

Mack, Tracy. *Drawing Lessons*. New York: Scholastic, 2002.

Maia, Love. *DJ Rising*. New York: Little, Brown Books for Young Readers, 2013.

Marcus, Kimberly. *Exposed*. New York: Random House, 2011.

Marsden, Carolyn. *Silk Umbrellas*. Cambridge, MA: Candlewick Press, 2004.

Martinez, Jessica. *Virtuosity*. Reprint ed. New York: Simon Pulse, 2012.

Matthews, Andrew. *The Flip Side*. New York: Laurel Leaf, 2005.

Mori, Kyoki. *Shizuko's Daughter*. New York: Random House, 1994.

Myers, Walter Dean. *The Autobiography of My Dead Brother*. New York: Amistad, 2005.

———. *Carmen: An Urban Adaptation of the Opera*. New York: Egmont, 2011.

———. *Monster*. New York: Amistad, 2001.

———. *Scorpion*. New York: Amistad, 1988.

Ness, Patrick. *A Monster Calls*. Based on an idea by Siobhan Dowd. New York: Candlewick, 2011.

Oneal, Zibby. *In Summer Light*. New York: Viking, 1985.

Padian, Maria. *Jersey Tomatoes Are the Best*. New York: Knopf, 2011.

Parry, Rosanne. *Second Fiddle*. New York: Random House, 2011.

Pixley, Marcella. *Without Tess*. New York: Farrar, Straus and Giroux, 2011.

Riggs, Ransom. *Miss Peregrine's Home for Peculiar Children*. Philadelphia: Quirk Books, 2011.

Sandell, Lisa Ann. *A Map of the Known World*. New York: Scholastic, 2009.

Schmidt, Gary. *OK for Now*. New York: Clarion Books, 2011.

Selznick, Brian. *Wonderstruck*. New York: Scholastic, 2011.

Sepetys, Ruta. *Between Shades of Gray.* New York: Speak, 2011.

Shanahan, Lisa. *The Sweet, Terrible, Glorious Year I Truly, Completely Lost It.* New York: Delacorte, 2008.

Sharenow, Robert. *The Berlin Boxing Club.* New York: HarperTeen, 2011.

Skovon, Jon. *Struts and Frets.* New York: Amulet Books, 2009.

Sloan, Holly Goldberg. *I'll Be There.* New York: Little, Brown, 2011.

Sonneblick, Jordan. *Curveball: The Year I Lost My Grip.* New York: Scholastic, 2012.

Southgate, Martha. *Another Way to Dance.* New York: Laurel Leaf, 1998.

Spiegler, Louise. *The Jewel and the Key.* Boston: Clarion, 2011.

Staples, Suzanne Fisher. *Shabanu: Daughter of the Wind.* New York: Random House, 1989.

Stork, Francisco X. *Irises.* New York: Scholastic, 2012.

Tashjian, Janet. *My Life as a Book.* Cartoons by Jake Tashjian. New York: Holt, 2010.

———. *My Life as a Stuntboy.* New York: Holt, 2011.

Vega, Denise. *Rock On: A Story of Guitars, Gigs, Girls, and a Brother (Not Necessarily in That Order).* New York: Little, Brown Books for Young Readers, 2013.

Velchin, Eugene. *Breaking Stalin's Nose.* New York: Holt, 2011.

Violi, Jen. *Putting Makeup on Dead People.* New York: Hyperion, 2012.

Wealer, Sara Bennett. *Rival.* New York: HarperCollins, 2011.

Wenberg, Michael. *Stringz.* Lodi, NJ: Westside Books, 2010.

Wesselhoeft, Conrad. *Adios, Nirvana.* Boston: Houghton Mifflin, 2010.

Westerfield, Scott, and Keith Thompson. *Manual for Aeronautics: An Illustrated Guide to the Leviathan Series.* New York: Simon Pulse, 2012.

Wolff, Virginia Euwer. *Make Lemonade.* New York: Scholastic, 1993.

Woodson, Jacqueline. *I Hadn't Meant to Tell You This.* New York: Bantam Doubleday Dell, 1994.

Yoo, Paula. *Good Enough.* New York: HarperTeen, 2008.

Zadoff, Allen. *My Life, the Theater, and Other Tragedies.* New York: Egmont, 2011.

Secondary Sources Cited

Baumeister, Roy F., Jennifer Campbell, Joachim Krueger, and Kathleen Vohs. "Exploding the Self-Esteem Myth." *Scientific American* 292 (January 2005): 84–91.

Baumrind, Diana. "The Influence of Parenting Style on Adolescent Competence and Substance Use." *Journal of Early Adolescence* 11, no. 1 (1991): 56–95.

———. "Parenting: The Discipline Controversy Revisited." *Family Relations* 45, no. 4 (1996): 405–14.

Belifiore, Elizabeth S. *Tragic Pleasures: Aristotle on Plot and Emotion.* Princeton, NJ: Princeton University, 1992.

Bettis, Pamela J., and Natalie G. Adams. "Landscapes of Girlhood. " In *Geographies of Girlhood: Identities In-Between,* edited by Pamela Bettis and Natalie Adams, preface. Mahweh, NJ: Erlbaum, 2005.

Bloom, Benjamin. "The Role of Gifts and Markers in the Development of Talent." *Exceptional Children* 48 (1982): 510–22.

Chao, Ruth K. "Beyond Parental Control and Authoritarian Parenting Style: Understanding Chinese Parenting through the Cultural Notion of Training." *Child Development* 65 (1994): 1111–19.

Choi, Namok. "Self-Efficacy and Self-Concept as Predictors of College Students' Academic Performance." *Psychology in the Schools* 42, no. 2 (2005): 197–205.

Copland, Aaron. *Music and Imagination.* New York: Mentor Books, 1952.

Cornett, Claudia. *Creating Meaning through Literature and the Arts: Arts Integration for Classroom Teachers.* 4th ed. Boston: Allyn & Bacon / Pearson, 2010.

Dennis, Tracy A., Pamela M. Cole, and Carolyn Zahn-Waxler. "Self in Context: Autonomy and Relatedness." *Child Development* 73, no. 6. (2002): 1803–7.

Erikson, Erik. *Childhood and Society.* 2nd ed. New York: Norton, 1963.

Henderson, Nan, and Mike Milstein. *Resiliency in Schools: Making It Happen for Students and Educators.* Updated ed. Thousand Oaks, CA: Corwin Press, 2002.

Kroger, Jane. *Identity Development: Adolescence through Adulthood.* Thousand Oaks, CA: Sage, 2000.

Kübler-Ross, Elisabeth, and David Kessler. *On Grief and Grieving: Finding the Meaning of Grief through the Five Stages of Loss.* New York: Scribner, 2007.

Marcia, James E. "Representational Thought in Ego Identity, Psychotherapy and Psychosocial Developmental Theory." In *Development of Mental Representations*, edited by Irving E. Sigel, 397–421. Mahwah, NJ: Erlbaum, 1999.

McLeod, Julie, and Lyn Yates. *Making Modern Lives: Subjectivity, Schooling and Social Change.* Albany: State University of New York Press, 2006.

Renzulli, Joseph, and S. M. Reis. "The School-wide Enrichment Model: Developing Creative and Productive Giftedness." In *Handbook of Gifted Education*, edited by N. Colangelo and G. A. Davis, 184–203. Boston: Allyn & Bacon, 2003.

Ryan, A. "The Peer Group as Context for Development of a Young Adult's Motivation and Achievement." *Child Development* 72 (2001): 1135–50.

Schunk, Dale H., Paul R. Pintrich, and Judith L. Meece. *Motivation in Education: Theory, Research, and Application.* 3rd ed. Upper Saddle River, NJ: Merrill/Pearson, 2008.

Stover, Lois Thomas. *Teaching the Selected Works of Katherine Paterson.* Portsmouth, NH: Heinemann. 2008.

Strickland, Bonnie, executive ed. "Catharsis." In *Gale Encyclopedia of Psychology*, 116–17. Farmington Hills, MI: Gale, 2000. http://en.calameo.com/read/00019357488c28fdf44f5.

Vygotsky, Lev. *Thought and Language.* Cambridge, MA: MIT Press, 1962.

Westerfield, Scott. "ALAN Breakfast Speech." Presented at the National Council of Teachers of English Conference, Las Vegas, NV, November 17, 2012.

Woolfolk, Anita. *Educational Psychology.* 12th ed. Upper Saddle River, NJ: Pearson, 2013.

Zitlow, Connie S. "Sounds and Pictures in Words: Images in Literature for Young Adults." *ALAN Review* 27, no. 2 (2000): 20–26.

———. *Teaching the Selected Works of Walter Dean Myers.* Portsmouth, NH: Heinemann, 2007.

Zitlow, Connie S., and Lois T. Stover. "Portrait of the Artist as a Young Adult: Who Is the Real Me?" *ALAN Review* 38, no. 2 (2011): 32–42.

Index

About the Authors

Lois Thomas Stover is a former middle and high school teacher of English and drama. A graduate of the College of William and Mary, she earned a master of arts in teaching from the University of Vermont and a doctorate in education from the University of Virginia. She serves as dean of the School of Education and Human Services at Marymount University, Arlington, Virginia. A former president of the Assembly on Literature for Adolescents of the National Council of Teachers of English, she is the author of *Creating Interactive Environments in Secondary Schools*, *Young Adult Literature: The Heart of the Middle School Curriculum*, *Presenting Phyllis Reynolds Naylor*, *Presenting Jacqueline Woodson: The Real Thing*, *Teaching the Selected Works of Katherine Paterson*, and numerous book chapters and articles on young adult literature. She also coedited the thirteenth edition of the council's annotated bibliography for high school readers *Books for You*.

* * *

Connie S. Zitlow, a former English and music teacher, is professor emerita at Ohio Wesleyan University. A graduate of Wittenberg University, she earned a doctorate at The Ohio State University, where she served as a visiting assistant professor. At Ohio Wesleyan, she taught courses in young adult literature, content area literacy, and secondary teaching methods and served as director of the Adolescence to Young

Adult and Multi-Age Licensure programs. She is former president of the Assembly on Literature for Adolescents of the National Council of Teachers of English and the Ohio Council Teachers of English Language Arts. She coedited the *Ohio Journal of English Language Arts*, and she edited the "Professional Links" column of *English Journal*. She is the author of *Lost Masterworks of Young Literature*, *Teaching the Selected Works of Walter Dean Myers*, and numerous articles and book chapters on young adult literature, including chapters in *Adolescent Literature as a Complement to the Classics*, coauthored with Lois Stover.